NEVIS ISLAND
A Unique View of Its Early History

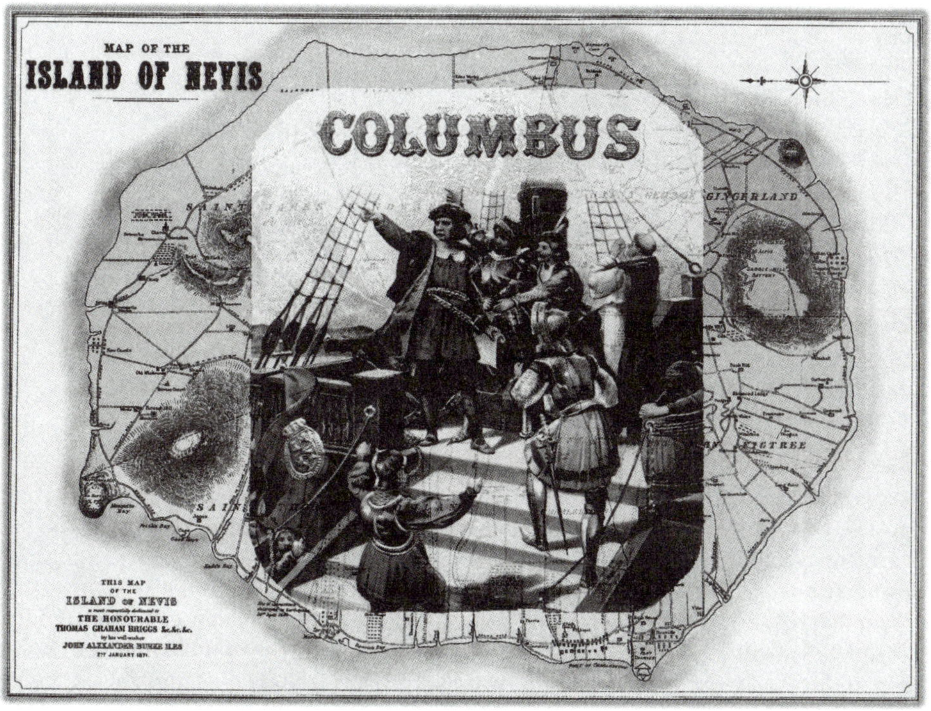

By: Msgr. Prof. [Dr. of Med.] Charles McWilliams
Produced and written in Nevis, West Indies
© 2017

NEVIS ISLAND
A Unique View of Its Early History
Msgr. Prof. [Dr. of Med.] Charles McWilliams © 2017
POB 553, Charlestown, NEVIS, West Indies • panamint@sisterisles.kn

CONTENTS

	Page No.
FOREWORDS	2
CHAPTER 1. A Pre-history of Nevis & the Amerindians	7
CHAPTER 2. The Arrival of the Conquistadors from Christendom (Christopher Columbus)	23
CHAPTER 3. The First British Settlement of Nevis	32
CHAPTER 4. The Knights of St. John Colonize the Americas	40
CHAPTER 5. Caribbean Migrants	51
CHAPTER 6. The Queen of the Caribe – Sugar, Air and Water	59
CHAPTER 7. From the Bush (Living off the Lands)	74
CHAPTER 8. The Pirates of Nevis	90
CHAPTER 9. Emancipation	114
CHAPTER 10. Independence - "Bones in our rice, pepper in our soup"	126
CHAPTER 11. The Culture of St. Kitts/Nevis	142
CHAPTER 12. SUMMARY	149
APPENDIX	154

FOREWORDS

Most people living in the northern climes always dream of that Caribbean vacation with sandy beaches, day upon day of glaring sunlight, ocean breezes, rum punch, beach towels, suntan lotion and sunglasses, all the features of a tropical vacation, yes!
But how about a Caribbean vacation with eyes wide open to its people?
Would you ever be able to guess why indigenous Caribbean people are so friendly, with least attitudes, so 'laid back,' able to readily 'live off the land' so to speak, yet can endure frequent power outages, watch store items that come and go, can make do without, as well as struggle through devastating hurricanes as if it were just a long traffic jam. I dare say most do not have a clue what makes a Caribbean Man or Woman so resilient and salted?

Ans. It is because of our history.

That is one purpose of this book. Read this book first, and your yearning trip to the Caribbean will be forever enriched with a knowledge base fewest visitors come to learn. And better, make that trip to an enchanted island called 'Nevis,' a Caribbean island like none other. This book will take you beyond the rum punch, Cuban cigars, hot sauce, suntan lotion, and conch fritters. You will learn about our people, our story, and our history unique to no other place on planet earth.

Good historical research requires seeing matters through documents, artifacts, and accounts generated around the time of events. Developing curiosity and intrigue with readers using folklore and considering mysteries from tales and old books makes for the lasting impressions that takes the reader away from the mundane, drab, and dreary popular notions which may well, one day, be relegated to urban legends of previous cultures. Those were my thoughts from the outset of this book. Having read all books available on amazon about my island, all of them left me empty, considering I have lived on Nevis for over twenty-eight years. No fair-skinned observer could possibly understand and appreciate the diversity and uniqueness of the Caribbean community without living here at least one decade of their life. Caribbean life hardens an individual through its sunburn, parched thirst, practical necessities, hurricanes, and ozonated air. Consider these facts about the Caribbean:

- There are at least 28 island nations and more than 7,000 individual islands in the Caribbean, which includes islands off the coasts of South and Central America as well as those in the Leeward and Windward Islands and the major islands of Cuba, Jamaica, Hispaniola (home to Haiti and the Dominican Republic, the Bahamas, and Puerto Rico. Only about only 2% of these islands are inhabited!
- The Caribbean is an area populated by a diverse polyglot of peoples in every combination of race, religion, language, and culture coexisting peacefully, dwelling on islands large and small, some poorly endowed with natural resources, others abundantly. Yet, no other region of the world is so richly varied, peaceful, and non-racial.
- Christopher Columbus was looking for a western route to the Orient, and he carried with him letters of introduction to the Great Khan of China. His mission was to convince the Great Kahn to join forces and reclaim Jerusalem under the Christian Flag.
- Much has been published of Columbus' connections with the Knights Templar. He was married to a daughter of a former Grand Master of the Knights of Christ, a Portuguese order that had emerged after the Templars had been driven underground. It's been noted as significant that Columbus navigated ships whose sails carried the distinctive Red Cross 'patte' of the Templars.
- All of the significant Caribbean islands were first discovered by Knights (and Conquistadors) from Europe. Most people think in terms of the "Crusades" having been conducted in the Holy Land of Jerusalem from the eleventh through the thirteenth centuries. However, the Crusades actually continued throughout the sixteenth century into the New World.
- During the Age of Discovery, the conquistadors were Knights that sailed beyond Europe to the Americas, Oceania, Africa and Asia, claiming territory and opening trade routes. They colonized much of the world for Britain, Spain, the Dutch Republic, and Portugal in the 16th, 17th and 18th centuries.
- Jamaica was the first commercial producer of bananas in the Western Hemisphere.

- The sole tropical rain forest in the national forest system in the U.S. is located in Puerto Rico.
- Haiti, the former French colony of Saint-Domingue on Hispaniola, was the first Caribbean nation to gain independence from European powers in 1804.
- Most of the people of the Caribbean live in sovereign nations, independent of colonial rule.
- The reggae music of Jamaica and the Afro-Caribbean traditions of various other islands are some of the most popular genres of music in the world.
- The production of sugar in the 17th century was the greatest on Nevis, and became vital for trade dollars for the interests in the American colonies and the developing British Empire.
- Jamaica has more churches in a single square mile than any other country in the world for a total of 1,600+.
- Alexander Hamilton was born and spent his childhood in Charlestown, the capital of the island of Nevis.
- Anthony Hilton, the first governor of Nevis, was a buccaneer. Nevis would become a pirates haven in the 17th century.
- Wars were fought, lands were conquered; weapons, cookware, and tools manufactured; and people enslaved, all to gain control over the production of sugar in the face of a burgeoning rise of consumption in Europe. Sugar became worth its weight in gold and the Nevis was the engine of production and growth in the 17th century.

Folklore always adds color to historical accounts and lends inflective hues to the black and white print. Later written accounts are likely to be written with the benefit of hindsight or influenced by the thinking of that later period and the author's gestalt. History (account, tale, or story) is thus written through either through the prism of the time or by the vision of an author(s). The writer of this book is not a visitor to Nevis, but rather a resident and citizen over decades of time with a medical practice of over 6,000 patients, largely from the people of these islands. This editor was also accepted as a 'citizen' of the Boriken Sovereign Peoples of Puerto Rico who struggle for some autonomy and independence.

We are composing this book as a fresh, up-to-date account with new historical evidence brought to light recently. The archaeological evidence from Nevis reflects a great complexity of Caribbean prehistory. The abrupt and historically recent beginning of the human history of the Caribbean, coupled with the brutal modes of occupation, piracy, hurricanes, and desolation among the colonizing forces of the conquistadors has led many scholars to conclude that the Antilles is virtually "historyless". This book examines more carefully this unique history of the early Americas and its attendant effect on the shaping of Caribbean history.

The research in this book relies on such critical materials as articles, books, as well as known folklore published in the literature of this area of the world. In the end, it is discovered that as a result of the popular stories of this area, much of the works and criticism of the history and literature of this region is often jaundiced and myopic. Popular Caribbean history can exert a meager influence on its actual vibrant history, yet the reader can now view the ravages of history and transcend this by reading about this time period in all its suspense and splendor. Respecting prior works but casting a broad prism, not a microscope, on the wonderment of this most unique island, and wonderful people we live with daily, reveals a very different story.

What we wish to convey here is, were it not for *renaissance colonization* of the isles of the Caribbean, the Americas as we know it today would simply not be!

Forewords

By Dr. Jose' V. A. Humphreys MD, MSc IM (Edin), FICPS
Antigua, West Indies

The heights by great men reached and kept were not attained by sudden flight, but they while their companions slept, were toiling upward in the night.
Henry Wadsworth Longfellow (US Poet 1807-1882).

About 20 years ago, I met a brilliant, unassuming gentleman who captivated my attention and plunged me into a world where I dared to dream the impossible dream, and challenge all I ever knew in a concerted effort to become who I am today. My appetite for knowledge and passion to pursue the same grew exponentially. I realized through his excellent mentorship that knowledge was only limited by ones ability or willingness to pursue it. Professor Dr. Charles McWilliams (Doc) is a giant of a man and profound academician.

When Doc asked me to write the foreword for his latest book, my heart fluttered with excitement. It is my esteemed pleasure to pen these lines.

This book gives a unique overview of the history of Nevis; its colonial settlements, its struggles and conquests. The resilience and adaptability of the people cannot be overlooked.

Doc has created another literary masterpiece! Its captivated accounts woo the reader to learn more. What more can I say but how extremely proud I am of Professor Dr. Charles McWilliams, a brilliant physician, scientist, author, inventor and humanitarian, with an incalculable passion for helping others.

Dr. Jose Humphreys is a qualified doctor of medicine. He holds a Masters degree in Internal Medicine from the University of Edinburgh (Edinburgh Medical College) and the Royal College of Physicians of Edinburgh. He is a Fellow of the Inter-American College of Physicians and Surgeons. He is a graduate of the PanAmerican School of Natural Medicine of Nevis.

Rev. Minister Dr. Marwen Saab
Grand Chancellor and Grand Priory of CURAÇAO

This book is a celebration on its self.
My gratitude to our Grand Master Mgrs. Charles Prof. Dr. McWilliams for his beautiful inspiration, utmost and inexhaustible work for this Magnum history book of the Medical Knights in the Caribbean.
This beautiful inspiration arose from the goodness within our Grand Master that projects the history of the Caribbean, especially the beautiful island of Nevis at large about the origin of the Medical Knights as Hospitallers.
This book will inspire the reader to explore the fascinating and almost infinite moments of the past to understand profoundly the unique multicultural people of the present in the Caribbean.
It is our duty to disseminate the teachings of our ancestors, especially the Medical Knights through the Islands of the Caribbean and the whole world.
God bless you Grand Master.

I have know Dr. Charles McWilliam for many years and we share mutual interest especially in the value of Christian Order. He kindly asked me to write few words on the occasion of the publication of this new book on the history of Nevis and the Knight Hospitallers. No much more can be said about Dr. Charles McWilliam and his accomplishment either in the field of medicine, research, teaching and especially his devotion to Monastic medicine which indeed he gave a new dimension. I am just astonished of what he had accomplish so far.

His new book project the history of the original Hospitaller Order of St-John of Jerusalem created in 1048 and its venue in America and the Caribbean area and especially Nevis. As Bailiff and International Grand Master of the Sovereign Order of St-John of Jerusalem- Knights of Malta- the hereditary Order which headquarters is Malta, I may say that we are the guardian of human value today badly needed in our world. Today more than ever we need value, we need courage, we need more honesty, we need to be good with other brothers and give some sense to our life. Teaching is something important, giving some of your time, your life to help and to embrace both medicine and religion is not easy but probably a personal achievement by Dr. McWilliam especially with the rebirth of Monastic Medicine, SMOCH and the history of Hospitaller Knights in America . I guess such men need to be honored but God will not forget and may I say how I am proud to know him and have him as colleague and to share his accomplishment.

Prof. Doctor Serge Jurasunas (M.D.A/M) N.D., M.D. (Hom)
Academician, Pioneer in Natural medicine, Professor of Naturopathic Oncology
Grand Master of the Sovereign Order of St-John of Jerusalem (Malta)
Commander of the Royal and Military Order of St-Brigitte of Sweden
Commander of the Order of the Temple of Jerusalem.

"How does one man manage to accomplish so much? Its obvious it is passionate mission on earth. And we are the beneficiaries. Professor Charles historically colourful writings on Nevis and the wider Caribbean are the latest installment of his prolific ability to capture and share critically important information for future generations to come. Doc Style..!!

Stu Jemesen DNM Ph.D.
Tasmania

CHAPTER 1. A Pre-history of Nevis & the Amerindians

The Caribbean
The Caribbean Sea is filled with numerous, delightful tropical islands, and each country with their own unique culture and history. The region takes its name from that of the Caribs, an indigenous people of the Lesser Antilles and parts of adjacent South America at the time of the Spanish conquest. The Caribbean brought the Western world sugar, chili peppers, Cuban cigars, Pirate tales, rum, barbeque, and calypso. They are of course popular tourist destinations today and many people refer to the *Antilles* when speaking of certain islands in this archipelago (chain of islands) yet no island country has the name 'Caribbean' within its title. Within this large collection of islands are three main groups: the Bahamas, the Greater Antilles and the Lesser Antilles.

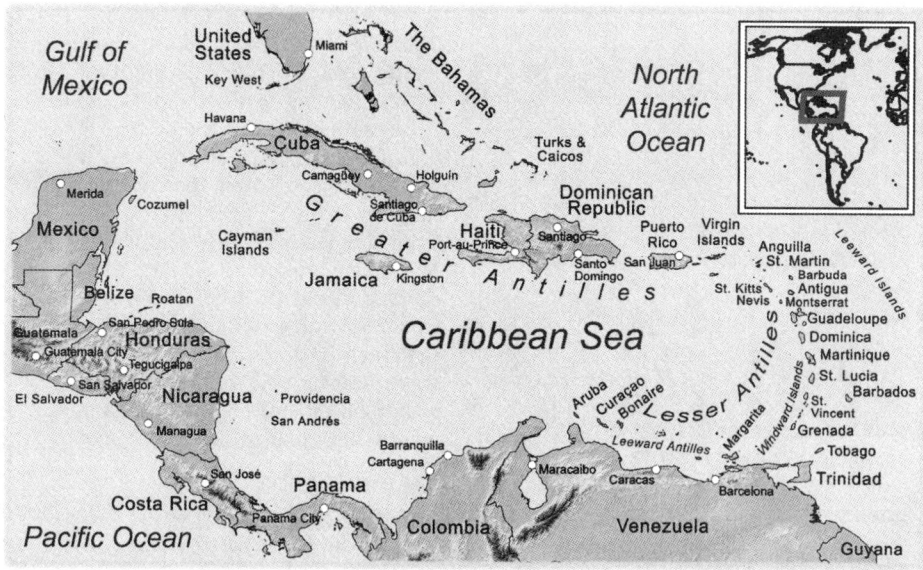

The Bahamas include over 3000 islands and reefs on the north and east side of the Caribbean Sea, beginning just off the coast of Florida. To the south are the islands of the Antilles. The Greater Antilles are the four largest islands in the northwestern portion of the Caribbean Sea. This includes Cuba, Hispaniola (the nations of Haiti and the Dominican Republic), Jamaica and Puerto Rico. The Lesser Antilles include the smaller islands of the Caribbean to the south and east of Puerto Rico with the British and U.S. Virgin Islands, extending to and extends south to Grenada. Trinidad and Tobago, just off the Venezuelan coast, are also included, as is the east-west chain of islands that stretches to Aruba.

The name 'Antilles' refers to a semi-mythical land once called *Antilia*, the Island of Seven Cities, which can be found on many medieval maps. Antillia was a phantom island that was imagined during the 15th-century before the age of exploration, to lie in the Atlantic Ocean, far to the west of Portugal. The term *Antillia* is probably derived from the Portuguese "Ante-Ilha" ("Fore-Island", "Island of the Other", or "Opposite Island"). It may be a reference to the belief that an island lay directly "opposite" from mainland Portugal, consistent with the Seven Cities story. Its size and rectangular shape is a near-mirror image of the Kingdom of Portugal itself. Some suggest the ante-ilha etymology might be older, possibly related in meaning to the "Aprositus" ("the Inaccessible"), the name reported by Ptolemy for one of the *Fortunate Isles*. The geographer Toscanelli, in his famous letter to Columbus, recommended Antillia as likely to be useful to Columbus as a way station before reaching India. When the great explorer reached Hispaniola, he was supposed to have discovered this mysterious island, hence the name of *Antilles* was given to the group. Some geographers, noting that the shape of Puerto Rico resembles the shape of Antilla on early maps, have associated the two islands. Of course, in time, the name Antilla became Antilles, and is still in use today.

Antilla appears on the far left of this 1455 map by Pareto. Spain and Africa are on the right.

Antilla makes its first explicit appearance as a large rectangular island in the 1424 portolan chart of Zuane Pizzigano. Thereafter, it routinely appeared in most nautical charts of the 15th century. After 1492, when the north Atlantic Ocean began to be routinely sailed, and became more accurately mapped, depictions of Antillia gradually disappeared. It nonetheless lent its name to the Spanish Antilles. According to an old Iberian legend, set during the Muslim conquest of Hispania c. 714, seven Christian Visigoth bishops seeking to flee from the Muslim conquerors embarked with their flocks on ships and set sail westwards into the Atlantic Ocean, eventually landing on an island (Antilha) where they founded seven settlements.

Stories of islands in the Atlantic Ocean, legendary and otherwise, have been reported since classical antiquity. Utopian tales of the *Fortunate Islands* (or Isles of the Blest) were sung by poets like Homer and Horace. Plato articulated the legend of Atlantis which has resulted even today in scores of books, speculations, folklore, archaeological dives, and legends. Ancient writers like Plutarch, Strabo, and, more explicitly, Pliny the Elder and Ptolemy, testified to the existence of the Canary Islands off the coast of Africa. The peoples of the Iberian peninsula, who were closest to the real Atlantic islands of the Canaries, Madeira and Azores, and whose seafarers and fishermen may have seen and even visited them, articulated their own tales. Given the tendency of the legends of different seafarers – Greek, Norse, Irish, Arab and Iberian – to cross-fertilize and influence each other, the exact source of some legendary Atlantic islands – such as the mythical islands of Brazil and the Isle of Mam – are impossible to disentangle.

The Caribbean Sea is also known as the *Sea of the Antilles.* The *West Indies* received its name because Christopher Columbus thought he had reached the Pacific islands near Asia (known as the East Indies at the time) when he sailed west from Spain. Of course, he was famously mistaken, though the name has remained.

Caribbean History

History can refer to the academic discipline which uses a *narrative*, theme or story, upon which to examine and analyze a sequence of past events, and objectively determine the patterns of cause and effect that determined them. For Caribbean history, this turns out to be vital – it is a theme or story of this region that is actually a *gestalt* – an organized whole that must be perceived as more than the sum of its parts. This book examines this history that leads to the present times. This book examines more carefully this unique history of the Caribbean, in particular Nevis Island, and its attendant effect on the shaping of the history of not only the island itself, but the Americas and the world at large, which it dramatically did. American history, in fact, was pivotally shaped by the activities on Nevis beginning at the age of exploration.

From a standpoint of world history, the Caribbean poses an abrupt and recent beginning, coupled with the brutal modes of occupation, agriculture, slavery, piracy, hurricanes, and desolation among the colonizing forces beginning with the Vikings and later the Knights or the Christian Military Orders and the Iberian Conquistadors who sailed to the Americas. History (from Greek ἱστορία, historia, meaning "inquiry, knowledge acquired by investigation") as defined "is the study of the past as it is described in written documents." And on this note, we have fortunately new documents, so scholars would argue fewest, upon which to base a thorough study of Caribbean history. However, as this book unfolds, we do have significant history and reports to obtain a most interesting facet and story of the human experience of the Caribbean that one is able to piece together.

Caribbean Beginnings

From the second millennium BC humans made their way along this island chain from South America. The first to do so were a group of hunter-gatherers known to archaeologists as the *Ciboney*. Following, in the early centuries of the Christian era more sophisticated tribes of Neolithic farmers, the Arawak, move gradually north through the islands pushing the Ciboney ahead or out of them. Arawaks altered the shape of their heads by depressing their skulls in childhood with a wooden frame. These islanders were tall and moved gracefully, and they had fine dark eyes and friendly smiles. They were a benign, happy, and pleasure-loving people overall. Their principal foods were vegan - cassava, a starchy root, and maize or corn.

Columbus was charmed by these native islanders upon first contact. Columbus said of them in his report to King Ferdinand and Queen Isabella of Spain, "So lovable, so tractable, so peaceful are these people that I swear to your Majesties that there is not in the world a better nation nor a better land. They love their neighbors as themselves and their discourse is ever sweet and gentle and accompanied by a smile." These were the Arawaks (aka Taínos), a people now virtually extinct in the Caribbean, except for descendants in the Bahamas, Hispaniola, Puerto Rico and Cuba. Arawaks also still inhabit tropical forests in South America, especially north of the Amazon River, in Guyana and Venezuela. Their Island Carib language appears to have been Arawakan like that of their relatives, the Taíno.

From about 1000 AD, a third group, the Caribs, begin to exert the same pressure on the Arawak, expanded their territories by ruthless warfare. The Caribs were described as tall and brown, with long, shiny black hair, which they dressed daily with great care. They only cut their hair short when in mourning. Like the Arawaks, they altered the shape of their heads, but in an opposite manner. In childhood, they placed boards on the forehead and on the back of the head, so that their heads came to have a boxlike look. They scarred their cheeks with deep incisions, which they painted black.

Around their eyes the Caribs inscribed black and white circles, and many perforated their noses and inserted fish bones or pieces of tortoise shell. They made bracelets for their arms and ankles out of the teeth of their dead enemies. Carib boys were taught the early use of the bow and arrow by having their food suspended from a tree out of reach, so that they would have to go hungry until they had learned to shoot it down. The Spaniards, the next group to arrive in the islands, were alarmed and fascinated by them. News of them spread rapidly in Europe, resulting in a misnomer of their behavior – *cannibal*, as the Caribs had a reputation as warriors who raided neighboring islands ruthlessly. Early Europeans claimed that they practiced cannibalism – which they did not.

The Archeological Evidence
The history of the world is effectively the memory of the past experiences of Homo sapiens sapiens, as that experience has been preserved, meagerly in written records like the Sumerian texts, Vedas (sacred scriptures of Hinduism), Tao-te-ching (Taoism book of philosophy), Bahagavad Gita (Indian Hindu epic poem), the Egyptian papyri, the Bible, etc. By "prehistory", historians mean the recovery of knowledge of the past in an area where no or fewest written records exist, or where the writing of a culture is not understood. That status is certainly is the case of Caribbean history. By studying painting, drawings, carvings, pottery, and other artifacts, some information can be recovered even in the absence of a written record. So kindly bear with me, so we can explore briefly the necessary archeological evidence to piece together the pre-history of the Antilles.

Archaeology (or archeology) is the study of human activity through the recovery and analysis of material culture. The archaeological record consists of artifacts, architecture, biofacts or ecofacts, and cultural landscapes. Archaeology can be considered both a social science and a branch of the humanities. The discipline of archaeology is by no means a simple nor a singular study of the past. Due to the wide range of evidence within the archaeological records, from organic to inorganic, many different methods and approaches are taken in order to deal with the wide spectrum of differing evidence. Nevertheless, the study of *pottery* is without doubt one of the most important tasks taken on by any archaeologist. A great wealth of information can be gained from the study of pottery, despite its inanimate state because it is preserved relatively intact, like bones and teeth. Pottery is the craft of making ceramic material into pots or pottery wares using mud. Pottery is to culture what bones are to existence. Archaeologists have often been called 'bone diggers,' and we can add to that they are also 'pottery diggers' for very good reason. It is for this very reason that this book will attempt to explore and explain the multitude of study that archaeologists have applied to pottery to reconstruct Caribbean history.

It is believed from the discovery of archaeological sites in Trinidad and Antigua, and the greater Caribbean islands, although hundreds of thousands of years old, were only first inhabited, perhaps some 6,000 years ago, by a race of hunter-gatherers, now categorized as the *Ortoiroid* people (after the name of the site at Ortoire in Trinidad), who gradually spread through the island chain from South America northwards, to reach as far as Puerto Rico by about 1000 BC.

Alternately, some anthropologists believe people apparently first came first into the Caribbean from the Yucatan peninsula of Mexico first. Archaeological remains dating to around 4000 to 3500 B.C. have been found in Cuba, Haiti, and the Dominican Republic and comparable lithic (stone) artifacts that have been found in Belize. These artifacts, called *Casimiroid*, represent these migrants, hunter-gatherers (nomads) who exploited both the marine resources of the coasts and the wild plants and animals of the land interiors. Thus, these people appeared more adaptable and resourceful. By around 2000 B.C. their descendants had produced stone tools with several distinctive regional variants. They had also arrived in Puerto Rico, and had moved into or at least traveled to the Lesser Antilles. On Nevis, a group of stone vessels and other objects, called the "17th hole cache" for its place of discovery on the Four Seasons Resort property on the west coast of Nevis, is comparable to the Casimiroid stone artifacts of the Greater Antilles, but also is comparable to Archaic material from the Windward Islands also.

So thus we have two sets of earliest archeological evidences of the Caribbean:
1. Casimroid pottery from Mexico; and
2. Ortoiroid pottery, indicating a second migration to the Caribbean islands appeared around 2000 B.C. These people came from the South American mainland and established sites throughout the Lesser Antilles, although not in great numbers. The name "Ortoiroid" comes from Ortoire, a shell midden site in southeast Trinidad.

The rather amorphous lithic assemblages known as *Ortoiroid*, are found as far north as the island of Puerto Rico, with many sites known from the island of Antigua. After 500 B.C. one or more groups of migrants moved north into the

Lesser Antilles. From the areas of the Orinoco drainage and other interior river systems of northeastern South America (Venezuela), they lived in permanent villages and cultivated food plants, a first mark of civilization. Their distinctive ceramics, with either white-on-red painting (known ""wor" ware) or patterned incision are called Saladoid (a unique pottery style), a pre-Columbian indigenous culture of territory in present-day Venezuela and the Caribbean that flourished from 500 BCE to 545 CE. Although these movements probably involved more than one mainland group, and possibly several, within a few centuries after their arrival a relatively homogeneous archaeological manifestation identifiable as *Saladoid* had emerged.

How, when and why the first people arrived in the islands of the Caribbean are questions that cannot be answered. According to legend, the first inhabitants, aboriginals known as the *Ciboney*, were followed in turn by a more highly developed peaceful people called *Arawaks*, who in turn were displaced by a more developed but warlike race called *Caribs* by the time Columbus arrived in the Caribbean is the popular story, greatly over-simplified and historically misleading.

Arawakan, the peaceful and developed people, was their language found among the people of South America living in and between the Orinoco and Amazon river basins, and it was successive groups of Arawakans who, from around 400 BC moved into the islands north of Trinidad next to Venezuela. Whether the first such migration displaced the earlier inhabitants, or the migrants found the islands unoccupied is not known. These were the forerunners of people who, ever since the European discovery of the Caribbean, have been called 'Arawaks'.

The Saladoid people (as they are called after a style of pottery found at Saladero in Venezuela) were more advanced than the earlier Arawakan inhabitants, with a more settled way of life marked by agriculture and the use of pottery. By AD 1000 they had spread through the entire region as far as Cuba, Puerto Rico, and the Bahamas. They had also evolved a far more advanced social organization and way of life, leading in modern times to their being given a new identity as the ' Taíno' people with a distinctive Tainan culture including written symbols and religious practices. They were a peaceful people, as opposed to the war-like Caribs.

Saint Kitts and Nevis
Saint Kitts and Nevis have one of the longest written histories in the Caribbean, both islands being among Spain's and England's first, occupied colonies in the archipelago. Eight days after Columbus' second voyage from Spain, landing first on Guadeloupe, he sailed past Redonda and on November 11th, 1493, he landed on a small island he called *Saint Martin*, which remained its name for twenty to thirty years until it was changed to **Nievis** by Spanish map makers. Saint Martin's Day, also known as the Feast of Saint Martin, is celebrated on November 11th of which Columbus in reverence named the island. Despite being only two miles apart and quite small in land mass size, Saint Kitts and Nevis were widely recognized as being separate entities with distinct identities until they were forcibly united in the late 19th century by the British, and some would insist continues to this day.

The original Latin name of the island of *Nievis* was originally *Qualie*, or Ouilia, thought to be of Taíno (some say Kalinago or Island Carib) origin and means *Land of Beautiful Water*. Nevis proper, it is said, derives its name from the Spanish phrase "Nuestro Señora del las Nieves" -- *Our Lady of the Snows*. Columbus had first settled first upon this island and called it *San Martin* (as he sighted the island of Nevis on that saint's feast day), and the persistent, daily halo of white clouds shrouding the island's central peak suggested a snow cap to the later Spanish sailors and map makers, and thus now its official state name due to them – *Nevis* (locally pronounced nee-vis, *not* nev-is).

People have lived on the small West Indian island of Nevis for only 3,000 years of record. The islands of the Caribbean were settled for over 4,000 years (estimate) before European arrival in 1492. The Eastern Caribbean islands were then dominated by two main cultural groups: the Arawaks and the Caribs (Kalinago or Callinago as they called themselves). Some say, the first settlers to arrive to the islands, almost 3,000 years B.C., were a pre-agricultural, pre-ceramic people, who migrated down the archipelago from Florida, but anthropologists point to the Yucatan (first migration) and Venezuela (second migration) and generally agree upon a southern migration from the Orinoco and Amazon river basins as the predominant influence of early island settlements of substance and record.

Known as *Island Caribs*, the Kalinago are an indigenous people of the Lesser Antilles in the Caribbean and were making bride-capturing raids on Puerto Rico against the Taíno's by the time of Columbus' arrival, Columbus had heard from the Taino - "All the people I have met here," he entered in his diary, "have said that they are greatly afraid of the 'Caniba' or 'Canima'.". Over the two centuries leading up to Christopher Columbus' arrival in the Caribbean archipelago in 1492, the Kalinago mostly displaced the peaceful Taínos by warfare, extermination, and assimilation. The Taíno had settled the island chains earlier in history, migrating from the mainland of South America, but they spoke an unrelated Arawak language and used their own symbols in writing. They lived throughout the Windward Islands, Dominica, Cuba, Puerto Rico and possibly the southern Leeward Islands, Nevis, and even the coast of Florida south of Tampa. These were the forerunners of people who, ever since the European discovery of the Caribbean, have been called 'Arawaks'. The names by which they were known to themselves or others at the time are of course unknown.

These Saladoid, Taíno people (as they are called after a style of pottery found at Saladero in Venezuela) were more advanced than the earlier inhabitants, with a more settled way of life marked by agriculture and the use of pottery. By AD 1000 they had spread through the entire region as far as Cuba, Florida, and the Bahamas. They had also evolved a far more advanced social organization and way of life, leading in modern times to their being given a new identity as the 'Taino' people with a distinctive Tainan culture which is well known in Cuba and Puerto Rico. Today we call them Taínos since thousands of descendants still identify themselves on the isles of Cuba and Puerto Rico. Their identity or bloodline can only be spotted if you have lived a long time in the Caribbean in the Spanish-settled isles. The Taíno bloodline exhibits a calming and peaceful nature to the personality as opposed to the more aggressive Spaniard lineage. Taino is known as the name of the Arawak Indian tribes of the Caribbean which means "kindness" because of their hospitality and living in harmony with nature.

The Arawâks formerly inhabited the whole of the West Indian Islands. Those in the Lesser Antilles were exterminated by the Caribs, before the discovery of America by Columbus. The inhabitants of the larger island perished soon after that event, under the oppression of the Spaniards. The few Arawâks who dwell near the coast of Guiana and whose legends are here given are now the only known representatives of a gentle and once numerous race. [WILLIAM HENRY BRETT, B.D., Missionary in connection with the S. P. G.; Chaplain to the Lord Bishop of Guiana; and Late Rector of the Parish of Holy Trinity, Essiquibo.]

The smoke not only cooked the fish, it kept away flies and animals, and preserved it for storage.

The first tribesmen Columbus encountered were Arawaks, and the Spaniards documented their language and their habits. Arawaks cooked outdoors and one of their favorite methods was to place food on a wooden frame above the fire. It was built of green wood so it would not burn, had four vertical poles to hold up a grid of more green wood cross pieces, and was usually tall enough to prevent the wood and food from incinerating.

The word for this device was *barbacoa* and the *Diccionario de la Lengua Espanola* (2nd Edition) of the *Real Academia Espanola* traces the origin of the word to the Taino dialect of the Arawak Amerindians. The Spanish explorer Gonzalo Fernández De Oviedo y Valdés traveled extensively in the Caribbean and what is now Florida in the 1500s, and he was the first to use the word in print when, in Spain in 1526, he first described the *barbeque* devices.

Having identified the uniqueness of the Taínos settling in the various islands, history records within a century or two, circa 1200 AD, yet another group of Arawakan-speaking peoples who began their Caribbean journeys. By 1493, when Columbus sailed for the first time through the Eastern Caribbean, these *Calina, Kallipina or Kalinago* peoples had already controlled all the Lesser Antilles and were making warring raids as far as Puerto Rico to the west. Columbus became aware of the fear they created among the Taínos of the Greater Antilles as a result of their warlike activities, but unfortunately for the Kalinago (the term generally adopted) and their descendants, completely misinterpreted the tales he was told involving words like 'caniba', 'carima' and 'carib'. So the myth arose that the Taínos had described a tribe called the Caribs who practiced according to the emerging false legend, *cannibalism*. As a result, from 1493 until very recent times the world at large considered a *Carib* a cannibal. In fact, however, there is no evidence they ate human flesh as part of their diet. Further, there never were people in any of the islands who knew themselves or each other as 'Caribs' or 'Arawaks', and nor was there such a clear-cut division between Amerindian inhabitants. Today 'Carib' is accepted as the official name of a group of people living on the island of Dominica and a much larger group in the South America mainland proper. Those who were in the islands during the European contact period are now generally referred to as 'Island Caribs' or Kalinago.

Arawak woman by John Gabriel Stedman.　　Carib family by John Gabriel Stedman 1818.

Let's just say for lack of more documented history, the Caribbean island's earliest inhabitants appeared nomadic, fished and collected wild foods; and probably had historical and hereditary connections with the South American mainland, particularly Venezuela. These people from the Orinco region established small settlements on Nevis and several other islands. Later, around 2,000 years ago, another group of South America Indians colonized the Lesser Antilles, Cuba, and Puerto Rico. Unlike their predecessors, these peaceful people cultivated food crops like manioc and corn, developed language and social customs, and lived in permanent villages, and today we call them Taínos, the most advanced and cultured Amerindians.

During the European explorations of the 1500s Arawak tribes were not native to areas now in the United States, but some Arawak tribes moved into southern Florida during the mid-to-late 1600s. In fact, a barbacoa used by Amerindians in the mid 1580s is recorded in what is today North Carolina. It was done by the European engraver and publisher Theodor de Bry and based on a watercolor by a settler, John White. Similar illustrations were made in the 1560s by the first European artist in North America, Miles Harvey and in 1564 by Jacques le Moyne. The DeSoto National Memorial in Bradenton, FL, the place where the Spanish explorer is believed to have landed in 1539 with 400 soldiers, horses, and 300 hogs, the first to inhabit North America, has a small replica *barbacoa* on display.

The archaeological evidence from Nevis also reflects this great complexity of Caribbean prehistory finding evidence of *Casimiroid* hunter-gatherers and a name thought to be of Taíno origin. Although the broad outlines of the region's chronology are fairly well established, there is considerable variation and uniqueness from island to island which remains to this day. Thus both Casimroid pottery from Mexico; and Ortoiroid pottery from peoples of the South American mainland can be excavated, and only time will tell a more definitive history, unique to each island. The history of recent importance, however, is from the arrivals from the East that established the colonizations of the Americas and today's Caribbean population estimated to be over seven (7) million people:

Anguilla	Dominican Republic	Saint Martin (France)
Antigua and Barbuda	Grenada	Saint Vincent and the Grenadines
Aruba	Guadeloupe	
Bahamas	Haiti	Sint Maarten (Kingdom of the Netherlands)
Barbados	Jamaica	
British Virgin Islands	Martinique	Trinidad and Tobago
Caribbean Netherlands	Montserrat (UK)	Turks and Caicos Islands
Cayman Islands	Puerto Rico	
Cuba	Saint Barthélemy	United States Virgin Islands
Curaçao	Saint Kitts and Nevis	
Dominica	Saint Lucia	

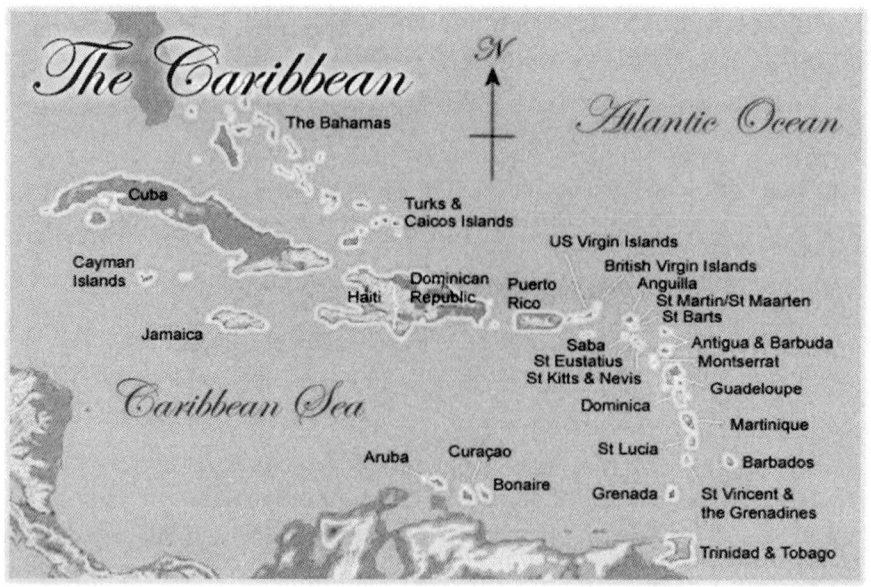

The Saladoid people are among the ancestors of the Taíno, who were the dominant people living in the Greater Antilles when Europeans arrived in 1492 with

Columbus. There is strong continuity in certain symbolic aspects of the Saladoid and Taíno material repertoire, such as the triangular carved figures known as three-pointed stones, trigonolitos, or zemis. There is also continuity in ceramic technology, vessel forms, and other attributes from Saladoid to later ceramic artifacts.

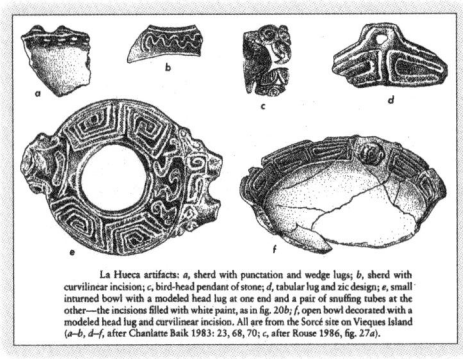

La Hueca artifacts: *a*, sherd with punctation and wedge lugs; *b*, sherd with curvilinear incision; *c*, bird-head pendant of stone; *d*, tabular lug and zic design; *e*, small inturned bowl with a modeled head lug at one end and a pair of snuffing tubes at the other—the incisions filled with white paint, as in fig. 20b; *f*, open bowl decorated with a modeled head lug and curvilinear incision. All are from the Sorcé site on Vieques Island (*a–b, d–f*, after Chanlatte Baik 1983: 23, 68, 70; *c*, after Rouse 1986, fig. 27*a*).

La Heuca Artifacts | Taíno Pottery

La Hueca

Another group or subgroup, adding to this complex picture, which occupied parts of the northern Lesser Antilles and Puerto Rico at the same time as the Saladoid people, may have some bearing on the complexity of the prehistory of Nevis. Its archaeological remains are best known from the site of *La Hueca* on the island of Vieques next to Puerto Rico, one of the most important archaeological areas in the Caribbean. Since 1978, the Center for Archaeological Investigation at the University of Puerto Rico has conducted important excavations there. La Hueca and Sorcé were sites of significant indigenous activity. Cultural material, including clay artifacts, stone and shell tools; weapons and a particularly impressive array of corporal adornments made of a variety of local resources as well as "imported" semi-precious stones, make up a treasure of Vieques' Indian artifacts currently under analysis at the Univeristy of Puerto Rico laboratories.

At La Hueca itself there are none of the distinctive white-on-red painted ceramics characteristic of the Saladoid series, although such pottery can be found on the adjacent site of Sorce. The pottery at *La Hueca* is modeled and incised, and unpainted. Vessels were decorated by fine-line incision in a cross-hatch pattern, perhaps as a way of helping pigments to stick to the pottery after firing in a kiln. The crosshatching was usually laid out in more deeply incised zones, so archaeologists have called this pottery zone-incised crosshatched, or "zic," ware. La Huecan culture is extraordinary in that it contains this pottery exclusively. It also has a remarkable lot of exotic stone artifacts—small pendants of jade, greenstone, or other semiprecious stones depicting raptorial birds holding human heads, as well as many amulets of frogs and other animals. Another site similar to La Hueca, *Punta Candelero*, was found on the island of Puerto Rico across the 7 km ocean passage that separates it from Vieques island.

On Nevis *zic* pottery (Huecan) digs are also found in association with Saladoid pottery just as on the small island of Vieques. The presence of the La Hueca material side by side and with the Saladoid material on these digs raises challenging questions for understanding Caribbean and Nevisian prehistory. It could relate to the interaction between early nomads from the South American mainland and Archaic groups already living in the islands. Saladoid people settled Puerto Rico extensively, occupying the rich river valleys and coastal plains. They also crossed the Mona Passage between Puerto Rico and Hispaniola, establishing settlements in what is now the eastern Dominican Republic. There, for centuries, they lived in contact with the Casimiroid (~4190-2165 BCE) descendants of the first migrants from Central America. The Ortoiroid people were the second wave of human settlers of the Caribbean who began their migration into the Antilles around 2000 BCE. They are believed to have originated in the Orinoco valley in South America, migrating to the Antilles from Trinidad and Tobago to Puerto Rico.

Other Saladoid sites that have been extensively excavated, such as the Golden Rock Site on St. Eustatius and Maisabel on Puerto Rico, which show that Saladoid villages consisted of a few large circular huts over 10 meters in diameter, other auxiliary structures, cemeteries, and a central open plaza. The houses were pole and thatch structures similar to those known ethnographically and historically from lowlands of South America. From island to island, there is no great variability in the size or organization of Saladoid settlements; meaning they probably all represent autonomous communities without hierarchies of political control above the village level. The villages undoubtedly interacted with each other, but they were likely autonomous political entities, particularly in the Leeward Islands.

Between A.D. 500 and 1000 several changes took place throughout the Caribbean. The distinctive Saladoid patterns of ceramic decoration—white-on-red painting and zoned-incised-crosshatched incision—were lost and apparently there was a significant growth in the overall populations. Post-Saladoid settlements were larger and more numerous on most islands. The 18 post-Saladoid sites on Nevis are located at nearly every source of fresh water on the island, meaning our island had quite a few hundred to thousands of inhabitants. This pattern also holds true on the islands around Nevis, especially those in the arc of volcanic islands that includes Saba, St. Eustatius, St. Christopher, and Montserrat.

A more dramatic change apparently took place around 600 A.D. The ceramics of a horticultural people dramatically expanded their area of settlement in the Greater Antilles, moving into the highlands of Puerto Rico, and into the Dominican Republic and Haiti, Jamaica, and Cuba which became the main population bases for the Taíno people. They also began colonizing the Bahamas archipelago and even Florida's southern west coast. There is archaeological evidence for the emergence of complex societies in the Caribbean shortly after this, including the construction of ball courts or bateys, leveled and stone-lined plazas where dances and ceremonies were held and a 'ball game' was played. This indicates a peace-loving peoples of which today the vestige of Taíno people and their culture are appreciated with state parks in their honor in Puerto Rico and Cuba.

Reproduction of a typical Taino village, Cuba

With expansion into the Greater Antilles west of Puerto Rico, the population apparently grew rapidly and continued to grow until the time of the European invasions and colonizations. Complex, multi-tiered political entities emerged, consisting of dozens of villages allied under the leadership of an individual chieftain or lineage. Archaeological evidence of village layout, funerary goods, and symbols of personal status and rank show the increasing social differentiation between commoner and elite segments of society. These are the groups that scholars have designated today as the *Taíno Indians*. Recently, National Geographic published a study confirming that current Puerto Ricans have a significant amount of Taíno DNA.

When Columbus arrived in the Caribbean they encountered complex chiefdoms consisting of as many as one hundred villages and tens of thousands of people. Villages with thousands of inhabitants fed themselves through intensive forms of successful agriculture, an indigenous form of medicine, and some organized division of labor. The Taíno people of Hispaniola farmed manioc, maize, pineapples, potatoes, beans and squash; engaged in inter-island trade; and lived in villages presided over by Caciques (chiefs). Although they were able to mount considerable resistance to the Spanish, mobilizing armed forces of tens of thousands, ultimately disease and severe economic disruption led to the collapse of Taíno society in the wake of the germs, guns and ammo of the Spaniards.

When complex Taíno societies were flourishing in the Greater Antilles, the organization of post-Saladoid societies on Nevis and in the Leeward Islands remained relatively unchanged. Between A.D. 600 and the time of the latest prehistoric sites on Nevis, artifact assemblages show continuity up to the most recent sites. There is some evidence for trade or other interactions with the Greater Antilles on Saba and Nevis. Finally, ceramics similar to the late prehistoric Chicoid ceramics of the Greater Antilles have been found on both islands. The latest radiocarbon dates from Nevis are from the 12th century AD, meaning at this point they vanished before Columbus arrived in 1493 (November 11th).

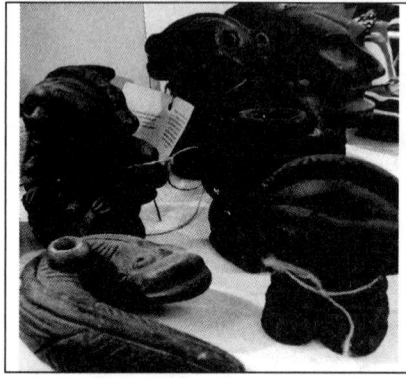

The Taino had rich artistic traditions in ceramics, carved wood and textiles. They believed the supernatural world was peopled with zemis (spirit allies) who might be enlisted for various purposes by the privileged people who understood their secrets. The zemi was the all-important contact of the spiritual world. For this reason, the Taino fashioned zemi images on their pottery, ornaments, and furnishings.

Columbus Arrives
From the earliest European encounters, the Leeward Islands were scarcely inhabited. On his second voyage Columbus found people living on the larger islands between his landfalls on Dominica and Puerto Rico. His fleet anchored off the leeward coast of Nevis in November 1493, but made no record of any inhabitants, apparently not staying long. The difficulty of encompassing ethnicity, identity, colonialist hegemony and the construction of their villages is to determine who these people were. From their earliest experiences in the Caribbean, Europeans discussed the existence of "Caribs," warlike and threatening inhabitants of the Lesser Antilles. Clearly this emergent view simplified what was almost certainly a complex cultural geography of ethnic diversity into a perception of indigenous people as "warlike Caribs" and "peaceful Arawaks" (the Taíno). The portrayal of the Caribs as hostile, and even cannibalistic, historians now generally agree that it was politically and economically motivated, for cannibals could legally be enslaved, justifiably by the conquistadors, even against the wishes of the Queen of Spain, Isabella, and even Columbus himself.

Thus, the unique identity of the Island Caribs has received considerable attention from scholars. Historians argue that there cannot be a single or definitive identity of Island Caribs since there is compelling evidence that both the Greater and Lesser Antilles were characterized by a great deal of ethnic and linguistic diversity at the time of European colonizations and conquests, and in fact can better be seen as a cultural mosaic rather than a region controlled on one side by the named groups – the Arawaks or Tainos and Caribs. The shifting situations were chaotic and dangerous in the late 16th and early 17th centuries, with groups of indigenous people moving among island to island, with maroons, mariners, soldiers, pirates and buccaneers roaming the seas, while the indigenous peoples were attempting to withstand the European assault on their archipelagos. Thus, from historical citations it is hard to say whether the people European observers saw on Nevis were temporary nomads or permanent inhabitants, but most likely the former, as Nevis did not pose ready, abudndant made sources of food.

The Taíno, we believe, was a beautiful culture from all historical accounts. They were aware of a Divine presence they called *Yocahu*, and to worship and give thanks was a major part of their lives. They had a social order that provided the leaders and guidelines by which they all lived. They hunted, fished, cultivated crops and ate the fruits provided by nature. They were clever and ingenious and had everything they needed to survive. They had beautiful ceremonies that were held at various times - birth, death, marriage, harvest, naming and coming of age, to name a few. They had special reverence for the Earth Mother (Atabey) and had respect for all creatures knowing that all living things are interconnected. There was little need for clothing due to the tropic heat, but upon reaching puberty both males and females would wear a small woven loincloths to cover the privates. Puberty was also the time at which they were considered old enough to be married. The population estimates for the Taíno people across the Caribbean at the height of their culture are as high as 8,000,000, nearly greater than the Caribbean as it is today. That was in 1492....

The story that the Europeans and Conquistadors gathered and developed concerning a Carib "invasion" of the Lesser Antilles is not supported by the archaeological evidence, which shows neither a marked late prehistoric or historic change that could be interpreted as a "Carib horizon," nor the arrival of a new population. But archaeological remains such as only pottery are often poor indicators of cultural identity, and so evidence does not tell us who the earliest historic inhabitants of Nevis and the Leewards perceived themselves to actually be, other than a peace loving peoples, scratching out a living with tubers, berries, herbs, fodder, clams and fish.

The Black Carib Wars
Freedom, Survival, and the Making of the Garifuna
CHRISTOPHER TAYLOR

Throughout the 17th century there was bitter warfare between Europeans and the indigenous people of the Lesser Antilles. In a complex political environment involving British, French, Dutch, Spanish invaders and Pirates, indigenous people sought to build the most advantageous alliances possible, often playing one European power against the others. Demographically overwhelmed, however, they had ceased to be a military power and stake their claim in the islands early on. Like the Indians to the North, they were to become a conquered people. In time, they would band together with escaped slaves and live with a marooned people, high in the island mountains.

The Taíno have been considered extinct as a distinct population since the 16th century, even though many people in the Caribbean have Taíno ancestry. A 2003 mitochondrial DNA study under the Taino genome project determined that 62% of people in Puerto Rico have direct-line maternal ancestry to Taíno or Arawakan ancestors!

References
- Antillia. From Wikipedia, the free encyclopedia. https://en.wikipedia.org/wiki/Antillia
- Dyde. Brian. Out of Crowded Vagueness: A History of the Islands of St. Kitts, Nevis And Anguilla. Interlink Publishing Group. 2006.
- Higginson, Thomas Wentworth. Tales of the Enchanted Islands of the Atlantic. 1898
- Kwabena, Roi. About the Caribbean. 1986. (A self-published guide)
- Vilar, Miguel. Genographic Project DNA Results Reveal Details of Puerto Rican History. July 25, 2014. VOICES-Ideas and Insight From Explorers.
- Saint Kitts and Nevis. From Wikipedia, the free encyclopedia
- Wentworth-Higginson, Thomas. Tales of the Enchanted Islands of the Atlantic, Gyldernscroft, Marlow, England.1899.
- Wilson, Samuel Meredith. The Prehistory of Nevis, a Small Island in the Lesser Antilles. Yale University Publications in Anthropology, 2010.

CHAPTER 2. The Arrival of the Conquistadors from Christendom

Christopher Columbus - Knight of Christ - Caribbean Arrival - 1492

On This Day: Columbus Lands in Caribbean • October 12, 1492

His historic voyage ignited the age of exploration and cross-Atlantic expansion by European settlers.
Shortly after 2 a.m. on the morning of Oct. 12, 1492, a crewmember aboard the Spanish ship *Pinta* spotted land. They had achieved their goal: to find the continent west of the Atlantic Ocean. Columbus named the new land San Salvador and claimed it for Spain. He continued sailing among what are now considered to be the Bahamas, and visited Hispaniola (now Haiti and the Dominican Republic) and Cuba, the latter of which he mistakenly took to be the mainland of Asia.
Columbus discovered Nevis on his second voyage in 1493, November 11th.

Columbus, The Apocalypse, the Knights, and the New Jerusalem
Most people think in terms of the "Crusades" having been conducted in the Holy Land of Jerusalem from the eleventh through the thirteenth centuries. However, the Crusades actually continued throughout the sixteenth century including an *American Crusade* led by Christopher Columbus who was at least related, if not one himself, a Knight of one of the religious, military Orders and carried on his own crusade to what is now known as American and Caribbean Soils.

Crusade from *croisade* (1570s), in a figurative sense became of "campaign against a public evil" and that included not only in the view of Christendom the expelling of the Moors but now the conquest of the black plague with ravaged Europe in the years 1346–1353. The death rate was as high as 60% in all of Europe, greater than all wars. The Spanish sought new medicines and spices to prevent recurrences and other pestilences including typhoid fever, malaria, yellow fever and tuberculosis.

The Christian military orders were monastic but with a military purpose originally established as Catholic religious societies during the medieval Crusades for protection of Christians against violent persecution by the Islamic conquests (623- to date) in the Holy Land, the silk routes, the Iberian Peninsula, as well as by Baltic Eastern Europe. Most members, often titled Knights, were laymen cooperating with the clergy, sometimes even taking religious vows such as poverty, chastity, and obedience; according to monastic ideals. As such, it was in the military orders that the Medieval concept of *chivalry* reached its apogee and under *Just war* theory, they became a formidable military discipline with Christian virtues. Prominent examples include the Knights Hospitaller of St. John, the Knights

Templar of Christendom, the Teutonic Knights in the Baltics, the Knights of Lazarus of Jerusalem, the Knights Santiago of Spain, and the Knights of Christ of Portugal. Their important roles in history are often not portrayed as they should.

In the middle of the seventeenth century, apart from such leading powers as Spain, Portugal, England, France, and the Netherlands, the crusader Orders of the Knights Templar, Santiago, the Knights of Christ, and St. John not only joined in the global race for colonies, but were even there long before. Much has been made of Columbus's connections with the Knights Templar. He was married to a daughter of a former Grand Master of the Knights of Christ, a Portuguese order that had emerged from King Denys after the Templars had been driven underground. It's been noted as significant that Columbus navigated ships whose sails carried the distinctive *red cross pattée* of the Templars. Well documented, in 1651 the Order of St. John of Jerusalem acquired the islands of St. Christopher, St Martin, St Bartholomew, and St Croix, and in spite of many obstacles, and made them profitable. The history of these events not only sheds light on the international, indeed worldwide, networking of these Orders but also on the ambitions and need of a new 'globalized' age after the Black Plague and conflicts had ravaged much of Christendom. This book presents the long overdue short story of this, until now only scarcely researched, yet a colorful episode in the long and chequered history of the Antilles and the Americas. [Also see *Hospitallers of the Americas* book]

The original historic Knights Templar were a famous, Christian military order, originally the Order of the *Poor Fellow Soldiers of Christ and of the Temple of Solomon,* that officially existed from the 12th to 14th centuries to provide warriors and protectors in the Crusades, the legacy of which would extend to the Crusades to the Americas, an amazing revelation. Authors Wallace-Murphy, Hopkins, and several others, have advanced that the Templars ventured across the North Atlantic, following a similar path as the Vikings, and traded with the Native American populations of northeastern Canada and America (Rhode Island).

It is well known that the crusades of the Levant had a direct impact on the later, newer crusades and the discoveries of Americas. The Fourth Crusade which resulted in the sacking of Constantinople (1204) resulting in the fatal weakening of the Byzantine Empire became pivotal. With the eventual fall of Byzantium to the Ottoman Turks (1453) and the collapse of the Mongol Empire to the East, Europe's trading access to China and the Far East was lost with the disintegration of the all important *Silk Road* of commerce. These Templars were famous, highly influential, and wealthy in the late Middle Ages. They became the envy of those in need of money, and the Order was brutally disbanded by King Philip IV of France and Pope Clement, who took action against the Templars in order to avoid repaying their own financial debts by plundering their riches and burning many members at the stake. They accused them of heresy, ordered the arrest of all Templars within his realm in 1307 and had many of them imprisoned. The Grand Master, Jaques de Molay, was burned at the stake after his arrest on *Friday the 13th* under the inquisitors infamous torture schemes. The dramatic end of the Templars combined with the treacherous Albigensian Crusade against fellow Christians in southern France (1244) led to many conflicts, stories and legends developing about them over the following centuries.

Since their papal dissolution following accusations of heresy in the 14th Century, the Knights Templar have been associated with some of the most mysterious and intriguing legends in history. A military order which sprang out of the famous Order of the Temple of Jerusalem, would set sail to Spain, Portugal, the Americas, and even Madagascar. As Portugal was the first country in Europe where the Templars settled (in 1128) after its inquisition in France, it had been one of the last to preserve a remnant of that order under King Denys and was reformed as the *Knights of Christ* whose cross can be found the ships of the conquistadors that settled colonies in Cuba, Hispaniola, Florida and other Caribbean islands.

The Templars had been granted lands in Scotland 100 years before by the great King David I. They were given about 100 properties from which they collected rents. Despite the trial of the Templars in Paris these lands were not seized by the Scottish government of Robert the Bruce. Scotland's link with the Templar mysteries is through Rosslyn Chapel in the village of *Roslin* near Edinburgh. Even though the chapel was built over a century after the formal suppression of the Order, many believe that the ornate carvings in the chapel hold the key to the secrets of the Templars, and that Rosslyn Chapel may hold some of the Templars' fabled treasure, said variously to include the Ark of the Covenant, the Holy Grail, lost teachings of Jesus or even the mummified head of Christ.

In 1398, almost one hundred years before Columbus arrived in the New World, the Scottish prince Henry Sinclair, Earl of Orkney, had already sailed to what is today Nova Scotia, where his presence was recorded by Mi'kmaq Indian legends about

Glooskap, according to author William F. Mann. This was the same Prince Henry Sinclair who offered refuge to the Knights Templar fleeing the persecution unleashed against the Order by French king *Philip the Fair* early in the fourteenth century. With evidence from archaeological sites, indigenous legend, and sacred geometry handed down by the Templar Order to the Freemasons, author William F. Mann has now rediscovered the site of the settlement established by Sinclair and his Templar followers in the New World. Details of these findings have been filmed by the History Channel and can be found on youtube.com.

The real history of the Caribbean is indeed peculiar. It does not evolve gradually, organically, and naturally out of a remote mythological and archaeological past, but begins abruptly with the landing on the Bahamas in 1492 by Christopher Columbus. Except for him, the following European adventures called the *Age of Exploration* in the Caribbean was primarily motivated by economic considerations which led to plundering, piracy, and slavery; and secondarily to those seeking religious freedom. Yet, all this activity would change the face of humanity *forever.*

Cristoforo Colombo of Genoa, whose uncle was a Knight of Christ, had access to the Vatican library which it is believed housed maps of the new world which were passed onto him. The true motivation for Columbus's voyages to the Americas is very different from what is commonly assumed in the popular storybooks. Recent historical studies shows that he was inspired to find a western route to the Orient not only to obtain vast sums of gold and spices for the Spanish Crown but primarily to help form a new crusade to take Jerusalem from the Muslims once and for all—a goal that sustained him until the day he died. Rather than an avaricious glory hunter, Columbus was a man of deep passion, patience, and religious conviction. He followed the Queen's instructions to be patient and passionate with any contacts of the native Americans and islanders. He was neither a greedy imperialist nor a quixotic adventurer, as he has lately been ill-depicted, but rather a man driven by an abiding religious passion to reclaim the Holy Land. That *is* the story of the American Crusade which would pivotally involve our blessed Nevis.

Just two years after his birth, the sacking of Constantinople by the Ottomans barred Christians from the trade route to the East and the pilgrimage route to Jerusalem. The Portuguese were occupying the trade routes down the coast of Africa, so a new route had to be found. The failure of multiple crusades to keep Jerusalem in Christian possession; the crises and deaths of the Black Plague; the impending reformation and schisms in the Church; and the constant plights with the Moors occupying Spain provided, *Cristoforo Colombo*, an Italian, had the impetus to set sail for the New World. Columbus's belief that he was destined to play a decisive role in the retaking of Jerusalem - a force that drove him to petition the Spanish monarchy to fund his journey, even in the face of ridicule about his idea of sailing west to reach the East. In the drama of the four voyages, bringing the trials of ocean navigation vividly to life and showing Columbus for the master navigator that he was, was a man of legacy. Judging Columbus from a contemporary, historical perspective rather than from the values and stories of his own time, his motivations and his accomplishments offers this more realistic perspective. In what would follow from his identification and sailing route to the Americas, more knights would follow, with Ponce de Leon establishing Florida and the legend of the Fountain of Youth; DeSoto a Knight of Santiago, would colonize Florida and go on to explore Georgia, Alabama to the Mississippi river; Menendez de Aviles, also a Santiago Knight, would colonize America's oldest city, St. Augustine; Ovando of the Knights would colonize the Dominican Republic and establish the first hospital of the Americas; Hernán Cortés would exploit Mexico; Vasco da Gama (1460 –1524), a Portuguese explorer and Knight of Christ, was the first European to reach India by sea, linking Europe and Asia for the first time by ocean route. These are the stories and sagas of the Knights of the Military Orders of Christendom after conquering and reclaiming Europe from Muslim rule.

Columbus set forth on his voyage with the intention to deliver letters to the Grand Khan from Queen Isabella and King Ferdinand, asking the Grand Khan to convert to Christianity since many of his council of Mongolians had already become Christians. He wanted then to convince the Grand Khan to give aid to an attack on Jerusalem, and to set up a trading post to trade for the gold and spices he had read about in Marco Polo's travels. The stated purpose of that trade was to obtain enough gold to finance a crusade to retake Jerusalem from the Muslims as a prerequisite for rebuilding the temple for Christ's return before the end of the world. That vision led to the founding of St. Christopher and Nevis.

Because events of the fourteenth and fifteenth centuries had heightened expectations of an imminent, decisive, confrontation between good and evil, stemming from apocalyptic beliefs of those times, the approaching end of the world and return of the Savior, his project was seen as eminently worthwhile by his contemporaries as well as by the enormously wealthy King and Queen of Spain. Columbus did not intend to supplant the native peoples with Europeans or steal their lands; but later, faced with rebellions, he capitulated to the settlers' demands, and Isabella eventually approved land grants to them. He surely did not intend to commit genocide, of which he has been accused. He wanted to enlist the Grand Khan and his people on his side, not to conquer anyone but the muslims. Nor was his intention to obtain slaves; there was no possibility of enslaving the people in the civilized, luxurious world of the Grand Khan. When he first met the native people of the islands, he thought that they were attractive and intelligent and because they had no false pretense, he thought they were already natural Christians. "I believe that in the world there are no better people or a better land. They love their neighbors as themselves, and they have the sweetest speech in the world; and [they are] gentle and are always laughing" (Diario, p. 281).

There is no question about the terrible devastation and depopulation that was visited upon the native people of the Caribbean due to disease and hardships brought by other conquistadors who followed. Likewise, the conquistadors suffered from tropical yellow fever, malaria, cholera, and having contracted yaws and taking back syphilis to Europe which would again change its landscape as did the plague. Atrocities often occurred on the islands when Columbus was not even there or was on board ship when his men disobeyed his explicit orders and went on rampages of which he continually complained to the Queen. Columbus repeatedly asked for friars who would learn the native language and instruct the natives in culture, Christianity, and language. Columbus was neither an angel nor a felon; he was a man of his time, and his grandiose ideas and goals were formed in that context of his ideals. An extraordinarily talented navigator and seaman, he was ill prepared to manage an unruly and mixed colony and was often disgusted by the behavior of his men. Deeply devout, he fervently believed in his Christian, crusader mission that would later be called the *American Crusade*.

The Role of the Printing Press upon the Americas
Just prior to the launch of Columbus' adventures, Johannes Gutenberg invented the printing press with moveable wooden or metal letters completed by 1440. This method of printing can be credited not only for a revolution in the production of books, but also for fostering rapid development in the sciences, arts and religion through the bulk transmission of texts, maps, and illustrations which had previously only be scantily available and harbored by the monasteries. The Gutenberg press with its movable type printing brought the Bibles to the New World in many languages. In the early 1600's, the Geneva Bible became the first Bible to be taken across the Atlantic to America.

In 1517 Martin Luther posted his "theses" at Wittenberg, a move that would challenge the Catholic Church's hegemony over faith and fables. Luther also translated the Bible from Latin into German so that those who could read their own language might see how far the pope and his followers had strayed from biblical teachings. To accompany the text, he commissioned paintings and a series of double woodcuts from Lucas Cranach that juxtaposed the pope's actions with those of Jesus. One of the woodcuts showed Jesus kneeling as he washed the feet of a leper while the other showed the resplendent pope sitting on his throne while supplicants kneeled and kissed his feet. Clearly, the people of the times knew something was wrong with that picture.

Luther's translation of the Bible into the vernacular meant that the people themselves could interpret its meaning and no longer had to depend on their Latin priests for interpretations. Effectively, the printing press was a moment in time of great change then, as is the internet has done today. This led ultimately to the *reformation* and the fragmentation of the church into numerous denominations. The apocalyptic scenario, which has always been an integral theme in Christianity, receded into the background as it became more prominent and transformed into a number of the Protestant churches. With the Hugenots and Puritans they made the earliest transatlantic crossings after Columbus and became firmly planted in the northern American landscape. Leaving what they saw as a corrupt world, the Puritans had crossed the ocean to establish a godly city, a "new Jerusalem" in 'New' England. For the Puritans, Jerusalem became a metaphor, a symbol—a crusade to capture the ancient holy city was no longer necessary; they would build a new and better one for Christ's return in a Western, protestant tradition.

Columbus's vision was transformed as his torch was transferred to American shores to the north being settled mainly by Protestants while to the south remained mainly Catholic, creating a great divide. America was to be the place of redemption, and the "city on a hill" would be a light unto the nations. This idea persisted even as it underwent secularization when Enlightenment ideas began to take hold of some of the influential thinkers in the new republic. The Enlightenment fostered the idea that human reason, rather than religion, was the source of authority, especially after the episode of the Salem witchcraft trials. The belief that the new American nation has a divinely supported manifest destiny, sometimes referred to as *American exceptionalism*, not only legitimated its expansion westward and the suppression of the native peoples, but also ordained its global mission to spread the American way of life and its values around the world, sometimes at the point of a sword or gun. Despite the separation of church and state, mandated by the founding fathers, many Americans believed the United States was a God-supported, if not explicitly a Christian nation. Since 1954, our Pledge of Allegiance has reminded us of "one nation under God"; presidents and jurists take their oaths on the Bible, and until recently, witnesses had to swear they were telling *the whole truth and nothing but the truth* "so help me God." Even our money proclaims "In God We Trust."

The discovery of America by Columbus gave the western nations vast opportunities for conquest, trade, and colonization, but the two great powers of Spain and England, were foremost in this revolution. Although both nations had a similar background of Christian western culture, their systems of colonization were rooted in very different religious and political philosophies, and that the state of their cultural and religious practices in those two countries varied according to their development and its rulers.

A striking characteristic of the Spanish Americas are the numerous expeditions undertaken during the colonial period aimed at enlarging the knowledge of natural resources by the friars. Historians seldom appreciate the fact that one of the motives for Columbus's voyages was the Spanish need to secure the medicinal spices and oriental drugs so as to avoid dependence on the Venetians for items of high importance in the preservation of the food and health of the Spanish armies. The conquistadors and their writers described the New World not only as the sources of gold and precious stones, but also as the land of the marvelous Balsam to cure wounds, the cathartic Jalap root and the exotic Coca leaf. These three were well known to the Indians as also were the anthelmintic properties of Chenopodia, and the anti-dysenteric action of Ipecac. Circa 1650, the physician *Sebastiano Bado* declared that Peruvian (quinine) bark had proved more precious to mankind than all the gold and silver that the Spaniards had obtained from South America, and the world confirmed his opinion. Spanish medicine due to Islamic influence during its occupation, had become dramatically more superior to the rest of Christendom, especially in terms of surgical care.

Until Columbus, the only beans known in the Old World were soybeans and some uncommon species. Other types of beans widely used today—shell, string, kidney, lima, and pea beans—were cultivated by indigenous peoples of the Americas. Such products as tobacco, corn, cassava, potato, tomato, and most species of beans were unknown in Europe before the voyages of Columbus. As the early explorers encountered these exotic items in the Americas, they brought them to Europe and Africa, where they eventually revolutionized eating habits worldwide to this day.

The Portuguese brought crystal sugar and the Spaniards introduced chocolate to Europe where they quickly became exotic luxuries. In 1657 a London store began selling chocolate and started a lasting trend. What is known in the U.S. today as corn is actually maize, or was sometimes called Indian corn. In England, "corn" meant wheat, while in Scotland and Ireland it referred to oats. Indians cultivated several varieties of true corn—white, yellow, red, blue, sweet corn, popcorn, and corn to make corn meal. Corn as a food is actually a mixture of several types of wild grasses. From its origins among the Inca of the Andes Mountains, potato cultivation spread through wide areas of the Americas, where it was often adopted a staple crop. The Spanish introduced it to Europe but the English first began to grow potatoes on a large scale. English settlers brought the potato with them to North America after 1600, thus reintroducing it to the New World. In Europe, the potato became a staple in many areas. Failure of the Irish potato crop in the mid-1800s prompted a massive migration to the Americas.

Suffice it to say, the religious, military Orders of the Knights 'discovered' and settled the Americas. They were both military and hospitaller Orders. On every ship, Columbus brought physicians and friars, as did DeSoto, Ovando, and Cortez. From St. Augustine, Tampa, Hispaniola, Mexico and Cuba, they were settled by the Knights of Santiago who had established earlier five hospitals in Spain. The mandate of the Council of Nicea (325 AD) held that hospitals should be established in every colony and that was part of the mission of the conquistadors as well as the pursuit of medical spices and herbs. Thus, the title of my book: THE HOSPITALLERS OF THE AMERICAS should be a must read for those of sincere interest in Caribbean and world medical history.

Nevis and Columbus
On November 11th, 1493, Columbus, with 17 ships and over 1,000 men, anchored overnight on an island he called San Martin which would one day be called *Nevis*. This is certain by the earliest map drawn by Columbus' cartographer Juan de la Cosa in 1500. The route followed by his fleet from Guadeloupe, where it first landed on his second voyage had remained for a few days to replenish water supplies, went to the north-west, passing Montserrat, the uninhabited islet of Redonda, and then landing on San Martin (Nevis), all bear the names given to them by Columbus. Having sailed past Redonda, the fleet anchored overnight on the next island, to which it is fairly certain Columbus gave the name *San Martin*. This then became the name by which Nevis was known to the Spanish for the next twenty to thirty years. In the early 1520s the Spanish carried out a complete survey of the region, and as a result many of the

original names on maps were changed or given to other islands. After about 1525 the names of all the islands were very much as they are today.

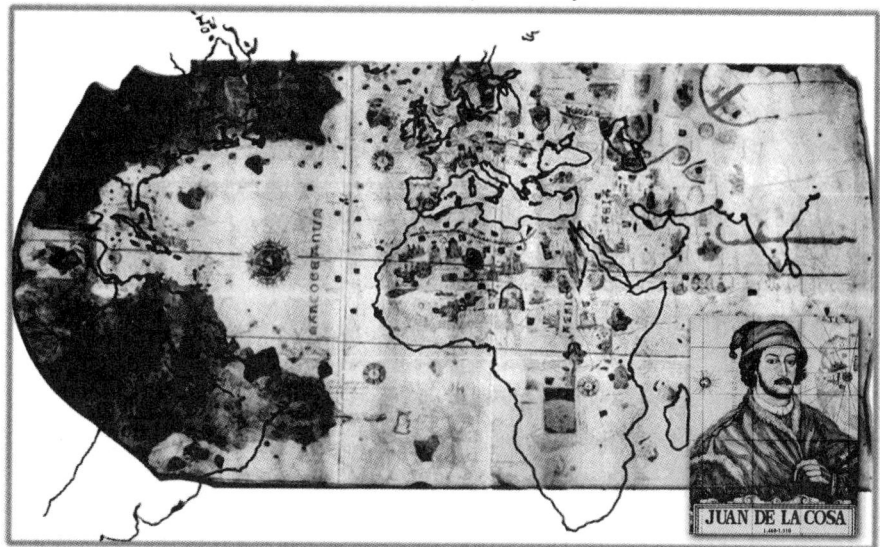

The map or chart of Juan de la Cosa is a *mappa mundi* painted on parchment, 93 cm high and 183 cm wide. This map is the earliest undisputed representation of the Americas.

There is a theory that Spanish seafarers, seeing the island under the morning haze, thought it looked as if it were covered by snow, and therefore called it "La isla de los nieves" ("the island of snows"). The famous Sefardi poet, Daniel Levy de Barrios, still refers to that idea in a poem he wrote two generations later, "Nieves" ("Snows").

References

- Burns, Sir Alan. History of the West Indies , London, 1954.
- Cameron. Thomas W. M. M.A., D.Sc. The early history of the Caribee Islands (1493 to 1530). Scottish Geographical Magazine. Vol. 50, No. 1, 1934.
- Delaney, Carol. Columbus and the Quest for Jerusalem: How Religion Drove the Voyages that Led to America. Free Press, 2012.
- Dyde, Brian. Out of Crowded Vagueness: A History of the Islands of St. Kitts, Nevis And Anguilla. Interlink Publishing Group, 2006.
- Freller, Thomas; Zammit, William. Knights, buccaneers, and sugar cane : the Caribbean colonies of the Order of Malta. Malta: Midsea Books, 2015.
- Kongstam, Angus. Piracy the Complete History. Osprey, 2008.
- Konstam, Angus. Pirates: Predators of the Seas. Skyhorse Publishing, 2007.

CHAPTER 3. The First British Settlement in the Nevis

A waggish observer in the 17th century West Indies once wrote that when new colonies were established, the first thing the Spanish did was to build a church, the Dutch to build a fort, and the English to build a tavern. From what we know of the character of some early settlers in Nevis, there was more than a little truth to this allegation. (Swords, Ships and Sugar: A History of Nevis to 1900. Vince Hubbard, a friend of the author)

Colonialism by definition is the establishment of a colony in one territory by a political power from another state, and the subsequent maintenance, expansion, and exploitation of that colony by the occupier. The term is also used to describe a set of unequal relationships between the colonial power and the colony and often between the colonists and the indigenous peoples or slaves and this dramatically is exemplified by the *Colonization of the Americas*.

The European colonial period was the era from the 16th century to the mid-20th century when several European powers claimed lands and established colonies in Asia, Africa, and the Americas. At first, the countries followed a policy of exploitive mercantilism, designed to strengthen the home economy at the expense of rivals and the lands so occupied. The colonies were usually allowed to trade only with the mother country which in turn fostered piracy and lawlessness. By the mid-19th century, however, the powerful British Empire gave up mercantilism and trade restrictions, and introduced the principle of free trade, with few restrictions or tariffs. Colonies were then granted various forms of independence.

The first non-Spanish settlement attempt in the Caribbean occurred on Saint Kitts, when French Huguenot refugees from the fishing town of Dieppe, Northern France, established a harbor on the island's north coast, which they also named Dieppe, in 1538. However, only months after the founding, the settlement was raided by the Spanish and all the inhabitants were deported. The remains of one of the buildings is now the basement for the Main house in the Golden Lemon Hotel (left), once owned by a gracious patient of the author, Arthur Lehman.

Though the Spaniards claimed Nevis and St. Christopher as part of their empire early on with Columbus' landing, they never settled their claim on the two islands having assumed correctly they offered no gold nor spices. There are also no recorded reports of Amerindians living on either St Christopher or Nevis before the early years of the seventeenth century. The privateer Sir Francis Drake found them uninhabited in 1585 when he landed his sick and fumigated his ships, and no sighting of 'Indians' was recorded by the first wood-cutters in the 1590s. However, there is evidence that Caribs had moved onto both islands soon after this, evidently as a roving band settlement. Thus, Nevis was one island that was not 'stolen' by the Conquistadors, it was genuinely 'discovered.' By the increasing use of the islands being made by the sailors and pirates as replenishment and repair bases, most of the islands either, like Nevis and St. Christopher, supported a small Carib community or, like Anguilla, were occasionally visited by roving bands of hostile Caribs.

In Nevis in 1603, Caribs are reported as having sold tobacco to Bartholomew Gilbert, the master of a ship called the *Elizabeth* which had landed for three weeks to cut the coveted wood from the lignum vitae tree. According to Oviedo, the early historian and writer, the Spanish word *tabaco* comes unchanged from a Haitian Taíno word for the *pipe* used for smoking it. Gilbert sailed on to Virginia to seek out survivors of the Roanoke settlement in what is now North Carolina. Four years later, when Captain John Smith, on his way to establish the colony of Virginia, spent five days on Nevis, the Caribs were reported to be wary and had no dealings with him or his men. How many there were it is impossible to know. In 1607 Smith documented the many hot springs in Nevis, whose waters had remarkable curative abilities against skin ailments, joint pains, and poor health. That site would later become the famous 'Bath Hotel,' the first Spa of the Caribbean. This was the voyage of English explorers took which founded Jamestown, the first permanent English settlement in the New World.

Of special interest to Nevisians is the route the Jamestown colonists of Smith took to Virginia. In the ships of the early 17th century it was easier to set sail to the islands between the mainland continents of what is now North and South America and then travel north via the Gulf Stream currents to the Atlantic seaboard. The islands, except for the Greater Antilles – Hispaniola (today Haiti and the Dominican Republic), Cuba, Puerto Rico and Jamaica – had no European settlers at this time. It was typically a seven-week sail from the Strait of Dover (off the east coast of England) to the West Indies. After the Canary Islands, their first landfall for supplies and water was the isle of Martinique on February 21st, 1607. Then next they went ashore on Guadeloupe where they found the spring near the active volcano too hot for comfortable bathing. "Our Admiral Captaine Newport, caused a piece of pork to be put in it, which boiled it so, in the space of half an hour, as no fire could mend it".

They sailed past Montserrat to Nevis, the same route Columbus took in 1493, where Captain Newport ordered six days ashore to rest and cure his men of scurvy and other ills which were inevitable with sea voyages at that time. Exact dates are not given but four days out from Nevis on April 7, 1607, the fleet had passed San Juan, Puerto Rico thus we can guess that they were on Nevis the last three days of March and the first three days of April. Their account leads us to believe that they anchored off Gallows Bay, Nevis as they developed skin rashes due to the manchineel trees that grow there even today. The tree John Smith described was the red mangrove, but the mangrove does not produce a skin irritation. However manchineel trees still grow at Gallows Bay and horrible rashes develop when rain or dew hits the manchineel and falls on the skin. Their account tells of bathing in hot and cold springs, apparently the Bath House Stream, to relieve the discomfort of the skin rash. No mention again is made of any encounters with the indigenous people who inhabited Nevis at that time.

After six days in Nevis, they sailed past St. Eustatius and Saba and then west to the Virgin Islands. They describe an excellent harbor there, probably Road Town, Tortola where they complained of the lack of fresh water. By the time they got to the island of Mona between Puerto Rico and Santo Domingo, the water they had taken on board in Nevis had begun to smell so bad no one was able to drink it and so they happily filled their casks with fresh water once again.

St. Christopher
On another arrival of an English ship in 1622 was a man who was on his way home after having been on an unsuccessful expedition to Guyana which had left England two years earlier. When Thomas Warner stepped ashore on St. Christopher, nearly 130 years after Columbus, he thought it would be a very good place for planting of tobacco. Warner's return to England was made in order to obtain official sanction for his settlement of St. Christopher and Nevis. Thomas Warner returned as Governor in 1626 with three ships, provisions, and more than 100 new settlers. The third ship had about 60 slaves and no record of where they came from. In October 1627, another ship, the *Hopewell*, arrived with a provision of arms, ammunition, Warner's wife and several women. Also on board, the first group of white laborers from Ireland. Among them, a ship's captain *Anthony Hilton* who started a small tobacco farm on a remote side of the island. He took his product to London and found a ready market and returned with a man named Thomas Littleton accompanied with more than 100 settlers. Returning to start a plantation in Barbuda, it turned out unsuitable for planting tobacco. On July 22, 1628, Hilton and his men landed on Nevis near Charlestown. Warner in the meantime had established an 'autocratic' rule on St. Christopher, and in time, many dissatisfied settlers left for Nevis. Thus, Nevis was destined to become a settled British isle.

In 1625, a French captain, Pierre Belain d'Esnambuc, arrived on the island. He had left France hoping to establish an island colony after hearing about the success of the English on Saint Christopher, but his fleet was destroyed in a clash with the Spanish navy, leaving him with only his flagship. Warner took pity on the French settlers and allowed them to settle on the island as well, thus making Saint Christopher the site of the first permanent French colony (St. Christophe) in the Caribbean as well. French settlers lodged themselves again in the town of Dieppe after the previous Hugenots failed to stay in the previous century. Gov. Warner also willingly accepted the French, it is said, in an attempt to out-populate the local Carib (Kalinago) Indians, of whom he was growing suspicious of their activities and behavior.

As the European population on Saint Christopher continued to increase, Kalinago Chief *Ouboutou Tegremante* grew hostile to the foreigners. Given the proximity of this early European settlement to the petroglyphs of the Wingfield and Stonefort River, an affront to Kalinago spiritual sensitivity may have been a cause of contention. Warner was accompanied by Master John Featly, an Anglican minister, who had hopes of good relations between the colonists and the indigenous indians, and might have wanted to see their conversion to Christianity. Plans to oust the European intruders, whose numbers were rapidly growing, were soon in the making, however by the Kalinago (island Caribs).

In 1626, a secret raid Tegremante plotted would ambush the European settlements. The plan was revealed to the Europeans, however, by an Arawak woman named *Barbe*. She had only recently been brought to St Christopher as a slave-wife after a raid on an Arawak island. Barbe despised the Kalinago and had fallen in love with Warner, and thus told him of the planned ambush. The Europeans acted by attacking the Kalinago first. Large numbers of Caribs from Dominica and other neighboring islands were said to have been summonsed to St. Christopher to help get rid of the settlers. According to Du Tertre (1667, *Histoire Generale des Antilles*, I:6), between 100 and 120 Caribs were killed in their beds that night, with only the most beautiful Carib women spared death to serve as slaves. At a site now called *Bloody Point*, in Trinity Palmetto Point Parish, Saint Kitts, which housed the island's main Kalinago settlement, over 2,000 Kalinago men were reported to have been massacred. Having thus rid themselves of the local Caribs, the French and English subsequently divided the island between them and set about fortifying the island against the expected invasion of Caribs from other islands. In the ensuing battle, three to four thousand Caribs allegedly took up arms against the Europeans. Du Tertre gives no precise information on the number of Caribs killed, but mentions that the fallen Amerindians on the beach were piled high into a mound. The English and French suffered at least 100 casualties (Du Tertre 1667 I:6). It is said that the blood of the Caribs ran down Bloody River for three days. This is why the area was named *Bloody Point*.

After the *Kalinago Genocide* of 1626, the island was formally partitioned between the English and the French by treaty, with the French gaining the ends, Capisterre in the north and Basseterre in the south, and the English gaining the center of the island. The 1629 English colonization was led by George Donne. Both powers then proceeded to colonize neighboring islands from their bases. The English settled Nevis (1628), Antigua (1632), Montserrat (1632); and later Anguilla (1650) and Tortola (1672). The French colonized Martinique (1635), the Guadeloupe archipelago (1635), St Martin (1648), St Barths (1648), and Saint Croix (1650).

Basseterre, today's capital, was founded on Saint Kitts in 1627 by Pierre Belain d'Esnambuc. Saint Christopher suffered heavily from a Spanish raid in 1629, from which most all of the island's inhabitants fled as the Spaniards pillaged. Later in the same year they also attacked the isle of Tortuga (Hispaniola) where many of the settlers sought refuge also from Nevis. They returned to St. Christopher shortly after, however, and developed a series of fortifications along the Caribbean coast.

The island soon became a center of production of tobacco. The English planters grew prosperous. However, when the colony of Virginia of the Americas began to dominate world tobacco production and profits started declining, the island switched to producing sugar cane, starting in 1640. To provide the large amounts of labor needed for the industry, African slaves started to be imported in large numbers in St. Christopher and Nevis. The slaves had very harsh living conditions, and thousands perished either en route from Africa or working the fields.

Nevis

The early history of Nevis was less tumultuous than in St. Christopher. The island governor, Sir Thomas Warner, acting in the title of the *Earl of Carlisle*, gave permission to Anthony Hilton in 1625 to settle Nevis and appointed him its lieutenant governor. An earl is a member of the nobility. The title is Anglo-Saxon in origin, and means "chieftain", particularly a chieftain set to rule a territory in a king's stead. Earl of Carlisle is a title that has been created three times in the *Peerage of England*, the first creation came in 1322. The second creation came in 1622 when James Hay, 1st Viscount Doncaster, was made Earl of Carlisle. He was a great favorite of James I. He was knighted and taken into favor by James VI of Scotland, brought into England in 1603, treated as a "prime favourite" and made a *gentleman of the bedchamber*.

It appears that Charles I made an arrangement with the Earl of Carlisle (family name Hay) concerning proprietorship of certain Caribbean Islands including Barbados. On 30 August 1620, James 6th of Scotland - James I of England asserted sovereignty over Nevis by giving a Royal Patent for colonization to the Earl of Carlisle. However, actual European settlement did not happen until 1628 when Anthony Hilton moved from nearby Saint Kitts following a murder plot against him and destruction of his plantation by island Caribs.

According to "An Armourial for Westmoreland and Lonsdale" printed for the *Cumberland and Westmoreland (England) Antiquarian and Archaeological Society*, the Hiltons of Hilton (village) are "traditionally descended from the Barons Hylton of Hylton Castle", in North East England. During the Civil War in England, it would appear that many of the Hiltons took the side of the Royalists, and many still remained loyal to the catholic religion. In the court records of Appleby in Westmoreland, England in 1667 it was recorded that "the jurors found on their oathes that the following Roman Catholics have not attended the Parish Church (Anglican) or Chapel within 12 months contrary to the Statutes. They are ordered to go before some magistrate and give security for their appearance of the next sessions to be held at Appleby (held each quarter), or a warrant will issue to take them into custody". The Maryland colony in America had been set up as a refuge for Catholics at this time and any of the above could have chosen to migrate to the Americas as well. With members of the *Hylton of Hylton Castle* family already well established in the Caribbean - Nevis & St. Christopher, Virginia, and New England by then, to the younger members of the Hiltons, the Americas could well have been an opportunity not to be missed. Thus the tone for religious tolerance in Nevis was established by its first governor and budding buccaneer, Anthony Hilton.

The original number of settlers of Nevis was augmented by people coming from the island of Barbuda where they had been raided time and again by the Caribs, and from St. Christopher, prompting them to move to peaceful Nevis away from Warner's autocratic rule. In 1628, the original plantation of Anthony Hilton on the island of St. Christopher was destroyed by Carib Indians and then moved to Nevis. Some of the settlers, in addition to their attempt to gain a livelihood through planting, turned to buccaneering which led to repeated attacks by the Spanish and the destruction of the first plantations in 1629. At this point, Nevis was becoming a refuge for pirates for the next 100+ years.

Buccaneers were essentially pirates of the Caribbean Sea who challenged Spanish hegemony in the region. By attacking and looting Spanish ships and sacking coastal settlements during the 17th and 18th centuries, constant war and conflicts ensued. Sanctioned from London (the Queen), buccaneering became a low-budget mercenary war against England's rival - Spain. So, the English crown licensed buccaneers with *letters of marque*, legalizing their operations in return for a share of their profits. Before long, however, they became full-fledged pirates and a threat to non-Spanish settlements as well, and the target of the *anti-piracy crusades*. It is now at this juncture of history we turn to murky waters, as the Caribbean now develops into the "The Wild, Wild West(ern Europe)".

The term 'buccaneer' derives from the Caribbean Arawak word *buccan*, a wooden frame on which Tainos and Caribs slowly roasted or smoked barbeque meats. Also believed to be derived the French word *boucane* and hence the name boucanier for French hunters who used such frames to smoke meat from feral cattle and pigs on Hispaniola (now Haiti and the Dominican Republic). English colonists anglicised the word *boucanier* to buccaneer.

The Spaniards considered the English in St. Christopher and Nevis as trespassers, heretics, and pirates. Thus, when Spanish Admiral *Fadrique de Toledo* appeared in Nevis (7th Sept. 1629) with 30 armed vessels, the English indentured servants, being badly treated by their masters, deserted to the enemy and Nevis had to surrender. Anthony Hilton slipped away and left for the island of Tortuga and there would become a buccaneer before the infamous pirate Captain Morgan.

The Spanish left abruptly and the settlers moved back, and Nevis quickly grew very profitable from tobacco trading, and was able to secure prime investments from England. It was able to evade much of the conflict and devastation that nearby islands suffered, and its riches were so great it was later nicknamed "Queen of the Caribees." In 1640, Nevis, like St Christopher, began to change over to sugar cane planting and production and its wealth continued to grow. By 1660, it was officially the most profitable colony in the English crown per capita. Its gross profits were great as well, as they surpassed that of all 13 American colonies combined despite being thousands of times smaller in land mass. Nevis' riches however, made it a target for pirates and other European nations.

The Puritan rebellion in England, and troubles in Barbados with the jews, sent many exiled loyalists to the West Indies, and Nevis acquired a group of prominent and affluent English and Jewish families who became successful plantation owners. The existence of healthy mineral springs (still extant) made Nevis, by the 18th century, "a center of West Indian social life, rivaling in pomp and circumstances at Bath and even London itself." Jews moved into Nevis as sugar merchants, and some settled as planters, as early as the 1650s. The heavy export tax in Barbados as well as the limitations and disabilities imposed on the Jews at various levels of life yielded a movement of Barbadian Jews taking up settlement in Nevis. Nevis thus became attractive due to its peacefulness, affluence, and religious tolerance.

As a result, Nevis was actually considered an overpopulated island in the 17th century (according to one account). In 1640 the combined population of St. Kitts and Nevis reached 20,000. Nevis settlers attempted settlements in Antigua, Montserrat, St. Lucia, and Marie Galante, but ferocious attacks by Carib Indians coupled with French attacks and the ultimate occupation of St. Lucia and Marie Galante by the French made the desired island sites more than unsettled. During the 17th century the French, based on Saint Kitts, launched many attacks also on Nevis, sometimes assisted by the Island Caribs, who in 1667 sent a large fleet of canoes along in support. Letters and other records from the era indicate that the English on Nevis hated and feared the Amerindians. In 1674 and 1683 they participated in attacks on Carib villages in Dominica and St. Vincent, in spite of a lack of official approval from The Crown for the attacks.

On Nevis, the English built Fort Charles and a series of smaller fortifications to aid in defending the island against Carib attacks. Fort Charles repeatedly also came under attack by various European powers also, including the Dutch, the Spanish and the French, but only the French would end up taking the fort. In 1706, the entire island was overrun by forces under Pierre Le Moyne d'Iberville. During this action, Fort Charles was outflanked and taken from the landward entrance. By 1854, all forts on Nevis were abandoned. Currently the Fort Charles site is largely overgrown; there remains an old wall, a cistern, a powder magazine, and several cannons. Toward the end of the century, in 1680, the first of a series of disasters visited the island in the form of a devastating earthquake.

During the century that followed, there was one violent occurrence after another: hurricanes, warfare, starvation, and epidemical disease contributed to the erosion of Nevis' early prosperity. During the same period, St. Kitts was transformed into one of the most successful of Britain's Caribbean sugar colonies. Despite this reversal of fortunes, Nevis island continued to administer itself apart from St. Christopher.

In 1690, another massive earthquake and tsunami destroyed the city of Jamestown, then the capital of Nevis on the northern point east of the airport. So much damage was done that the city was completely buried in ash, abandoned and remains to this day. It is reputed that the whole city sank into the sea, but since then, the land has moved over at least 100 yards to the west. That means that anything left of Jamestown would now be underground or underwater. The island capital was moved south to the town of Charlestown where it remains to this day, and the island's successful sugar and slave trade quickly returned.

This concludes the highlights of the beginning of the settlement of Nevis from the 17th century. With sugar production as its main economic activity, Nevis would enter the 18th century as a slave, plantation society, wealthy and productive. The island, under the Governorship of Anthony Hilton, we know now to be have become a buccaneer, operating also out of Tortuga, naturally attracted privateers to Nevis, however, the written records are sparse. As Anthony Hilton appears to be quite a chequered character, it would only make sense to allow the privateers to operate out of Nevis, providing a private mercenary force that would protect the island during such hostile times, especially with Carib Indians roaming the islands. Thus, Nevis did not suffer the same amount of turmoil as St. Christopher and as its small land mass appeared less attractive to colonizing European monarchies. We also see that religious tolerance was an early premise of Nevis' settlement as well as the tolerance for buccaneers. More evidence will unfold on the Chapter – Pirates of Nevis.

References

- Burns, Sir Alan. History of the West Indies , London, 1954.
- Colonialism. From Wikipedia, the free encyclopedia
  https://en.wikipedia.org/wiki/Colonialism
- Du Tertre, Jean Baptiste, 1667: Histoire Generale des Antilles... 2 vols. Paris: Jolly.
- Dyde, Brian. Out of Crowded Vagueness: A History of the Islands of St. Kitts, Nevis And Anguilla. Interlink Publishing Group, 2006.
- European colonization of the Americas. From Wikipedia, the free encyclopedia.
  https://en.wikipedia.org/wiki/European_colonization_of_the_Americas
- Hamber and Greenwood (1985). Emancipation to Emigration.
- Hillman, Richard .S. & D'Agostino, Thomas, J. (2003). Understanding the Contemporary Caribbean. Jamaica: Ian Randle Publishers.
- Hubbard, Vince. Swords, Ships and Sugar: A History of Nevis to 1900. Premiere Editions Intl. 1996.
- Konstam, Angus. The Great Expedition, Sir Francis Drake on the Spanish Main 1585-86. Osprey Publishing. 2011.
- Lamberton, E. W. "The Hiltons of Hylton Castle" complete family pedigee of the Hylton Castle family from 1172-1769 published by Family Heritage International, Dreamlane Limited.
- Mohammed, J. (2007). CAPE Caribbean Studies: An Interdisciplinary Approach. Malaysia: Macmillan Publishers Limited. Chapter 4

CHAPTER 4. The Knights of St. John Colonize the Americas

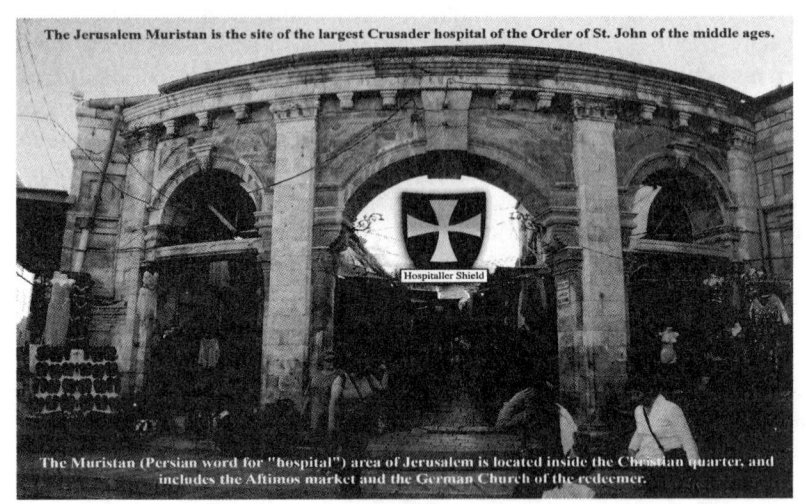

The Jerusalem Muristan is the site of the largest Crusader hospital of the Order of St. John of the middle ages.

The Muristan (Persian word for "hospital") area of Jerusalem is located inside the Christian quarter, and includes the Aftimos market and the German Church of the redeemer.

The Knights of St. John, also known generally as 'Hospitallers', is a religious order founded in Jerusalem (c. 1049) before the First Crusade in 1099, dedicated mainly to caring for the sick and to the defense of Christendom (today known as the territory of *Europe*). Their descendants today are recognized as the various orders of St John — the Sovereign Military Order of Malta; the Johanniter orders in Germany, in the Netherlands and Sweden, and their associate bodies in Finland, Switzerland, Hungary and France; and in Britain, the Most Venerable Order of the Hospital of St John of Jerusalem; in the United States as the Sovereign Orthodox Order of the Knights Hospitaller; Sovereign Order of Saint John of Jerusalem (SOSJ) - the International Grand Priory of Malta, also known as 'the Maltese Langue of The SOSJ, The Hereditary Order'; and various sundry fraternal organizations.

There have come to be known, three great historic periods in the lengthy, centuries old History of the Orders of St. John:
1. Ancient, from the beginnings of Christendom, to the Hospitals in the Holy Lands, to the expulsion by the Muslims in 1187 A.D.
2. Medieval, from the occupations of first Cyprus, then Rhodes, and then Malta until their expulsion by Napoleon in 1798; and
3. Contemporary, mainly groups of Hospitallers of different langues (tongues), having taken residence in Italy, Russia, Germany, England, and other parts of Europe and the Americas.

From its very beginnings, the Order was founded by the pilgrims of laity. Their hospital established in Jerusalem before the crusades from the 11th century and first adopted the policy of receiving all needy patients, Mohammedans and Jews, as well as Christians. Christian monasticism, as it has been written, was the creation of masters of religion who in the third century had withdrawn from the world to lead a spiritual life in the Egyptian desert like the Essenes, but the idea came to be widened to include those who lived in a way which combined 'withdrawal' with the active work of pastoral care or charity, which is why the word 'religious' is often used to describe those who share the belief that men or women can only grow spiritually if they are disentangled from earthly cares but do not necessarily divorce themselves entirely from their earthly chores. Pope Paschal II confirmed on February 15, 1113 through the bull "Pie postulatio voluntatis" the hospital community as a religious order, and he took on the protectorate of the hospital and confirmed the acquisitions and donations of the order in Europe and Asia.

Although historically of a Catholic origin, the Order seems to have always had a separate mandate from the direct ties to the Roman Church, described by some as autonomous *privileges*, if not *supraconfessional*. The character and aims of the Order inevitably altered once it obtained effective sovereign power in the Levant. I am convinced, that the conception of charity as worship of God for man, which represents the essential aim of the Order, was the motivating force which preserved the Order until today through the heavy storms of its history, its many divisions, victories and defeats, contrary to other religious orders of chivalry. The Order of St. John was the first religious Order which made medical hospitality its main task and has been called the eldest, as for centuries it was the only regular relief organization of the occident who no doubt fostered the formation of the contemporary Red Cross. Rightfully it deserves the honor of being the oldest hospital order of the world.

The Hospitallers and the Knights Templar became the most formidable military orders in the Holy Land. Frederick Barbarossa, the Holy Roman Emperor, pledged his protection to the Knights of St. John in a charter of privileges granted in 1185. In 1248 Pope Innocent IV (1243-54) approved a standard military dress for the Hospitallers to be worn during battle. Instead of a closed cape over their armor (which restricted their movements), they wore a red surcoat with a white cross emblazoned on it. Many of the more substantial Christian fortifications in the Holy Land were built by the Templars and the Hospitallers. At the height of the Kingdom of Jerusalem, the Hospitallers held seven great forts and 140 other estates in the area. The two largest of these, their bases of power in the Kingdom and in the Principality of Antioch, were the *Krak des Chevaliers* and *Margat* in Syria. The property of the Order was divided into priories, subdivided into bailiwicks, which in turn were divided into commanderies. Pope Clement V maliciously dissolved the Hospitallers' rival order, the Knights Templar, in 1312 with a series of papal bulls, including the *Ad providam* bull that turned over much of their property to the rival Hospitallers.

After the fall of the Kingdom of Jerusalem in 1291 (the city of Jerusalem had fallen in 1187), the Knights were confined to the County of Tripoli and when Acre was captured in 1291, the order sought refuge in the Kingdom of Cyprus. Finding themselves becoming enmeshed in Cypriot politics, their Master, Guillaume de Villaret, created a plan of acquiring their own temporal domain, selecting Rhodes to be their new home, then part of the Byzantine empire. On Rhodes the Hospitallers, by then also referred to as the Knights of Rhodes, were forced to become a more militarized force, fighting especially against the Barbary pirates. They withstood two invasions in the 15th century, one by the Sultan of Egypt in 1444 and another by the Ottoman *Sultan Mehmed the Conqueror* in 1480 who, after capturing Constantinople and defeating the Byzantine Empire in 1453, made the Knights a priority target. In 1522, an entirely new sort of force arrived: 400 ships under the command of Sultan *Suleiman the Magnificent* delivered 100,000 men to the island (200,000 in other sources). Against this force the Knights, under Grand Master Philippe Villiers de L'Isle-Adam, had about 7,000 men-at-arms and their fortifications. The siege lasted six months, at the end of which the surviving defeated Hospitallers were allowed to withdraw to Sicily. Despite the defeat, both Christians and Muslims seem to have regarded the conduct of Villiers de L'Isle-Adam as extremely valiant, and the Grand Master was proclaimed a Defender of the Faith by Pope Adrian VI.

The Order Waxes

After seven years of moving from place to place in Europe, the knights gained fixed quarters in 1530 when Charles I of Spain, as King of Sicily, gave them the islands of Malta, Gozo and the North African port of Tripoli in perpetual fiefdom in exchange for an annual fee of a single Maltese falcon (the Tribute of the Maltese Falcon), which they were to send on All Souls' Day to the King's representative, the Viceroy of Sicily. The Hospitallers continued their actions against the Muslims and especially the Barbary pirates. Although they had only a few ships (which never lost a battle) they quickly drew the ire of the Ottomans, who were unhappy to see the order resettled. In 1565 Suleiman sent an invasion force of about 40,000 men to besiege Malta, the 700 knights and 8,000 soldiers and expel them from Malta and gain a new base from which to possibly launch another assault on Europe.

The Barbary pirates, sometimes called Barbary corsairs or Ottoman corsairs, were pirates and privateers who operated from North Africa, based primarily in the ports of Salé, Rabat, Algiers, Tunis, and Tripoli. This area was known in Europe as the Barbary Coast, a term derived from the name of its Berber inhabitants. The main purpose of their attacks was to capture Christian slaves for the Ottoman slave trade as well as the general Arabic market in North Africa and the Middle East. Corsairs captured thousands of ships and repeatedly raided coastal towns. As a result, residents abandoned their former villages of long stretches of coast in Spain and Italy. The raids were such a problem coastal settlements were seldom inhabited until the 19th century. From the 16th to 19th century, corsairs captured an estimated 800,000 to 1.25 million people as slaves.

In 1565 when the Ottoman Empire tried to invade the island of Malta, then held and governed by the Knights Hospitaller. Six months later, on 8 September, *The Great Siege of Malta*, one of the most decisive military actions of the world's naval history, ended and was the last action in which a force of Knights of St. John won a decisive military victory. When the Ottomans departed defeated, the Hospitallers had but 600 men able to bear arms. In 1607, the Grand Master of the Hospitallers was granted the status of Reichsfürst (Prince of the Holy Roman Empire), was awarded ecclesiastic equality with cardinals, and the unique hybrid post *His Most Eminent Highness*, reflecting both qualities qualifying him as a true Prince of the Church.

Suleiman controlled the greatest fighting force in the world at that time. Before him lay an armada of 200 ships ready to sail, an army of 40,000 troops on board. He planned to wipe the barren rock of Malta and the Knights of St John from the map. These knights had been living by raiding and disrupting his Ottoman shipping routes. The Sultan, however, did not expect undue trouble from the pitiful Knights by exacting his revenge. A mere 700 knights stood in his way. Scenes of heroism and horror abounded in the terrible days that followed. The once-proud Ottoman force scrambled in disarray for its ships, pursued across the island, cut down and picked off at every step. Thousands died and the waters of St Paul's Bay ran red. Of the 40,000 troops that had set sail in the spring from Constantinople, only some ten thousand made it home. Behind them they had left a scene of utter devastation and Ottoman defeat.

Almost the entire garrison commanded by *Jean Parisot de Valette* - after whom the city of Valletta is named - had perished. Now, after 112 days of siege, the exhausted handful of survivors limped through the blitzed wreckage of their lines. Malta was saved, for Europe and Christianity. The Knights of St John had won. The news of the Turkish defeat and withdrawal and the victory of the Knights of St. John, soon spread all over Europe and brought them fame and riches. The Knights Hospitaller would now be known as the Knights of Malta.

The Order Wanes
Following the Siege and the subsequent victory at the great naval Battle of Lepanto which swept the power of the Turks from the Mediterranean (1571), the Order went through a long period of depression. The Knights great achievements as the shield of Christendom were behind it. The Order beautified and enriched the island of Malta and developed its domains into a stable sovereign State, but its services as a fighting Order, as well as all the other Orders, were of less and less importance in the overall picture of European events. From this time on, the military Orders became more chivalric, honorific, and fraternal. The character of

the Order of St. John during this period, in keeping with the times, became increasingly more aristocratic. Its wealth, partly secured from contributions throughout Christendom and partly through trade, was enormous. The great palaces, churches, chapels, Auberges, the Great Library (founded in 1650) and the School of Medicine and Surgery (established in 1680), even the magnificent fortifications themselves were visible signs of the change in the character of the Order and of Europe, from a military role to the increasing luxury in the private lives of its members, which would seal its fate. On 1798, Napoleon invaded Malta, the second Siege of Malta, and dismantled the Order of Malta and its power of governance.

The days of glory of the old Order were not quite ended, however. In the middle of the 17th Century in a spurt of energy some new Caribbean islands were briefly added to the possessions of the Order. The Hospitaller colonization of the Americas occurred during a 14-year period in which the Knights of St. John possessed four Caribbean islands: **Saint Christopher**, Saint Martin, Saint Barthélemy, and Saint Croix. The Knights' presence in the Caribbean grew out of their order's close relationship with the French nobility and the presence of many members in the Americas as French administrators.

The Knights Head to the Islands
Saint Christopher had suffered heavily from a Spanish raid in 1629, from which nearly all of the island's inhabitants fled as the Spaniards pillaged in their usual fashion. The inhabitants returned shortly thereafter, however, and developed a series of fortifications along the Caribbean coast. The treaty between France and Britain was the provision made that St Christopher and S. Christophe - as the two settlements had now become known – would remain neutral in the event of England and France going to war, unless expressly directed otherwise by their sovereigns. Necessary as this may have seemed when the treaty was signed on 13th May, it represented little more than wishful thinking. There was never to be any love lost between the English people of St Christopher and the French of St. Christophe, and once each had a flourishing economy, neither side would waste any time before joining in any conflict taking place between their mother countries as time would tell.

Phillippe de Longvilliers de Poincy, founder of the Hospitaller colonies, began his career fighting the Turks in the Mediterranean and participated in the Sieges of the Isle of Ré and La Rochelle in 1627. In between, he served under Razilly in Acadia, commanding a fort. Poincy first went to Saint Christopher in 1639 as the appointed governor under the *Compagnie des Îles de l'Amérique*. On 12 January 1638 de Poincy set sail for the Caribbean on board *La Petite Europe*. On February 20 he took up his commission as Lieutenant Governor of the Isles of America and Captain general of the French at St Christophe. He arrived wearing the regalia of the Knights of St John and soon dispensed with the authority of the French king, declaring "The people of St Christophe will have no other Governor than De Poincy and will take no orders from the King of France."

King Louis XIII of France soon after made Poincy his Lieutenant-General for the entire Caribbean. Poincy began to invest heavily in building projects on the island of St. Chritophe. He extended French rule to other islands, establishing the first European settlement on Saint-Barthélemy in 1648, and founding a settlement on St. Croix in 1650-51. He sent an additional 300 men to reinforce and take over the small French settlement on Saint-Martin. There he negotiated the *Treaty of Concordia*, determining the boundary between the French and Dutch settlements that remains in place to this day.

	French Dutch Border • St. Maarten/St. Martin
	After the Spaniards abandoned the island in the mid-17th century, it was quickly populated by French and Dutch colonists. Rather than risk a military conflict, they negotiated the *Treaty of Concordia* in 1648. France now owns 20 square miles in the north while Netherland has the lower 13 square miles. This obelisk at the border celebrates the 300th anniversary of their agreement.

He instructed one of his followers, the Huguenot *Levasseur* with sixty buccaneers to drive out the English from Tortuga. Levasseur was successful and on 6 November 1640 a treaty was drawn up between de Poincy and Levasseur which allowed religious tolerations and trade between the two islands. Nevertheless, Poincy also established himself as the absolute ruler of the islands, resisting the authority of the failing company. He became embroiled in conflict with the Capuchin missionaries, who disapproved of the governor's consorting with local English, Dutch, and Huguenot Protestants, and of his refusal to liberate the children of baptized slaves. Poincy also provoked resentment at his harsh treatment of subjects who resisted him. He also drew disfavor from the Order of Malta when he used income from the Order's estates in Europe to pay for his grand style of living on the island. The company's directors decided to replace Poincy. They commissioned *Noëlle Patrocles de Thoisy*, a gentleman from Burgundy, to replace him, obtaining an order from the king summoning the governor back to France. Poincy refused to comply. His militia drove Thoisy off the island, and ultimately Thoisy was captured and sent back to France in chains. Thus, Poincy was a Knight commander to be reckoned with.

Seeking a way to keep his position, Poincy in 1649 suggested that the Order of Malta purchase the islands. By this time the Company was languishing but Poincy himself, by defying its authority, had shown its ineffectiveness. The Hospitallers, at the motion of Poincy with the approval of the Grand Master Lascaris of Malta, bought Saint-Christophe, along with Poincy's newly-established dependencies of Saint Croix, Saint Barthélemy, and Saint Martin. The Knights' ambassador to the

French court, *Jacques de Souvré*, signed the agreement. The Order's proprietary rights were confirmed in a treaty with France two years later - while the king would remain sovereign, the Knights would have complete temporal and spiritual jurisdiction on their islands. The only limits to their rule were that they could send only French knights to govern the islands, and upon the accession of each new King of France they were to provide a gold crown worth 1,000 écus.

Le Chateau de la Montagne

When he took over as governor of S. Christophe, de Poincy moved into the house d'Esnambuc had built on the eastern slopes of Olivees Mountain, a little over two miles inland of Basseterre. It must have been a modest building, well below the standard he considered befitted his wealth and status, because in 1642 he decided to replace it with something much grander.

In the *Histoire Proprietary Rule and its Demise Naturelle et Morale des iles Antilles de l'Amerique*, by Cesar de Rochefort, appeared the drawing above and it is doubtful if it was based on personal observations. According to author Dyde: "This illustration, showing a four-story, four-square mansion, surrounded by walled courtyards and formal gardens, and approached by a tree-lined avenue through pastoral surroundings, was accepted as a true representation of de Poincy's residence, not only by Richard Blome in 1672 but seemingly by most people ever since. In fact, the illustration can show no more than an artist's very fanciful impression of what de Poincy would have liked to build; either that, or what, on the opposite side of the Atlantic and working from hearsay and sketchy reports, de Rochefort imagined he had built." (Dyde, Brian. Out of Crowded Vagueness: A History of the Islands of St. Kitts, Nevis And Anguilla)

Poincy continued to develop the colonies. He built strong and impressive fortifications on Saint Christophe along with churches, roads, a hospital, stables, and his own grand residence. Outside the capital, Hospitaller rule was more precarious. The settlement on Saint Barthélemy suffered an attack by Carib people, and those who were not killed abandoned the island. Poincy sent a group of 30 men to replace them, which grew to 100 by 1664. In 1657 a rebellion overthrew the Hospitaller regime on St. Croix. Poincy sent a new governor to restore order, build fortifications and a monastery, and begin to clear much of the island's forests for plantation agriculture. To date we have no records of Poincy's influence over the governorship of Nevis.

The Beginnings of a Plantation Society
By the 1660s in both St Christopher and S. Christophe, and also in Nevis, more labor was being put into the growing of sugarcane than any other crop. Having been introduced into the region probably by the Dutch from Brazil, St. Christophe had begun to plant sugarcane in about 1640, and in Nevis two or three years later. Nevis lagged behind in its introduction, but by the 1650s sugar had become the island's staple and cash product. In 1652 it was reported that Nevis was 'the best island for sugar: 'it makes little of any other commodities, only some tobacco to windward, which is valued more than any of the English plantations'. This tobacco production was ignored for the place of sugar in St. Christophe, where more sugarcane was then being grown than in Nevis or English St Christopher. Before he died in 1660 de Poincy alone had six mills at work on two of his plantations.

Shortly before his death in 1660, Poincy signed a treaty of peace with the English and the Carib people of Saint Christopher. The peace did not last, however. De Sales succeeded Poincy as governor. In 1666, after the Knights had formally given up their control of the islands, and fighting broke out between the French and the English on the island. In a battle at Cayonne, de Sales was killed, but the French held on to their settlements.

Although sugar rapidly became the main product of both St. Christopher and Nevis, other crops continued to be grown commercially until well into the 1670s. Peter Lindestrom, the Swedish military engineer who visited St Christopher in 1654 (and was 'sumptuously entertained' by de Poincy) was most impressed by what was then being grown, recording a rare view of the island of the times:

"This is a very fertile island, there grow oranges, lemons sweet oranges, potatoes, bananas, sugar, tobacco, nutmegs, walnuts, chestnuts, grapes, red, blue, white and brown, pepper, ginger and innumerable quantity of all kinds of valuable and rare fruit. Ginger lay there in the fields in large heaps, like tumbled-over houses thrown together; if it was not carefully looked after and dug out in the fields, it would become so firmly and strongly rooted in, that it prevented all other fruit and roots from growing. On the ground all over, the fields were covered with oranges, lemons, pepper and all other kinds of fruit, which had fallen from the trees, like hail.... We threw oranges and lemons, like snowballs, at one another."

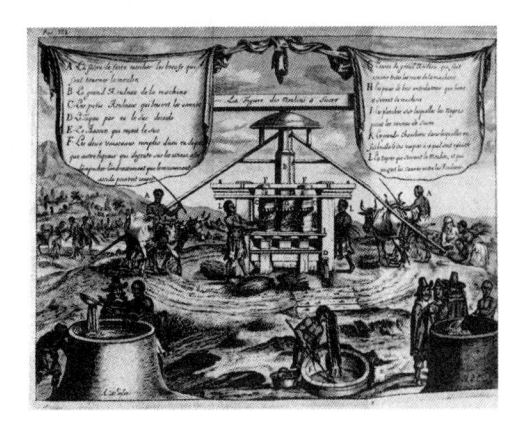

By the early 1660s, frustration was growing that the colonies were not turning a significant agricultural profit. The Order still owed money to France for the initial purchase of the islands, and on Malta the knights debated whether they should sell them back. Jean-Baptiste Colbert, much more interested in colonization than Mazarin, was now in power in King Louis XIV's court, and he applied pressure to the Knights to sell. In 1665, the Knights sold their colony to the newly formed company - *Compagnie des Indes occidentales*. That was the end of the rule of St. John in the Caribbean.

The national flower of St. Kitts and Nevis, the Poinciana or Flamboyant Tree (Delonix regia). Its local name is the "Shack Shack Tree". Native to Madagascar, it was called Poinciana for the French General de Poincy, Knight of St. John, the first French Governor of St. Kitts (1639-1660) who is said to have introduced it to the Americas. In the Indian state of Kerala, royal Poinciana is called kaalvarippoo which means the flower of Calvary. There is a popular belief among Saint Thomas Christians of Kerala that when Jesus was crucified, there was a small royal Poinciana tree nearby his Cross. It is believed that the blood of Jesus Christ was shed over the flowers of the tree and this is how the flowers of royal Poinciana got a sharp red color.

Conclusion

Little has been published in the past about the Hospitaller (St. Johns) colonization of the Americas occurring during a 14-year period when they possessed the four Caribbean islands of Saint Christopher, Saint Martin, Saint Barthélemy, and Saint Croix. The Knights' presence in the Caribbean grew out of their order's close relationship with the French nobility and the presence of many members in the Americas as French administrators. The key figure in their brief foray into colonization - *Phillippe de Longvilliers de Poincy*, was both a Knight and soldier, as well as the appointed governor of the French colonies in the Caribbean. Poincy convinced the Knights to purchase the islands from the bankrupt Compagnie des Îles de l'Amérique in 1651 and he stayed to govern them until his death in 1660. During this time, the Order acted as proprietor of the islands, while the King of France continued to hold nominal sovereignty. However, Poincy, as typical of an independent Knight, ruled largely independent of them both and initiated significant development of St. Christrophe including production of sugarcane. In 1665, the Hospitallers sold their rights in the islands to the new French West India Company, bringing their colonial project to an end.

The Knights of Malta would never establish another colony. However, members of the order remained active in France's navy and overseas empire. After Napoleon invaded Malta, the Grand Master von Hompesch surrendered and left Malta in shame writing "pathetic letters" to the Emperors in Vienna and St. Petersburg attempting to justify his surrender. On December 21, 1798 or January 1, 1799, the 'protector' Emperor-Grand Master Paul I of Russia issued a decree addressed to the Grand Priories of the Order in which he invited the whole Christian nobility of Europe to join the Order to combat the forces of revolution and 'Godlessness'. With this decree by its Grand Master, the Order became ecumenical and controversial. The Tsar then established within his Empire two Grand Priories. One of these was entitled "Russian Catholic Grand Priory" and was to consist of Catholics. The other was called "Russian Grand Priory" was comprised Christians of other than the Catholic Communion including the Orthodoxy and Protestants.

It was at this time that the Order of St. John first became pluralized and expanded the boundaries of beyond a single Roman Church. The right (de jure) in this position held by Paul I as Grand Master, even in a temporal sense, allowed the new branches of the Order that afterward came into being outside of the Catholic Communion to have valid succession from the old Order. Thus the 'langues' established Orders in different countries, some cooperate, most do not to this day. With this action, on February 9, 1803, the Order moved into its modern phase in which it was destined to come full circle back to an almost exclusive concern with hospital charity. Its military days over, its political mission ended, after a few decades required to redefine itself, it found that it had retained a vital role to play in the modern world in the care and succor of the sick and the needy once again and would go on to foster the formation of the Red Cross.

The short period of Hospitaller occupation is still remembered on the different islands. Poincy's rule on St. Kitts is remembered for the spectacle of his large, grand household, the servants all dressed in the emblem of the Knights, *cross pattée*. On St. Croix one can find frequent reference to the "seven flags" in the island's history, counting the Knights of Malta together with the United States and five European nations that have ruled it. St. Barthélemy has in its coat of arms a Maltese cross on a red fess, representing the period of Hospitaller colonization (left).

Coat of Arms: St. Barts

The Most Venerable Order of the Hospital of Saint John of Jerusalem (French: l'ordre très vénérable de l'Hôpital de Saint-Jean de Jérusalem) and also known as St John International, is today a royal order of chivalry first constituted in 1888 by Queen Victoria. It evolved from a faction of the Order of Malta that emerged in France in the 1820s and moved to Britain in the early 1830s, where, after operating under a succession of grand priors and different names, it became associated with the founding in 1882 of the St John Ophthalmic Hospital near the old city of Jerusalem and the St John Ambulance Brigade in 1887 in England.

St John of Jerusalem Eye Hospital Group

Author makes a visit and is obliged to a tour of the St. John Eye Hospital, Tel Aviv, Israel (2008)

As the Maltese (patée) cross, the symbol of the eight beatitudes of Christ's Sermon on the Mount, in refugee camps and on hospitals, on centers for medical research and ambulances, on institutions for civil defense and rehabilitation, on hospital trains for pilgrimages for the sick and on training facilities for nursing personnel, gives an eloquent witness, that the Order of St. John translates it's timeless motto "Protection of faith and obsequiousness to the poor" into contemporary works of Christian charity, we are reminded of the word of the founder of the Order, Blessed Gerard: "Our brotherhood will be everlasting, because the ground which this plant is rooted in, is the misery of the world - and because, God willing, there will always be people, which want to work towards the alleviation of these sufferings and making this misery more bearable."

May the Order of St. John, based on its spiritual foundation, continue to humbly serve the hungry and needy, the estranged and naked, the sick and imprisoned. Lord in all future, and thus become a sign of Christian faith, cheerful hope and apostolic love for the people. (Editor. Honorary Member of the Hereditary Order of St. John of Jerusalem, Italy)

References

- Dyde, Brian. Out of Crowded Vagueness: A History of the Islands of St. Kitts, Nevis And Anguilla. Interlink Publishing Group, 2006.
- Formhals, Robert. The White Cross. Sanghals Publishers, 1979.
- L'Abbe de Vertot. The History of the Knights of Malta. London, 1728.
- Knights Hospitaller. From Wikipedia, the free encyclopedia.
- https://en.wikipedia.org/wiki/Knights_Hospitaller
- McWilliams, Charles. The Medical Cross. The Achievements, Medical, Political and Social Works of the Orders of St. John of Jerusalem, Knights Hospitaller. SMOKH. 2007.
- Phillippe de Longvilliers de Poincy. From Wikipedia, the free encyclopedia. https://en.wikipedia.org/wiki/Phillippe_de_Longvilliers_de_Poincy

CHAPTER 5. Caribbean Migrants

Migrant is defined as "a person who moves from one place to another in order to find work or better living conditions." The term "migrant worker" has different meanings and connotations in different parts of the world. In the 360 years between 1500 and the end of the slave trade in the 1860s, at least 12 million Africans were forcibly taken to the Americas - then known as the "New World" to European settlers. This largest *forced migration* in human history relocated some 50 ethnic and linguistic groups, certainly not for better work and living conditions. Only a small portion of the enslaved - less than half a million - were sent to North America. The majority went to South America and the Caribbean. In the mid-1600s, Africans outnumbered Europeans in nascent cities such as Mexico City, Havana and Lima, Peru.

Caribbean by definition, means only pertaining to the Caribs, the Lesser Antilles, or the Caribbean Sea and its islands. There is no country with the name Caribbean. Being a collection of settler nations, the Caribbean has been shaped by waves of migration that have combined to form a unique blend of customs, cuisine, and traditions that have marked the socio-cultural development of its peaceful nation states. The Caribbean is usually visualized as an area populated by a diverse polyglot of peoples. There are so-called whites, blacks, browns, yellows, reds, mulattos, and an assortment of shades in between. There are Europeans, Africans, Asian Indians, Indonesian Javanese, Chinese, Aboriginal Indians, and many mixes. There are Christians, Hindus, Muslims, Jews, Rastafarians, Santería, Winti, Vudun, etc. People of the Caribbean speak in a multitude of tongues—Spanish, English, Dutch, French, English, and a diverse number of Creoles such as papiamentu, as well as Hindustani, Bhojpuri, Urdu, etc. In whatever combinations of race, religion, language, and culture; they cohere and coexist peacefully, they dwell on large and small islands, some poorly endowed with natural resources, others abundantly. Yet no other region of the world is so richly varied and non-racial. Remarked Caribbean scholar, Michel-Rolph Trouillot: "Caribbean societies are inescapably heterogenous... the Caribbean has long been an area where some people live next to others who are remarkably distinct. The region—and indeed particular territories within it—has long been multi-racial, multi-lingual, stratified, and some would say, multi-cultural."

St Kitts and Nevis' most significant characteristic, its most precious possession, is its people. The Caribbean is unique in the New World for our cosmopolitan population. Nevis was reported uninhabited when discovered and early on developed by the British as a tobacco, sugar, and cotton producing island to become *Queen of the Caribbean.* Nevisians today, are without exception, the descendants of migrants. The Spanish were brought here by the avarice for gold and spices; the Africans were abducted from their homelands; the French were displaced by the French Revolution and by the capture of other Caribbean islands by the British; the British came with the idea of colonial establishment; expats came here to escape oppression, crime, taxation, or sheer enjoyment; and the impoverished and disenchanted people from the Orient and Asia saw Nevis as a 'port of hope' in the New World. Even the Amerindians, whose unrecorded history came to a near end when the Europeans arrived in the Americas, had arrived at some point in time, coming from the Orinoco delta. Religious faiths on Nevis had early on been tolerated, establishing it as a peaceful island from the beginning. In this sense, Nevis itself was not 'colonized': "to settle among and establish control over the indigenous people of an area." Nevis was a 'frontier' settlement: "a region just beyond or at the edge of a settled area... an undeveloped area or field for discovery."

Slavery
The mining of gold and silver, and to a greater extent, the discovery of the great economic potential of sugar cultivation in the world market precipitated the institutionalization of slavery in the newly colonized West Indies. Economically, the Spanish were mining staggering amounts of silver bullion from New Spain and Peru. Their other trade was largely animal hides as the Spanish preferred ranching to plantations. The *Florida Cracker* is one of the oldest breeds of cattle in the United States, descending from Spanish cattle brought to the New World beginning in the early 1500s. As the Spanish colonized Florida and other parts of the Americas, they established low input, extensive cattle ranging systems typical of Spanish ranching. Slavery began in the 16th century with the British, French and Dutch plantations, and from that time onward, the fortunes of the Islands were greatly influenced by agriculture and the price of sugar, tobacco, cotton, and the availability of labor. It was the requirements of the sugar industry that really determined the nature and culture of the West Indian populations as it was the driving economic force of those times.

The Spaniards who were the original imperialists in the Caribbean, already had a system of slavery which made it easy for them to resort to this method of procuring labor for their gold and silver mines. Several sources of labor for the plantations, including aboriginal west Indians, indentured servants from Ireland, even white slaves and convicts were sought actually before others were brought into the West Indies from Africa. Negro slavery was initiated by the king of Spain on September 3, 1501 and began with the transportation of numbers of Christian negro slaves from Spain to the West Indies. In 1526, the Portuguese completed the first transatlantic slave voyage from Africa to the Americas, and other countries soon followed. Because of this diversity and lack of formal records, it is very difficult for scholars to write a complete history of the early peoples of the Caribbean.

Multiple forms of slavery and servitude had existed throughout Africa during history and were shaped by indigenous practices of slavery as well as the Roman institution of slavery, the Islamic institutions of slavery, and eventually the Atlantic slave trade. Slavery existed in parts of Africa (like the rest of the world) and was a part of the economic structure of some societies for many centuries, although the extent varied. Like most other regions of the world, slavery and forced labor existed in many kingdoms and societies of Africa for thousands of years. With the beginning of the Atlantic slave trade, demand for slavery in West Africa increased and a number of states became centered on the slave trade and slave captivity increased dramatically. Eighteenth century writers in Europe claimed that slavery in Africa was quite brutal in order to supply the Atlantic slave trade. Later writers used similar arguments to justify intervention and eventual colonization by European powers to end slavery in Africa. Africans knew of the harsh slavery that awaited slaves in the New World. Many elite Africans visited Europe on slave ships following the prevailing winds through the New World. African monarchs also sent their children along these same slave routes to be educated in Europe, and thousands of former slaves eventually returned to settle Liberia and Sierra Leone.

The wealth flowing from the New World to the Old started by the Spanish for the search for gold and spices was thus transformed largely by the cultivation of tropical crops like sugar, tobacco, and coffee. These crops figured importantly in European and world consumption. Profits for a plantation owner depended upon the success of cultivation and production of sugar, and on the number of laborers he controlled to make the product. The key to wealth for plantation owners depended upon the size of the estate in terms of land mass and by employing many laborers, while keeping costs low and peace within the plantation. Free European laborers demanded high wages. In the long run, the cost of slaves was lower. Slavery was quite simply - *all about the money*.

Initially Europeans tried enslaving native Amerindians. But the native peoples lacked genetic or acquired immunities to Old-World diseases like smallpox and suffered catastrophic mortality. It is estimated that over 90% of the native population of the Amerindians perished from Old-World diseases after contact. Africans, on the other hand, possessed the required immunities and brute strength. Europeans discovered this by the early 1500s and the Atlantic slave trade developed rapidly to fill the demand.

Indentured servitude was a form of debt bondage, established in the early years of the American colonies and Caribbean. It was sometimes used as a way for poor youth in Britain and the German states to get passage to the American colonies. They would work for a fixed number of years, then be free to work on their own. The employer purchased the indentured from the sea captain who brought the youths over; he did so because he needed labor. Some worked as farmers or helpers for farm wives, some were apprenticed to craftsmen. Both sides were legally obligated to meet the terms, which were enforced by local American courts. Runaways were sought out and returned. About half of the white immigrants to the American colonies in the 17th and 18th centuries were indentured servants.

Caribbean history demonstrates most clearly that a struggle for self-determination runs as a consistent theme of Caribbean living. History shows not only that slaves used a variety of methods to resist their masters and that strikes and riots were only some of the means used by African Caribbean people after emancipation to achieve full equality, but also piracy during its 'golden age', and that of US influence in the region in the twentieth century called for fierce resistance and independence.

The Slave Coast

In 1650 the British were minor participants in the slave trade. By 1700 Britain was emerging as the largest Atlantic slave trading nation, overtaking Portugal. The slave trade became so extensive in the 18th and 19th centuries that an "Atlantic community" of triangular trade was formed. The slave trade was facilitated by the Portuguese, the Dutch, the French and the British ships and companies. Slaves went to the New World, mostly to Brazil and the Caribbean with some migrating to the North.

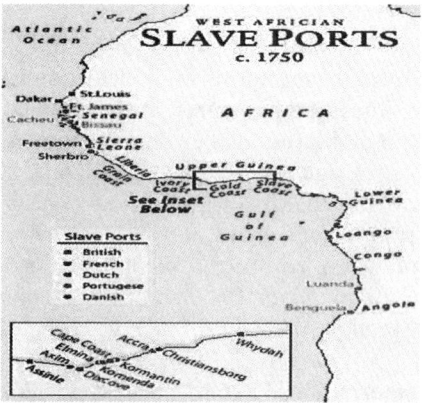

The Slave Coast is a historical name formerly used for parts of coastal West Africa along the Bight of Benin (Gulf of Guinea). The name is derived from February 1852 when the British established the Bight of Benin protectorate and became a major source of African slaves during the Atlantic slave trade from the early 16th century to the 19th century. Other nearby coastal regions historically known by their prime colonial exports are the Gold Coast, the Ivory Coast, and the Pepper Coast (or Grain Coast).

The Caribbean Triangulation of Sea Trade

In the notorious *triangular trade*, ships departed from Bristol, Liverpool and other ports in England carrying trade goods, such as beads, cloth, utensils, and guns to West Africa, where they exchanged their goods for enslaved Africans who were then transported to the Caribbean, South America, and American colonies to work on the plantations. The vessels returned home with sugar, tobacco, coffee, spices, and cotton, the produce of the enslaved workforces. Before 1820, over 80% of the people arriving in the New World were enslaved Africans. It is estimated that 12 million enslaved Africans were transported to the Americas.

The gate post of the slave market in Charlestown, Nevis.

As a consequence of these events, the size of the Black population in the Caribbean rose dramatically in the latter part of the 17th century. In the 1650s when sugar started to take over from tobacco as the main cash crop on Nevis, enslaved Africans formed only 20% of the population. By the census of 1678 the Black population had risen to 3,849 against a white population of 3,521. By the early 18th century when sugar production was fully established nearly 80% of the population was African.

The great increase in the Black population was feared by the white plantation owners and as a result treatment and punishments became even harsher as they felt a growing need to control a larger but discontented and potentially rebellious workforce. The death rate was therefore high. First they had to survive the appalling conditions on the voyage from West Africa, known as the Middle Passage. Nearly 350,000 Africans were transported to the Leeward Islands by 1810 but many died on the voyage through disease or ill treatment; some were driven by despair to commit suicide by jumping into the sea. Once they arrived in the Caribbean islands, the Africans were prepared for sale. They were washed and their skin was oiled. Finally they were sold to local buyers. Often parents were separated from children, and husbands from wives.

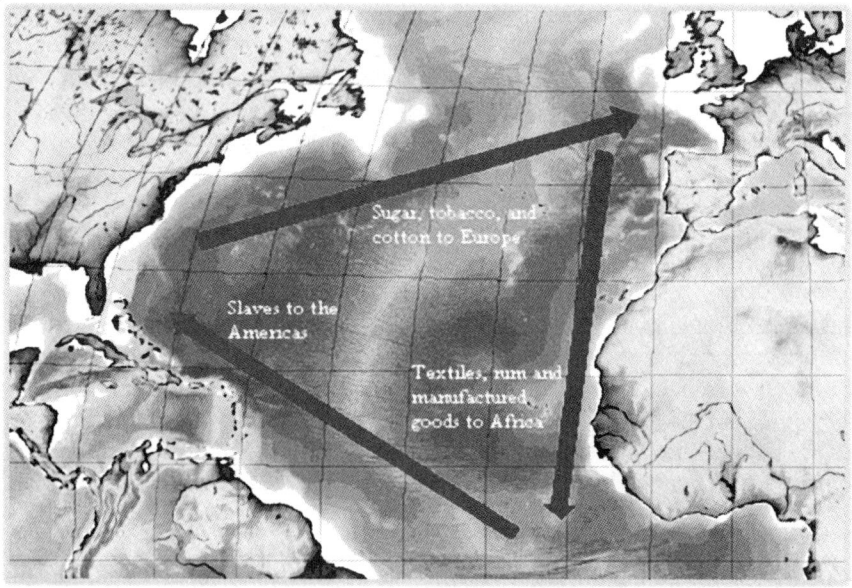

The Atlantic Community of Triangular Trade

By the end of the 17th century, the population of Nevis consisted of a small, rich planter elite in control, a marginal population of poor whites, a great majority of families of African descent, and an unknown number of *maroons*, people who had freed themselves from the exploitation at the plantations and escaped into the mountains. Between 1675 and 1730, the island was the headquarters for the slave trade for the Leeward Islands, with approximately 6,000-7,000 enslaved West Africans passing through on route to other islands each year. The *Royal African*

Company brought all its ships through Nevis for slave commerce. In 1780, 90 percent of the 10,000+ people living on Nevis were black. Some of the maroons joined with the few remaining Caribs in Nevis to form an ever present resistance force in the mountainous regions of the island. Memories of the Nevisian maroons' struggle against the injustices suffered by the Afro-Caribbean population under the plantation system are preserved in place names such as Maroon Hill, Nevis, an early center of resistance.

The words "Maroon" and "Seminole" share the same origin in the Spanish word cimarrón, meaning "wild" or "untamed". When runaway Blacks and Amerindians banded together and subsisted independently they were called Maroons. On the Caribbean islands, they formed bands and on some islands, armed camps. Maroon communities emerged in many places in the Caribbean (St. Vincent and Dominica, for example), but none were seen as such a great threat to the British as the Jamaican Maroons. The early Maroon communities were usually displaced. By 1700, Maroons had disappeared from the smaller islands.

In 1502, a mere 10 years after Columbus' first voyage, the first known African maroon escaped his captors and fled into the interior of the island of Hispaniola. The first enslaved Africans to be transported to the Spanish colony of Hispaniola are said to have rebelled and run away. From that time on, it is possible to speak of continual African resistance and rebellion. There were seven major rebellions in the British colony of Jamaica between 1673 and 1686, as well as several others during the same period in Antigua, Nevis and the Virgin Islands.

A typical maroon community in the early settlements usually consisted of three types of people. Most of them were slaves who ran away right after they got off the ships. They refused to accept enslavement and often tried to find ways to go back to Africa. The second group were unskilled slaves who had been working on plantations for a while but escaped. Those slaves were usually somewhat adjusted to the slave system but had been abused by the plantation owners, with excessive brutality even when compared to the normal standards. Others ran away when they were being sold suddenly to a new owner. The last group of maroons were usually skilled slaves with particularly strong ideals against the slave system. Otherwise, they could have chosen the easier way out by blending in with the locals.

Maroonage was a constant threat to New World plantation societies. Punishments for recaptured maroons were severe, like viciously removing an Achilles tendon, amputating a leg, castration, and even being roasted alive. Maroon communities had to be inaccessible and located in inhospitable environments in order to be sustainable. Maroon communities turned the severity of their environments to their advantage to hide and defend their communities. Disguised pathways, false trails, booby traps, underwater paths, quagmires and quicksand, and natural features were all used to conceal maroon villages. Maroon men utilized exemplary guerrilla warfare skills to fight their European enemies.

Work Conditions on the Plantation

The plantation relied almost solely on an imported enslaved workforce, and thus became an 'agricultural factory' concentrating on one profitable crop for sale. Enslaved Africans were forced to engage in a variety of laborious activities. The work in the fields was grueling, with long hours spent in the hot sun, supervised by overseers who were quick to use the whip. Tasks ranged from clearing land, planting, and harvesting canes by hand, to manuring and weeding.

Inside the plantation works, the conditions were often worse, especially the heat of the boiling house. Additionally, the hours were long, especially at harvest time. The death rate on the plantations was high, a result of overwork, poor nutrition, brutality, accidents, and disease. Many plantation owners preferred to import new slaves rather than providing the means and conditions (food and medical care) for the survival of their existing slaves. Until the *Amelioration Act* was passed in 1798, which forced planters to improve conditions for enslaved workers, many owners simply replaced the casualties by importing more slaves from West Africa.

The houses of the enslaved Africans were far less durable than the stone and timber buildings of European plantation owners. Slave houses in Nevis were described as 'composed of posts in the ground, thatched around the sides and upon the roof, with boarded partitions'. They were little more than huts, with a single story and thatched with cane trash. In the inventory of property lost in the French raid on St Kitts in February 1706 they were generally valued at as little as £2 each.

From the 17th century onwards, it became customary for plantation owners to give enslaved Africans Sundays off, even though many were not 'Christian' (baptized). Enslaved Africans used some of this free time to cultivate garden plots close to their houses, as well as in nearby 'provision grounds'. Provision grounds were often areas of land often of poor quality, mountainous or stony, and often at some distance from the villages which plantation owners set aside for the enslaved to grow their own food, such as sweet potatoes, yams and plantains. In addition to using the produce to supplement their own diet, slaves sold or exchanged it, as well as livestock such as chickens or pigs, in local markets. The location of the provision grounds at the Jessups estate, one of the Nevis plantations studied by the *St Kitts-Nevis Digital Archaeology Initiative*, is shown on a 1755 plan of the plantation. It is labeled as the 'Negro Ground' attached to Jessups plantation, high up the mountain.

By the early 18th century enslaved Africans trading in their own produce dominated the market on Nevis. In William Smith's day, the market in Charlestown was held from sunrise to 9 am on Sunday mornings where "the Negroes bring Fowls, Indian Corn, Yams, Garden-stuff of all sorts, etc." In Charlestown there is a place now known as the 'Slave Market'. We do not know whether this was the place where enslaved Africans were sold on arriving in Nevis or whether it is where slaves used to sell their produce on Sundays. However, the records show the market was enjoyed by all working people on Nevis, so it probably was the local produce market.

The abolitionists' humanitarian and religious arguments against slavery found a sympathetic popular audience in the Christian communities of England and America. One tool of the abolitionist movement was a boycott of slave-grown sugar, a consumer protest celebrated by contemporaries as a key component of abolition's success. The proponents of the boycott were given to liberal use of physical metaphor: in their writings sugar is equated with, or is figuratively imbued with, the *blood, sweat, and tears* of the slaves, and interpreted as a polluting substance - morally polluting the body politic.

Slavery was formally and finally abolished in the British Caribbean in 1834, the French Caribbean in 1848, the Dutch Caribbean in 1863, and in Cuba in 1886. By the turn of the twentieth century, the United States intervened in some territories in order to enhance stability and prevent European nations from increasing their hold over the Americas. US interventions in Cuba, Haiti, and the Dominican Republic, combines with a series of labor riots that took place in the Anglophone Caribbean in the 1930s, and put this part of the region on the road to independence. And while most territories became independent in the 1960s and 1970s, some became independent much earlier and others are still semi-dependent.

References
• J. H. Parry, P. M. Sherlock, and A.P. Maingot, A Short History of the West Indies, fourth edn. (Oxford, 1987); and J. Rogozinski, A Brief History of the Caribbean: From the Arawak and Carib to the Present (New York, 2000).
• J. J. MCusker and R. R. Menard, 'The sugar industry in the seventeenth century: a new perspective on the Barbadian "sugar revolution"', in Tropical Babylons: Sugar and the Making of the Atlantic World, 1450–1680, ed. S. B. Schwartz (Chapel Hill, 2004), 289–330.
B. Brereton, 'Searching for the invisible woman', Slavery and Abolition, 13.2 (1992), 86–96.
• Maroon (people). From Wikipedia, https://en.wikipedia.org/wiki/Maroon_people
• R. E. Reddock, Women Labour and Politics in Trinidad and Tobago: A History (London, 1994); M. Sheller, 'Quasheba, mother, queen: black women's public leadership and political protest in post-emancipation Jamaica, 1834–65', Slavery and Abolition 19.3 (1998), 90–117; and various articles in Gender and Slave Emancipation in the Atlantic World, ed. P. Scully and D. Paton (Durham, 2005).
• Slavery in Africa. From Wikipedia, https://en.wikipedia.org/wiki/Slavery_in_Africa
• Triangular trade. From Wikipedia, https://en.wikipedia.org/wiki/Triangular_trade

CHAPTER 6. The Queen of the Caribe - Sugar, Tropics, and Water

SUGAR CANE PLANTATION.

Sugar was originally known to medieval Europe (Christendom) as a rare and costly spice, but the growth of sugarcane production, first in the Mediterranean and then in the Atlantic, made sugar ever more available. Between the middle of the seventeenth century to the middle of the nineteenth, sugar was transformed from a luxury to a widely consumed commodity in England, Europe, and the United States. By the late nineteenth century it was a common article of diet, even a necessity, for all classes.

The cuisine of early Europe (c. 1500–1800) was a mix of dishes inherited from medieval cuisine combined with innovations that would persist into the modern era. Though there was a great influx of new ideas from the East, an increase in foreign trade and a scientific revolution, preservation of foods remained traditional: preserved by drying, salting, smoking, or pickling in vinegar. Fare was naturally dependent on the season availability and crop production, heavily weather dependent. Sugar became a highly prized and wanted sweetener.

In most parts of Europe two meals per day were eaten, one in the early morning to noon and one in the late afternoon or later at night. As in the Middle Ages, breakfast in the sense of an early morning meal, was largely absent. For most of Europe, the many varieties of grain were the most important crop and formed the daily staple for segments of society. Grain remained the undisputed main staple of early modern Europe until the 17th century. By this time the skepticism towards New World imports such as potatoes and maize had softened among the general populace, and the potato in particular found new appreciation in northern Europe, where it was a much more productive and flexible crop than wheat.

No parts of animals were wasted; blood was used in soups, for blood sausages, tripe was an ingredient in stews, soups or pies, and even cuts like the tongue, eyes, and testicles, that clearly reminded of the live creature, were readily consumed. European consumption of meat remained exceptionally high by world standards, while the poor continued to rely mainly on eggs, dairy products, and pulses for protein. Water as a neutral table beverage, digestive aid, and body cleanser did not appear in Europe until well into the Industrial era, when efficient water purification could ensure safe drinking water. All but the poorest drank mildly alcoholic drinks on a daily basis, for every meal; wine in the south, beer in the north, east and middle Europe. Naturally, digestive and kidney disease, as well as gout, were common.

Europeans came to crave the taste of sugar, especially as a sweetener for two other products from the Afro-Asian world, coffee and tea. These became popular additions to the European diet, especially valued as stimulants and comforts by workers in European factories, the products of which in turn fed the markets of the Atlantic world with cheaply manufactured goods, such as knives, belt buckles, machetes, hoes, shovels, rifles, buttons, and cast iron pots and pans.

A Sugar Love Story: In August 1492, Christopher Columbus stopped at *La Gomera* in the Canary Islands, for wine and water, intending to stay only four days. He became romantically involved with the governor of the island, *Beatriz de Bobadilla y Ossorio*, and stayed a month. When he finally sailed, she gave him cuttings of sugarcane, which became the first to reach the New World. The first sugar cane harvest was conducted in Hispaniola in 1501, and many sugar mills had been constructed in Cuba and Jamaica by the 1520s.

Naturally, with the importation of sugar now from the West Indies, during 18th century, sugar due to Caribbean production became one of the most popular foodstuffs ever, and constituted the world's most important and lucrative commodity in those times, as important as petroleum is today. Wars were fought, lands were conquered; weapons, cookware, and tools manufactured; and people enslaved, all to gain control over the production of sugar in the face of a burgeoning rise of consumption in Europe. Sugar became worth its weight in gold and the Caribbean was the engine of production and growth.

The average per capita sugar intake in England was 4 lb. (1.8 kg) in 1700 and 18 lb. (8.1 kg) in 1800, and it increased even more after the prime minister, William Gladstone, removed the sugar tax in 1874, which led to a mean consumption of 100 lb. (45 kg) in 1950. Deaths from tuberculosis increased dramatically in England and other sugar consuming countries. In 1776, Matthew Dobson confirmed that the sweet taste of urine of diabetics was due to excess of a kind of sugar in the urine and blood of people with diabetes.

To keep sugar, and its important by-products, molasses and rum, flowing steadily from the Caribbean, it took all the efforts of one of the few industries to be born in the colonialized world that became islands of near lawlessness, slavery and piracy.

Sugar had only become known to Europeans over the prior few hundred years. It had in medieval times been exceedingly rare, and was used mainly as a very expensive spice or medicinal compound used in syrups and elixirs to mask the taste of bitter drugs.

SUGAR PRODUCTION

Sugarcane (Saccharum officinarum L.) was first domesticated in New Guinea, and possibly also in Indonesia, as early as 8000 BC. The first references to actually making sugar occur in Sanskrit writings from India dating to around 400 BC. The invention of manufacture of cane sugar granules from the sugarcane juice in India a little over two thousand years ago, followed by improvements in refining the crystal granules in India in the early centuries A.D. Sugar making spread into the Mediterranean with the Muslim conquests in the 8th century AD. The Crusades brought sugar to the attention of Northern Europe, and an expansion of the sugar trade out of Palestine and Sicily in the 12th and 13th centuries. Known worldwide through the end of the medieval period, sugar was very expensive and was considered a "fine spice". The Knights Templar ran lucrative sugarcane plantations, sugar factories, and livestock and grain operations on their vast estates in the Levant, despite their commitment to monastic poverty. These activities, in the opinion of noted crusader historian, Jonathan Riley-Smith, made them a target of the Pope and King Philip IV in the years that followed leading to their persecution. Sugar production in Mediterranean collapsed shortly after the inception of the industry in the New World. The climate and soils of the Caribbean suited the cane, which thrived there, and it was much cheaper to produce in greater quantities than in Europe or the Levant. Thus, sugar has been associated with the system of colonial cash crop agriculture since the very beginning of European expansion.

White Gold, as British colonists called it, was the engine of the slave trade that brought millions of Africans to the Americas beginning in the early 16th-century. The history of every nation in the Caribbean, much of South America and parts of the Southern United States was forever shaped by sugar cane plantations started as cash crops by European superpowers.

In 1603, James VI, King of Scots, ascended (as James I) to the English throne and in 1604 negotiated the Treaty of London, ending hostilities with Spain. Now at peace with its main rival, English attention shifted from preying on other nations' colonial infrastructures to the business of establishing its own overseas colonies. The British Empire began to take shape during the early 17th century, with the English settlement of North America and the smaller islands of the Caribbean, first St. Christopher and Nevis, and the establishment of joint-stock companies, most notably the *East India Company*, to administer colonies and overseas trade. This period, until the loss of the Thirteen Colonies after the loss of the American War of Independence towards the end of the 18th century, has subsequently been referred to by some historians as the "First British Empire".

Kolossi Castle is a former Crusader stronghold west of the city of Limassol on the island of Cyprus. It held great strategic importance in the Middle Ages, and contained large facilities for the production of sugar and wine from the local sugarcane, one of Cyprus's main exports in the period. The original castle was built in 1210 by the Frankish military, when the land of Kolossi was given by King Hugh I to the Knights of the Order of St John of Jerusalem (Hospitallers). The island became an important refuge for the Knights after their defeat in the Holy Land in Acre. It was here the knights learned and yearned for the taste of wine and sugar.

Kolossi Castle Cyprus

Author and Wife

In the sixteenth and seventeenth centuries, European powers established the sugar colonies in the West Indies and along the Atlantic coast of South America. The first British sugar island was Barbados, followed by St. Kitts, Nevis, Antigua and Jamaica. In the nineteenth century, Puerto Rico, Grenada and Trinidad were added to the industrialization. Sugar dominated production on the islands. There were always some other crops grown, but after the plantation system was in full swing the planters preferred importing provisions to growing them locally so as to have the maximum amount of land planted and dedicated to sugar cane production, the cash crop of the Caribbean.

Nevis Sugar Production

Nevis was part of the Spanish claim to the Caribbean islands, a claim pursued until 1671, even though there were no Spanish settlements on the island. According to Vincent Hubbard, author of *Swords, Ships & Sugar: History of Nevis*, the Spanish caused many of the peaceful Arawak groups who were not ethnically Caribs to "be redefined as Caribs overnight". Records indicate that the Spanish enslaved large numbers of the native inhabitants on the more accessible of the Leeward Islands and sent them to Cubagua, Venezuela to dive for pearls. Hubbard suggests that the reason the first European settlers found so few "Caribs" on Nevis is that they had already been rounded up by the Spanish and shipped off to be used as slaves. However, there is no archaeological evidence to support this view as previously Columbus himself and Sir Walter Raleigh recorded no inhabitants on the island upon their arrival.

After the 1671 peace treaty between Spain and England, little Nevis became the seat of the British colony and the Admiralty Court also sat in Nevis. Between 1675 and 1730, the island was the headquarters for the slave trade for the Leeward Islands, with approximately 6,000-7,000 West Africans passing through on route to other islands each year. The *Royal African Company*, granted a monopoly over English trade with West Africa, brought all its ships through Nevis. This sleepy, quiet island was rapidly transformed into a bustling slave transshipment port. This "would have meant there was a lot of gold there at the time. It would have been Spanish colonial – Colombian mostly, I guess. And Mexican silver." (England Claimed Saint Kitts in 1630. By Bob Reis, World Coin News. May 26, 2011)

This early shift to sugar in Nevis appears to have been associated with the early role of Nevis' main town Charlestown as a slave trading center. Just as nearby St Eustatius was established as a Dutch trading center in the 1630s, Charlestown in Nevis developed as a major trading center, especially as the first Leeward Islands' slave market for the Royal African Company (1671-1752). The presence of English-based companies such as the Royal African Company strongly influenced the adoption of sugar by planters in the Leewards. As economic historian Richard Sheridan put it,

'the transition to sugar was facilitated by the presence of a mercantile community which was large by comparison with that of neighbouring islands. Not only did the merchants and factors of Nevis supply goods and services to the planters, but they also used their trading profits and principals' effects to acquire plantations of their own' (Sheridan 1973, 163)

Due to the profitable *Triangular Atlantic trade* and the high quality of Nevisian sugar cane, the island soon became a dominant source of wealth for Great Britain and the slave-owning British plantocracy. When the Leeward Islands were separated from Barbados in 1671, Nevis became the seat of the Leeward Islands colony and was given the nickname "Queen of the Caribees". It remained the colonial capital for the Leeward Islands until the seat was transferred to Antigua for military reasons in 1698. During this period, Nevis was the richest of the British Leeward Islands. The island outranked even larger islands like Jamaica in sugar production in the late 17th century. According to *The Economist*, in 1775, a ton of West Indian sugar was worth the equivalent of $5000 compared to $160 in 1990. The wealth of the planters on the island is evident in the tax records preserved at the *Calendar State Papers* in the British Colonial Office Public Records, where the amount of tax collected on the Leeward Islands was recorded. The sums recorded for 1676 as "head tax on slaves", a tax payable in sugar, amounted to 384,600 pounds in Nevis, as opposed to 67,000 each in Antigua and Saint Kitts, 62,500 in Montserrat, and 5,500 total in the other five islands. The profits on sugar cultivation in Nevis was enhanced by the fact that the cane juice from Nevis yielded an unusually high amount of sugar. A gallon (3.79 liters) of cane juice from Nevis yielded 24 ounces (0.71 liters) of sugar, whereas a gallon from Saint Kitts yielded 16 ounces (0.47 liters). Twenty percent of the British Empire's total sugar production in 1700 was derived from Nevisian plantations. Exports from West Indian colonies like Nevis were worth more than all the exports from all the mainland Thirteen colonies of North America combined at the time of the American Revolution.

Thus, the trade in sugar was vitally important to Britain's development as a trading nation and as an Empire. Throughout the eighteenth century, sugar from the colonies was England's most important import. It was the driving force in a network of trade that spanned the Atlantic, touching three continents. Historians debate whether and how much the capital accumulation made possible by the sugar industry was instrumental in financing the industrial revolution. It drove and benefited not only Europe but also the Americas. However, expanded networks of trade, such as those in which sugar was a force, certainly played a key role in stimulating industrialization.

Sugar was a transformative and successful commodity. Although the market was extremely volatile, with regular swings from scarcity to glut throughout the plantation era, production and consumption increased steadily throughout the world. Yet, it is impossible to study sugar production in the West Indies without considering slavery as an essential partner. The labor of enslaved Africans in the Caribbean was integral to the cultivation of the cane and production of sugar. Slaves toiled in the fields and the boiling houses, supplying the huge amounts of labor that sugar required. Overall some four million slaves were brought to the Caribbean, and almost all ended up on the sugar plantations. Conditions were harsh, and mortality rates were extremely high through all stages of a slaves' lives. In some sugar colonies the slave population was ten times that of Europeans, and slave uprisings were an ever-present fear for the planters.

The Skinny on Sugar
Tea and Coffee became staple beverages during the 18th century. By 1740 there were over 550 coffee houses in London alone. The coffee houses provided the bitter beverages, the bakeries the confectionaries, and an inviting environment for the rise in Britain's consumption of sugar. By the 1790s, on average, each Englishman ingested more than 20 pounds of sugar per year. Slavery allowed these products to become staples of British life, and in exchange for these goods, they found a market for their manufactured items. These goods included shoes, candles, felt hats, pewter, cottons, knives, buttons, and even beer. Even non-manufactured goods, such as beef, butter, sundry oats, cheese, and potatoes, found markets in the West Indies to feed the plantations and pirates. The result was Britain's extensive and almost unshakable economic intertwinement with the slave trade that built its Empire. Nevis stopped sugar cane production in 1960.

The Fountain of Youth
'Finding the Cure' two thousand years ago in Rome involved a sojourn at Baiae, on the shores of Vesuvius on the western shores of Italy (Naples) and taking the Baths. Historically, *taking the cure* after the collapse of the monasteries and the ravages of the plagues of Europe (16th century), meant a quest for healing waters: hot waters, cold waters, mineral waters, stinking waters, seawater, spring waters, or holy waters. It was *ancient hydrotherapy*, reborn, and sometimes a quest for healing muds or gases (pelotherapy). Found in most parts of the ancient world, myths of rejuvenation bring many fables. Some of these methods appear to be unique and others a continuation and variation from a previous story. In Baring-Gould's *Curious Myths of the Middle Ages*, we learn of the Icelandic Saga of the man who shed his skin every few centuries and always came out thirty years old. However, the commonest means of securing rejuvenation was to pray for it,

granted either by a deity, angel, saint, or a good-natured mortal who receives an unexpected power; or even a near fatal event saving one from a seemingly hopeless situation. There are the stories of magical cures, restoration to sight, and even of life, at the hands of Prophets and Hindu Yogis. In ancient India, the god Indra gives *Bharadvaja* a life-renewing science or formula granting one - "Never to come to old age " as the reward of living in a place especially holy. Or with a saint's aid as a spiritual protector the believer lives a long life.

A quest for Longevity. Five hundred years ago, the Spanish explorer Ponce de Leon drank his way around the Florida coast during his expedition to find the legendary Fountain of Youth. www.smoch.org

In the more alchemical sense, youth is also rendered by a special pearl which "removes poisons, devils, old age, and sickness," or a "heavenly fruit " which destroys "age and sickness". Indian literature abounds in tales of revivification by means of special balms, amulets, gems, and charms. For the attainment of " long life," various amulets or the grace of healing waters, are in common folklore from the earliest times in India.

In the West we find generally the *waters of life*, be it alchemical, blessed, saintly, holy, or ancient. Certain springs in the West were sacred, and the *sacred bath* and baptism was merged with Christian belief at an early date. Baptism is a Christian sacrament of admission and adoption in the 'kingdom', almost invariably with the use of water. The Fountains of Youth were to be found in those springs which had a beneficent and salutary effect on the health, pain relief, and complexion. At these locations reminiscent of the Spas of Rome, in these places one bathed before sunrise; or one collected water at these sacred springs for consumption. These tales would naturally find their way to the enchanted isles of *Antilia*, the mysterious, newly discovered Caribbean made popular by the return of Columbus.

What we find in Europe in these stories is the fairy-tale residuum not of old lore derived from remote Aryan ancestors, but more so of an Oriental myth brought to Europe which became united into one, that of the *waters of life* and of the *Fountain of Youth*. European tradition has in its tales of virtuous wells, the holy wells (sacred or prophetic), or the healing wells, and the wells of the natural *water of life*. English tales also has Celtic origins of waters that restores vigor.

The end of the military crusades in Europe paralleled the introduction of the black death and decades of fatal epidemics. In the 17th and the 18th centuries, while plagues had now been ravaging for centuries, the old crusade for religious territory was transformed into the crusade for health and medicine which not only involved the quest for spices and medicines of the new world, but was also to find the famed 'fountain of youth,' made famous in a Caribbean legend by Columbus' shipmate Ponce de Leon. According to this famous legend, the Spanish heard of Bimini from the Arawaks (Taínos) in Hispaniola, Cuba, and Puerto Rico. The Caribbean islanders described a mythical land of Beimeni or Beniny (aka Bimini), a land of wealth and prosperity, which became conflated with the fountain legend. By the time of Ponce de Leon, the land was thought to be located northwest towards the Bahamas (called la Vieja during the Ponce expedition). Sequene, an Arawak chief from Cuba, purportedly was unable to resist the lure of Bimini and its restorative fountain. He gathered a troupe of adventurers and sailed north, never to return. The legend of Bimini and its curative waters was widespread among the indigenous peoples of the Caribbean. The Italian-born chronicler Peter Martyr told of them in a letter to the pope in 1513, though he did not believe the stories and was dismayed that so many others did.

Juan Ponce de León and his explorers in Florida went looking for the Fountain of youth, according to a 19th century German drawing. It was Taino healing tales in Puerto Rico that got to Ponce de León believing in these waters giving youth. After sailing with Christopher Columbus on his second voyage to the New World in 1493 that discovered Nevis, Ponce de Leon remained on their next stop in Hispaniola (Santo Domingo), an island south of Florida, and would search for the fountain that was said when drunk would allow a person to never grow old. However, Ponce de León did not mention the fountain in any of his writings throughout the course of his expedition. The historical connection was made in Gonzalo Fernández de Oviedo's *Historia general y natural de las Indias* of 1535, in which he wrote that Ponce de León was looking for the waters of Bimini to regain youthfulness, yet arrived on the coast of Florida. A similar account appears in Francisco López de Gómara's *Historia general de las Indias* of 1551.

Ponce de Leon's Route in Quest of Fountain of Youth

In the Memoir of Hernando d'Escalante Fontaneda in 1575, the author places the restorative waters in Florida and mentions Ponce de León looking for them there. Fontaneda had spent seventeen years as an Indian captive after being shipwrecked in Florida as a boy. In his Memoir he tells of the curative waters of a lost river he calls "Jordan" and refers to de León looking for it. Herrera makes that connection definite in the romanticized version of Fontaneda's story included in his *Historia general de los hechos de los Castellanos en las islas y tierra firme del Mar Oceano*. Herrera states that local caciques (a Taíno word kassiquan, meaning "housekeeper") paid regular visits to the fountain. A frail old man, he observed, could become so completely restored that he could resume "all manly exercises... take a new wife and beget more children." Herrera adds that the Spaniards had unsuccessfully searched every "river, brook, lagoon or pool" along the Florida coast for the legendary fountain. Thus the mystique of the water's of the New World would spread all over Europe.

Even after years of search there is no trace of the fountain of youth, thus modern day researchers have claimed that this is a wishful thinking rather than reality. Many studies of cultures have led philosophers to interpret the fountain of youth as a metaphor for education and illumination.

Bath Springs, Nevis

Nevis is a small island in the Caribbean Sea that forms part of the inner arc of the Leeward Islands chain of the West Indies. Nevis and the neighboring island of Saint Kitts constitute one country - the Federation of Saint Kitts and Nevis. Nevis is located near the northern end of the Lesser Antilles archipelago about 350 km east-southeast of Puerto Rico (Boriken) and 80 km west of Antigua. Its area is 93 square Kilometres (36 sq mi) and the capital is Charlestown. Saint Kitts and Nevis are separated by a shallow channel known as "the Narrows".

Nevis is roughly conical in shape with a volcano known as Nevis Peak at its center. The island is beautifully laced on its western and northern coastlines by sandy beaches which are composed of a mixture of mostly white coral sand with some brown and black sand which has eroded and washed down from the volcanic rocks that make up the island. The gently sloping coastal plains have natural freshwater springs as well as volcanic hot springs especially along the western coast. Thus, Nevis was named *Dulcina* - "Sweet Island" - by the Arawaks and later *Oualie* - "land of beautiful waters" - by the Caribs. As both these peoples were rather nomadic, one can imagine having sailed the various islands under the hot sun, only to arrive thirsty. Finding these spring waters would have been a most welcomed relief.

Later in the 18th century Nevis became known as "Queen of the Caribees." The country name *Nevis* is originally derived from the Spanish - *Nuestra Señora de las Nieves* - which means Our Lady of the Snows - the name which first appears on Spanish maps in the 16th century. Nevis is also known by the sobriquet - Queen of the Caribees - which it earned in the 18th century when its sugar plantations created much wealth for the British and America.

Today mostly hidden away by a morass of vegetation, this is the spring where British naval hero Lord Horatio Nelson provisioned his flotilla of ships with fresh water. Located at Cotton Ground near the beach, the site no doubt is where the Arawaks landed and called Nevis *Dulcina*, "Sweet Island" later *Oualie* "land of beautiful waters" by the Caribs who some believe drove the Taino's off the island before Columbus' arrival. No doubt, Captain Kidd and other pirates also provisioned their ships here also.

Nelson's Spring, Nevis (c. 1973)

Captain John Smith, on his way to establish the colony of Virginia, spent five days at Nevis. The Carib Indians were reported to be wary and had no dealings with him or his men. How many there were, then or at any other time during the short period they were, it is impossible to know. In 1607 Smith documented the many hot springs in Nevis, whose waters would be found to have remarkable curative abilities against skin ailments, joint pains, and ailing health in general. *Taking the Bath* was already a popular healing movement in England and Europe and that site would later become the famous 'Bath Hotel,' the first Spa and Hotel of the Caribbean.

Nevis is blessed with an abundance of water and geothermal energy, both healing agents. For centuries, islanders, visitors and guests to the Queen of the Caribees have enjoyed the hot springs at Bath Village. Built in 1778, the Bath Hotel in Nevis was the first tourist hotel in the Caribbean. It was a rather grand "spa" hotel, and it rapidly became a very successful venture, attracting many wealthy European visitors who were hoping to treat their various ailments using the healing waters of the nearby volcanic hot spring, the "Bath Spring", and perhaps more importantly, to enjoy the social scene at this tropical spa hotel on what was then the busy colonial island of Nevis. Guests would visit by ship from throughout the West Indies and Europe for this pleasurable experience. So as the Caribbean islands became more settled, people from Europe started arriving not only for escape from religious persecution, but also as a quest for health and rejuvenation. The peacefulness of Nevis became the ideal location.

Bath is a small village on the island of Nevis, in Saint Kitts and Nevis. it is located on the west or Caribbean coast of the island, just south of Charlestown, near the southernmost end of Gallows Bay. The name of the village is derived from the fact that it is situated near a large volcanic hot spring, which has been used for healing therapeutic bathing for many centuries. During the 18th century, the Bath Hotel, an elegant hotel with a stone two-story bathhouse, was built near the hot spring source.

The Bath Hotel circa 1950.
Originally one walked through terraced gardens full of tropical flowers to reach the two-story stone bathhouse, which was supplied with water by a pipe that ran directly from the hot spring below.

Well-known photo of the early days at the Bath Hotel taken by Jose Anjo of Antigua.

The original main building of the Bath Hotel was constructed on a hillside above the spring, such that from one side the Bath Road meets the top story of the hotel, and from the other side the hotel is three, rather grand, stories high.

John Huggins, a merchant and aristocrat built the large, stone hotel at a cost of 43,000 "island" pounds, and surrounded it with lush landscaping, statuary, and goldfish ponds. The hotel was 200 feet long and 60 feet wide. Dignitaries such as Lord Nelson, Samuel Taylor Coleridge, and Prince William Henry, who was the Duke of Clarence, visited the hotel in its heyday.

With the downturn of the sugar industry, Nevis stepped into the world of tourism with this hotel, which flourished for about 60 years. Since then the hotel has had various uses, reopening as a hotel from 1912 until 1940. It was used as training center for the West Indian regiment during World War II, and most recently, the temporary headquarters of the Nevis police department while the new station was being built. Later in the 2000s it was used as government offices.

The Bath House, circa 1989

Within the compound of the Bath Hotel is the Spring House, a two story masonry structure which was constructed from local hand cut stones. This building sits on the upper bank of the Bath Stream. The facility comprises of five thermal baths whose source of water springs from the base of the house. The spring water contains minerals of medicinal value and is known to have cured many of chronic rheumatism and gout in those days. Its water temperature ranges from 104ºF to 108ºF hence the reason why the Spring House was used significantly by visitors and locals alike.

'One would think the English were ducks; they are for ever waddling to the waters,' complained Horace Walpole in 1790.

Horace Walpole, was a British politician and writer, noted for his collected letters and for having written the first Gothic horror novel, The Castle of Otranto (1764).

In the nineteenth century the medical emphasis switched to healing waters and climates, and for the Caribbean that fit the bill as well, filling the Bath Hotel and Nevis' private Beaches with guests. The essence of the operation was that one had to leave home in pilgrimage; which offered the excitement of travel, the change of air, scenery, routine and company, which remains an ancient custom to this day.

NEVIS' SPRING WATER, THE SOURCE

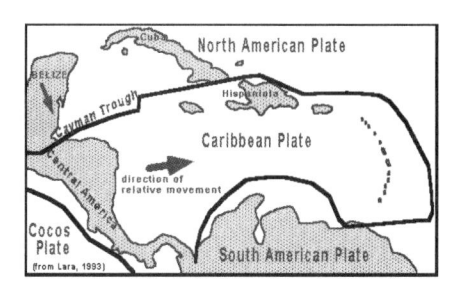

Since the Cretaceous period in geologic history (65 million years ago), the North Atlantic crustal plate has been moving westward and diving beneath the Caribbean crustal plate. Nevis is under laid exclusively by volcanic rocks. There are thought to be at least five main centers of volcanic activity on the island along with three other subsidiary centers. The oldest volcanic rocks at 3.34 million years old are thought to be those underlying Hurricane Hill in Newcastle on the northern tip of the island by the Crusader Museum and airport and thankfully the most recent eruptions occurred about 100,000 years ago at Nevis Peak.

Rain in the Caribbean islands increases with increasing elevation. Perennial streams are very rare in Nevis. Runoff only occurs when there is abundant rain during a very short period of time, such that the rate of precipitation exceeds the rate at which it can penetrate the soil, or when there is an extended period of rain as in the summertime, that results in a surplus runoff to the ocean after saturating the soil. The lack of runoff is due to the very permeable nature of the volcanic soils resulting in significant groundwater recharge but limited surface water flow. That is why we build cisterns to catch roof water to store in tanks.

Many of the volcanic islands in the Caribbean have relied on surface water or shallow groundwater supplies and as a result we suffer during drought. Both ground and surface water of these sources are susceptible to drought conditions. Recently scientists have discovered that there are plentiful sources of groundwater in deep volcanic aquifers on Nevis in the flanks of volcanic mountains. The development of these plentiful groundwater supplies is critical for the future expansion of an island's economy. The good government of Nevis has contracted with BEAD, LLC to develop 1.5 *migd* [Million Imperial Gallons per Day] from wells drilled into deep volcanic aquifers. The successful development of over a million gallons of groundwater per day from deep volcanic aquifers in Nevis was only the first step in the sustainable development of groundwater for long term growth. We can rest easy and the water quality from the recently commissioned water wells has been described as excellent.

The Original Source of Nevis' Island Water

Nevis' water supply comes mainly from mountain spring intakes, and is supplemented by several earthen dams. The country's entire population has some degree of access to domestic water supplies. No one goes thirsty or hungry on Nevis. For those who enjoy hiking, but may not want to go all the way to the Nevis peak, there's an alternative but challenging hike to 'the Source' which is the place that supplies water to much of the island. The final stretch to its top is a ladder that one must climb to access it. The walk up is exciting and dramatic; it's easy to see why Columbus named the place "Las Nieves," or snow, since the mountain is usually surrounded by a cloud cover.

This is a spot high up in the clouds along the slopes of Mt. Nevis (elevation: 3,232 feet) where the island's fresh spring water emerges from the ground. The trail appears on Nevis maps dating back to the 1600s when some very industrious, strong and incredibly determined English constructed an iron pipeline to bring the water from its source, high in the mountain, to the populace living below. The trail follows the pipe and is still used by government workers to access the pipe to make repairs.

The Source trail starts out quite wide at the bottom with the only challenges for us being the muddy ground and uneven footing on slick, moss-covered rocks of varying sizes. It's shady for the most part, not too steep, and fairly easy to hike. Then, about halfway up, things change. The path narrows considerably with a steep drop, slippery moss-covered concrete stairs and other natural hurdles testing your balance and agility most of the rest of the way. In a word, it's thrilling, especially if you, like us, get to experience *The Source* while hiking in a small group. You are able to listen to the sounds of the rainforest and feel the wonderment of nature in the islands. It's truly amazing hiking through the bush with clouds passing all around you, the temperature dropping as you climb higher and higher following an ancient, yet still vital pipeline for Nevis.

References
- Bandinel, James. Some Account of the Trade in Slaves From Africa. London: Frank Cass and Co., 1968
- Baring-Gould, Sabine. *Curious Myths of the Middle Ages*. Dover Books, 2005.
- British Empire. From Wikipedia, the free encyclopedia.
- https://en.wikipedia.org/wiki/British_Empire
- Elder, Melinda. The Slave Trade. Krumlin: Ryburn Publishing, 1992.

- Hicks, Dan. The Garden of the World: an historical archaeology of Eastern Caribbean sugar landscapes. Bar Intl. Series 1632, 2007.
- History of sugar. From Wikipedia, the free encyclopedia.
  https://en.wikipedia.org/wiki/History_of_sugar
  Hoag, Dr. Simultaneous Development Of Water And Energy For Sustainable Growth In Nevis. Integrating Water and Sanitation in Sustainable Development. BEAD, LLC.
- Hopkins, Washburn. The Fountain of Youth. Journal of the American Oriental Society, Yale University.
- Jackson, Charles Tenney. THE FOUNTAIN OF YOUTH. Outing publishing company, 1914
- Klingberg, Frank. The Anti-Slavery Movement in England. Hamden: Archon Books, 1968.
- Meide, Chuck. The Sugar Factory in the Colonial West Indies: an Archaeological and Historical Comparitive Analysis. Academia.edu. 2003.
- Riley-Smith, Jonathan. Templars and Hospitallers as Professed Religious in the Holy Land. University of Notre Dame Press, 2009.
- Turner, E. S. Taking the Cure. Quality Book Club. 1967.
- Water quality from new wells on Nevis described as excellent posted: Tuesday 1 July, 2008.
  http://www.sknvibes.com/News/NewsDetails.cfm/5670

Charlestown (Capital), NEVIS: Without a single traffic light nor even a hint of rush hour madness except around holidays, Nevis' population of just over 12,000 live by the mantra "Rush Slowly"; nothing is hurried is here. Yet despite its apparent charming appeal, Nevis offers far more than your average island escape.

CHARLESTOWN, NEVIS. A. M. Losada, Photo.

1950s

CHAPTER 7. From the Bush (Living off the Lands)

The Nevis Bush

We can imagine the landscape Columbus and the early settlers would have found by viewing the variable display of nature's splendor in the terrain around Nevis' peak. This remote area of Nevis is open for all to see, but only hiker's dare tread, from coastline to mountaintop, was once a continuously graceful sweeping display of microhabitat with variations and altitude conditioned biodiversity. Nevisians take obvious pride and have an innate understanding that the assembled landscape, both natural and man-made, constitute a remarkable resource, part of the national patrimony, and an asset of value that is priceless and remains relatively unexplored.

A View of Nevis from St Kitts by Nicholas Pocock. John Pinney commissioned this painting in 1790. Nicholas Pocock was an artist and sailor who drew pictures of ships, featuring slave trading on the coast of Africa. The picture depicts the landscape by the sea at turn of the 18th Century.

A View of Nevis in the background from Shitten Bay, St Kitts. The picture depicts the landscape by the sea at turn of the 20th Century. One can note the extensive deforestation of the coastal landscape as compared to Popock's painting above. Shitten's bay is one of the best snorkeling hot spots on St. Kitts. The waters are shallow and the array of colorful fish remarkable.

Nevis is situated some six degrees south of the Tropic of Cancer with temperature-moderating areas of open Atlantic ocean to the east, has a tropical marine climate, heavily influenced by steady northeast trade winds, which produces an environment ideal for human comfort. There are only small variations in temperature throughout the year, the average being 27.8 degrees C (79.6 F) and if below 18 degrees C (65 F), which is extremely rare, but enough to still knock your socks off. The prevailing winds hold fairly steady from the east, swinging seasonally between northeast and southeast with mean speeds ranging from 5.4 mph in November to 9.1 in July which translates to free water evaporation rates about five inches per month or 60 inches per year, which explains the general absence of open water impoundments and the need for tanks and cisterns for water storage. Rainfall is varies from 30 to 50 inches per year, the lowest on its Eastern side.

This distinguishing feature of the landscape of Nevis was shaped in its present form not just by nature but by the interaction of man, agriculture, and nature over time. Several centuries of unguided land cultivation, the damaging effects of plantation-based monoculture on sugar estates have left Nevis, at least until the 1950s, and since, with a scarred and ravaged landscape around the coastal communities. The natural vegetation that would have otherwise helped stem wind and water erosion, is eradicated from free-grazing goats, sheep, cattle, and pigs, and helped reduced the loss of sediments transported by run-off to coastal waters and reefs. As a result, the coastal areas appear rather barren and brown during dry seasons, what was once lush, tropical green landscape.

The agricultural soils of Nevis have been used extensively and intensively for over three hundred continuous years. Although the lowland soils of Nevis, in particular, show the ill effects of this and of other abuses, in general the soils have stood up amazingly well over the long period of cultivation. Chemical analysis of the country's soils as early as 1947 confirmed certain deficiencies. Low nitrogen and organic matter figures for the non-forest cane fields tend to confirm the negative impact of long continued cultivation, free ranging animals, leaving a rather barren landscape of weeds and shrubs.

The flora of the Lesser Antilles embraces about 2,000 species of flowering plants, of which, according to Beard (1949), 243 are trees (a tree being a woody plant capable of attaining a height of five meters at maturity). Of these 243 species of trees, St. Kitts and Nevis have approximately half or 121 species. The present vegetation of St. Kitts and Nevis gives evidence of great disturbance by human and grazing animal activity. In the lowland coastal areas, intensive land use has removed all vestiges of the natural vegetation. This has left today's gardening and landscaping challenging with irrigation, fertilizers, and frequent watering a vital necessity for year round, lush growth of fruits, vegetables, shrubs, and edible landscape. The importation of foreign plants has brought species of animals and reptiles unknown to the island.

Traditional Caribbean Medicine (TCM)

Traditional medicine (TM) refers to the knowledge, skills and practices based on the theories, beliefs and experiences indigenous to different cultures, used in the maintenance of health and in the prevention, diagnosis, improvement or treatment of physical and mental illness. Traditional medicine covers a wide variety of therapies and practices which vary from country to country and region to region. Traditional medicine has been used for thousands of years with great contributions made by practitioners to human health, particularly as primary health care providers (herbalists, 'barefoot doctors,' country doctors, midwives, barber surgeons, nurses, shamans, etc.) at the community level.

The World Health Organization (WHO) defines traditional medicine as "the sum total of the knowledge, skills, and practices based on the theories, beliefs, and experiences indigenous to different cultures, whether explicable or not, used in the maintenance of health as well as in the prevention, diagnosis, improvement or treatment of physical and mental illness." In some Asian and African countries, up to 80% of the population relies on traditional medicine for their primary health care needs. Practices known as traditional medicines in Africa include herbalists, diviners, midwives, Muti, Ifá, and generally, traditional African medicine. Core disciplines today which study traditional medicine include biology, herbalism, ethnomedicine, ethnobotany, pharmacognosy, and medical anthropology.

The term *folk medicine* refers to healing practices and ideas of body physiology and health preservation known to a limited segment of the population in a culture, transmitted informally as general knowledge, and practiced or applied by anyone in the culture having prior experience. All cultures and societies have knowledge best described as folk medicine.

Under colonial rule in Africa, traditional diviner-healers were usually outlawed because they were considered by the European nations to be practitioners of witchcraft and magic, and often declared illegal by the colonial authorities, creating a war against aspects of the indigenous culture that were seen as witchcraft. During this time, attempts were also made to control the sale of herbal medicines. As colonialism and Christianity spread through Africa, colonialists built general hospitals and Christian missionaries built private ones, with the hopes of making headway against widespread diseases. Little was done to investigate the legitimacy of these practices, as many foreigners believed that the native medical practices were pagan and superstitious and could only be suitably fixed by inheriting Western methods. During times of conflict, opposition has been particularly vehement as people are more likely to call on the supernatural realm for healing and solace. Consequently, doctors and health practitioners have, in most cases, continued to shun traditional practitioners despite their contribution to meeting the basic health needs of large segments of the population.

Considerations of health as a fundamental human right and the history of enslavement in the Caribbean as a toxic method of utilizing human labor, slavery guaranteed poor health outcomes and enduring problems in all of its geopolitical and historical contexts. The brutal acts of capture, incarceration, starvation, lack of hygiene, and forced transportation, all weakened health of the migrants. So too did the separation of families, disruption of communities and being held in captivity under constant surveillance, with labor coerced and closely supervised. Indeed, the health of the enslaved was constantly threatened by the rigid regulation of all aspects of daily life until emancipation arrived.

The health of slaves and servants was also vulnerable to the constant threat of violent punishment, dangerous and debilitating occupations, unhygienic living, poor nutrition, as well as environmental exposures. Poor housing, sanitation and inadequate food, water, and clothing put enslaved people at risk of a wide range of debilitating diseases. Throughout the history of their enslavement, however, Africans and immigrants vigorously resisted the destructive effects of oppression and pursued a struggle for health reliant upon their own knowledge, practices, and resources, absorbing new ways of healing through encounters and cross-cultural exchanges with missionaries and the indigenous peoples of the Americas. This led to new adaptations, innovations, and living practices, centered around living off the 'bush' as it came to be known. Thus, a new form of folk medicine emerged in the Caribbean, although never organized and scarcely documented.

A key factor for the survival of African slaves was their adaptive skills brought from their motherland. The plantation owners provided their workers with weekly rations of salt herrings or mackerel, sweet potatoes, and maize, and sometimes salted West Indian turtle. However, the enslaved Africans vitally supplemented their diet with other kinds of wild and cultivated food providing essential nutrients for survival. Enslaved Africans used free time to cultivate garden plots close to their houses, as well as in nearby 'provision grounds'. These were areas of land often of poor quality, mountainous or stony, and often at some distance from the villages which plantation owners set aside for the enslaved Africans to grow their own food, such as sweet potatoes, yams, salad greens, and plantains. In addition to using the produce to supplement their own diet, slaves sold or exchanged it, as well as livestock such as chickens or pigs, in local markets. The location of the provision grounds at the Jessups estate, one of the Nevis plantations studied by the *St Kitts-Nevis Digital Archaeology Initiative*, is shown on a 1755 plan of the plantation. It is labeled as the 'Negro Ground' attached to Jessups plantation, high up the mountain.

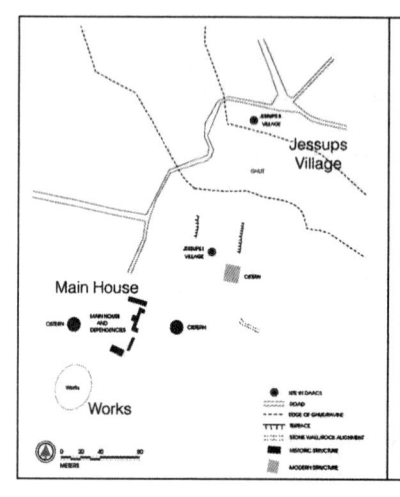

Located on the leeward side of Nevis, the Jessups Estate was an established sugar plantation of 180 acres in the early 1720s. By the mid-1700s, Jessups had grown to over 250 acres with an enslaved population of over 110 individuals. A number of evocative primary documents, including a richly detailed 1755 plat and a 1740 slave inventory, provide important glimpses into the landscape and demographics of the plantation.

Archaeological research has confirmed the location of two slave villages, the first village, Jessups I, dates from the mid-1700s to the early 1780s. A subsequent village, Jessups II, was located to the north of the first village and was occupied from the early 1780s through emancipation in 1834.

As capitalism emerged among the colonies in the Caribbean, there arose a new social system. Enslaved Africans were not simply labor to an estate, but had lives and communities of their own, interacting with other slaves and planters elsewhere on the island. Similarly, planters, merchants, and shipping companies were involved in intricate relationships of trade, credit, culture, and status. Citizens in Bristol or Liverpool England were as caught up in the economic web of Nevis as those living on the island. Wealth and population increase in these two cities grew in proportion to success in Nevis. Decisions made regarding planting, land sales, estate consolidation, price of goods, and the like had consequences reaching into people's live, how and where they lived, and the resources they could access. These are factors were examined by the archeological digs on Nevis.

Although the volcanic soils of the two islands of St. Christopher and Nevis were highly fertile, plantation owners and managers were so eager to maximize profits from sugar that they preferred to import food from North America rather than lose cane land by growing food. Salted meat and fish, along with building timber and animals to drive the mills, were actually shipped from New England, while ignoring the resources abundant, on and around the island of Nevis. According to the Methodist missionary Dr. Coke, fish were abundant off the shores of Nevis. This reflects on the ignorance and arrogance of the plantation owners.

Reverend Smith observed in 1745, "I have known some of them to be fond of eating grasshoppers, or locusts; others will wrap up cane rats, in bonano [banana] leaves, and roast them in wood embers."

On the Stapleton estate on Nevis, records show that there were 31 acres set aside to grow yams and sweet potatoes while slaves on the plantation had five acres of provision grounds at higher elevations, where they could grow vegetables and poultry. The plantation owner distributed to his slaves North American corn, salted herrings and beef, while horse beans and biscuit bread were sent from England on occasion.

Although the enslaved Africans were permitted provision grounds and gardens in the villages to grow food, these were not enough to stop them suffering from starvation in times of poor harvests and drought. A law was passed in Nevis in 1682 to force plantation owners to provide land for food crops to prevent starving slaves from stealing food. In the year 1706 there was a severe drought which caused most food crops to fail combined with the brutal attack of the French buccaneers. Many slaves would have died from starvation had not a prickly type of edible cucumber grown that year in great profusion (Smith 1745).

By the early 18th century enslaved Africans trading in their own produce dominated the market on Nevis. In William Smith's day, the market in Charlestown was held from sunrise to 9 am on Sunday mornings where "the Negroes bring Fowls, Indian Corn, Yams, Garden-stuff of all sorts, etc."

By 1750 St Kitts grew most of its own food but 25 years later, Nevis and St Kitts had come to rely heavily on food supplies imported from North America once again. At the outset of the American Revolution in 1776 trade was essentially closed between North America and the British islands, leading to disastrous food shortages. In 1777 as many as 400 slaves died from starvation or diseases caused by malnutrition on St Kitts and on Nevis.

Island Indigenous Medicine

Doctors on Nevis were historically in very short supply and worked on a fee basis, leaving little care for the common people. Plantation slaves were promised medical care, a small weekly ration of food including flour, corn or peas, and salted fish. However, the island was subjected to wars, drought, and political turmoil, thus local people were left to their rural medical system called *bush medicine*. As with any medical system, practice of bush medicine requires a three-fold knowledge.
- First, one must know the internal logic of the indigenous healing system, including concepts of normal body functioning and the body's response to the environment and various pathogens.
- Second, one must know treatments for maladies. In Caribbean bush medicine, locals treat the majority of recognized illnesses with medicinal plants, or *bush*. These are called 'simples,' the use of a tea bush for a cold or flu, ache or pain, nausea or vomiting, etc. A large part of this knowledge involved folklore; the collection, identification, and description of plant

species handed down through the generations; and good old common sense.
- Third, the healer should know the limitations of bush medicine, and when to seek help from outside the system of home-based care. Yet, Caribbean people generally take care of themselves much more often than they rely on a physician's care even today. Home cure treatment has the power to improve, palliate, or even exacerbate a medical condition. The native Amerindians, for example, were helpless in the wake of the epidemics of smallpox brought by the colonial invaders. Self-limited complaints like food poisoning could take a turn for the worse, especially in the elderly, small children or pregnant women.

There is little known of traditional African medicine and the role of New World Africans in establishing native plants on the plantations. It is little recognized that the vanishing Amerindian population of the Caribbean was replaced with African migrants who originated from tropical societies. Research attention has yet to elucidate fully how New World Africans drew upon their knowledge of tropical plant resources for food, healing, cultural identity and survival. West Africa and the New World, although separated by several thousand miles of ocean, shared some plant species before colonization. Slaves landing on Caribbean shores would probably have recognized some of the plants they encountered on the islands. Newly arrived shamans continued to employ the species as they had used in Africa, having brought seeds and knowledge.

Thus the foundation in tropical botanical knowledge provided Africans the critical knowledge for shaping Afro-Caribbean plant resources and surviving such harsh conditions. With the exception of the coffee plant and the oil of palm, as the British, French and Dutch apparently were not much interested in plants of African origin. The British, French, and Dutch colonists had little knowledge of plant medicines and nutrition, and medicine in general, as different from the Spanish who were looking for new medicines and spices.

While these two valued tree species, palm and coffee, would become minor plantation crops in the Caribbean, most plants indigenous to Africa depended upon New World Africans for their establishment, as arrogant whites did not consume them. Several factors, including soil exhaustion and deforestation, altered the balance of the ecology of the West Indies made matters even more difficult. Yet, by the 18th century, nearly all of the domesticated animals and cultivated plants in the Caribbean were ones that Europeans had introduced from other parts of the world. A better understanding of these conditions is portrayed by the movies *Mutiny* (Mel Gibson), *Cobra Verde* (Werner Herzog, Oscar winner), *Caribbean* (1952), and *Guiana (1838)*; and the documentaries *Slavery in Jamaica*; *The Slavery Business* (BBC).

One of the great food producers in its realm and widely known, at least by name, through its romanticized and dramatized history, the breadfruit, Artocarpus altilis Fosb. (syns. A. communis J.R. and G. Forst.; A. incisus L.f.) belongs to the mulberry family, Moraceae. The common name is almost universal, in English, or translated into Spanish as fruta de pan (fruit), or Breadfruit, Artocarpus altilis. The breadfruit tree is handsome and fast growing, reaching 85 feet (26 m) in height. In the green stage, the fruit is hard and the interior is white, starchy and somewhat fibrous. When fully ripe, the fruit is somewhat soft, the interior is cream colored or yellow and pasty, also sweetly fragrant.

The breadfruit is native to a vast area extending from New Guinea through the Indo-Malayan Archipelago to Western Micronesia.

It is said to have been widely spread in the Pacific area by migrating Polynesians, and Hawaiians believed that it was brought from the Samoan island of Upalu to Oahu in the 12th Century A.D. It is said to have been first seen by Europeans in the Marquesas in 1595, then in Tahiti in 1606. At the beginning of the 18th Century, the early English explorers were in its praises and fame by saving many thousands of people with several periods of famine in Jamaica between 1780 and 1786. It inspired plantation owners in the British West Indies to petition King George III to import seedless breadfruit trees to provide food for their slaves. They now grow all over the Antilles in crops and backyards. They serve readily as a substitute for Irish potato dishes in casseroles, soups, and salads.

There are some examples of Europeans, especially missionaries, relying on traditional herbal cures administered by enslaved people who in turn rejected the main European treatments of the time, which included bloodletting and purging, favorites among the European medics in those times. Africans often used their own traditional remedies to treat diseases they were already familiar with. A wide range of plants such as aloes, okra and even cottonseeds, was used to treat all sorts of illnesses such as water retention, piles, worms, stomachache and to heal wounds. Herbal remedies were also used against diseases such as malaria, yellow fever, cholera, and smallpox but with little recorded effects.

AFRICAN PLANTS ENTER THE NEW WORLD

African plants entered the Americas repeatedly over the 350 year period of the Atlantic slave trade in which millions of Africans were delivered into bondage. Arriving aboard slave ships as cultivars, seeds, food and medicines, the plants were grown by New World Africans on plantation provision fields, backyard gardens, and subsistence plots. In this manner, more than fifty species native to Africa became an essential part of the Caribbean botanical resources that have allowed the Caribbean peoples to thrive into the 21st century. An additional fourteen species of plants of Asian origin, but grown in Africa since antiquity, were also established by this colonization.

In the use of plants, African practices differed dramatically from those favored by Europeans. Herbal treatments were often prepared from living plants, rather than the dried concoctions, tinctures, syrups, elixirs, liniments, and balms favored in colonial and pirate medicine. Vitamin-rich greens formed a central component of the diet of New World Africans, and roots and herbs made into fresh infusions (bush teas) which remain to this day *central* to the traditional cures of the Caribbean. West Africa's rich tradition of using bush or herbal teas and greens for both food and medicine was the source of their continuing importance in the African Diaspora. In West Africa, the leaves of at least 150 species of plants are used as food, with 30 cultivated and over 100 collected gathered in the wild, with that tradition carried over to the Caribbean islands.

West African slaves brought not only herbal knowledge with them across the Atlantic but they also brought the actual seeds. Some wore necklaces of wild liquorice seeds as a protective amulet. Some knowledgeable Captains of slave vessels used native roots to treat fevers that decimated their human cargo. The ships' hellish holds were lined with straw that held the seeds of African grasses and other plants that took root in New World soil. Moreover, since the West African slave-coast climate is similar to the climate in the mid-Atlantic, slaves found some counterparts to their own plant species. And the herb lore of captive Africans was expanded by contact with Indian tribes as well as by interaction with European missionaries.

Europeans also introduced new food plants to the region. Of these, bananas and plantain and the famous Polynesian 'breadfruit' were a valuable addition to the food supply. Sugar and rice formed the basis of plantation agriculture, along with sugarcane, which juice provides valuable B-vitamins and is still sold as a tonic drink on the roadside in Latin countries where sugarcane is grown as in Columbia and Ecuador. New World foods from South America also found their way to Africa, such as the white potato, cassava and maize which moved across the Atlantic to Africa.

African domesticated plants, important into Caribbean cuisines, include the akee apple (Blighia sapida), wild spinach or pigweed (Amaranthus hybridus, Amaranthus spp.) along with bitter leaf (Vernonia spp.) and the mustard greens (Brassicas), the favored in Diaspora dishes providing valuable vitamins and minerals, and dietary fiber. Other African introductions include the baobab (Adansonia digitata); and the kola nut (Cola acuminate, C. nitida), a nonalcoholic stimulant with medicinal properties. By the early 1700s, African cola nut served as food and medicine for Jamaican slaves. The caffeine-containing nut smells a bit like rose petals, and has a taste that starts out bitter but eventually ends on a sweet note. Because kola nut has a long history of use in the preparation of beverages in African and Muslim cultures, John Pemberton, a 19th century American pharmacist, was inspired to combine kola with cocoa, sugar and carbonated water, giving the world the famous soft drink aptly named *Coca-Cola.*

Most West African cultivars traditionally served both food and medicinal purposes. Grains, fruits and tubers sustained the body while leaves, barks and roots ('the doctors') from the same plants, healed it. Because so many cultivars also served as medicines, introduction of Old World food plants to feed the growing slave populations supplied Africans with a familiar assortment of medicines that many Europeans would not eat. Common citrus species like lemon, originally used in Africa only for it curative properties, was being cultivated and used medically in Brazil by 1549 and would only later serve as the cure for ship's scurvy in the 18th century.

In the 1497 expedition of Vasco de Gama, the curative effects of citrus fruit were already known and confirmed by Pedro Álvares Cabral and his crew in 1507. The Portuguese also planted fruit trees and vegetables in Saint Helena, a stopping point for homebound voyages from Asia east of Rio de Janeiro, and left their sick, suffering from scurvy and other ailments to be taken home (if they recovered) by the next ship. However, it was not until 1747 that British surgeon James Lind formally demonstrated that scurvy could be treated by supplementing the diet with citrus fruit, in the first ever clinical nutrition trial. Thus all British ships began giving their crew limes to add to their afternoon provision of rum, creating the climate of 'limeys' that led to concoctions of rum punch and later an entire industry standard in liquor drinks rotating around a budding citrus and rum industry.

Overall, carried aboard slave ships, African plants contributed significantly to survival, health and economy in the Caribbean. Other early introductions of medicinal food crops included winged yam, pigeon pea, sorghum, oil palm, watermelon, akee and black-eyed peas. The African's use of okra, both as a staple and the seeds to induce abortion had been observed in the mid 18th century in Guyana. Okra pods were then taken to the colonies and became part of the cuisine of 'gumbo' stew of Louisiana. Okra is a hibiscus species with a pretty flower and grows easily in southern climates.

The journey across the Middle Passage also introduced African grasses used for bedding and as fodder for cattle, but also as 'weeds' that would dust their seeds onto the islands upon landing. Guinea grass, Megathyrsus maximus, was reported in Barbados in 1684 and introduced to Jamaica in 1745. It can be used as a long-term foraging grass for livestock. Many crops, given to the enslaved aboard the slave ships, also provided the means for New World Africans to establish these plants in plantation fields and their backyard gardens - these include African rice (Oryza glaberrima), yams (Dioscorea cayensis, D. rotundata), cow [black-eye] peas (Vigna unguiculata), pigeon (Congo) peas (Cajanu cajan), melegueta peppers (Aframomum melegueta), palm oil (Elaeis guineensis), sorrel/roselle (Hibiscus sabdariffa), okra (Abelmosclus esculentu), sorghum (Sorghun bicolor), millet (Pennisetum glaucum, Eleusine coracana), the Bambara groundnut (Vigna subterranean), and mangoes (Mangifera Indica).

One African plant, the Castor bean (Ricinus communis) was used for lamp oil, medicine and even as a hair tonic. Other prominent African medicinal plants introduced during the transatlantic slavery included (Momordica charantia) cerasse, (Kalanchoe integra) leaf of life, (Phyllanthus amarus) carry-me-seed, (Leonotis nepetifolia) leonotis, (Cola acuminate) kola nut and broomweed. The curative value of Kalanchoe is reflected in its common names 'long-life' and 'never-die', while 'maiden apple' or the 'African cucumber' (Momordica charantia) ranks as the single most important medicinal of African origin in the Caribbean to offset diabetes. It is also used in Asian medicine as an abortifacient, to treat snakebite, pain, high blood pressure and as an anti-inflammatory for rheumatism and arthritis. Another Old World plant esteemed for healing among population of the African Diaspora is Abrus precatorius, jumbie bread, a venerable south Asian ayurvedic medicine that had already diffused to the African subcontinent from India long before the onset of the transatlantic slave trade. Used as a febrifuge and expectorant by Caribbean diaspora populations, Abrus precatorius, wild liquorice, remains an esteemed herbal remedy throughout the Caribbean.

Table 2. TRAMIL Recommended Medicinal Plants Integrated in the Cuban National Health Systems

Allium sativum L.	Justicia pectoralis Jacq.
Aloe vera (L.) Burm. f.	Lycopersicon esculentum Mill.
Anethum graveolens L.	Manihot esculenta Crantz
Beta vulgaris L. *	Matricaria recutita L.
Bixa orellana L.	Mentha x piperita L.
Capsicum annuum L.	Myristica fragrans Houtt. *
Chenopodium ambrosioides L. *	Musa x paradisiaca L.
Citrus aurantifolia (Christm.) Swingle	Nicotiana tabacum L.
Citrus auratium L.	Ocimum basilicum L.
Citrus limetta Risso *	Ocimum gratissimum L.
Citrus sinensis (L.) Osbeck	Pimenta dioica (L.) Merr
Cocos nucifera L.	Plantago lanceolata L.
Coffea arabica L.	Plantago major L.
Cucurbita moschata Duchesne	Psidium guajava L.
Curcuma longa L.	Senna alata (L.) Roxb. *
Cymbopogon citratus (DC.) Stapf	Simarouba glauca DC. *
Eucalyptus citriodora Hook.	Solanum tuberosum L.
Eucalyptus globulus Labill.	Thymus vulgaris L. *
Foeniculum vulgare Mill.	Tradescantia spathacea Sw. (formerly Rhoeo spathacea [Sw.] Stearn) *
Guazuma ulmifolia Lam. *	Zea mays L.
Haematoxylon campechianum L.	Zingiber officinale Roscoe

* Included in the Cuban National Health Systems since 1991.

TRAMIL (Program for Applied Research and Diffusion of Medicinal Plants in the Caribbean)
The main form of traditional medicine in Cuba involves the popular use of plants as a means to resolve health problems. The roots of these practices are found in the historical and social development that resulted in the rise of the Cuban nation. The first reference to our medicinal plants occurred within ten days after the Spaniards arrival on the north coast of Holguín Province, in Cuba's eastern region. Under the date of November 5, 1492, Christopher Columbus' diary notes: "It is remarked that an Indian said, by sign, that almáciga is good for problems of the stomach".

Other plants of Old World origin were long established in Africa prior to their dissemination across the Atlantic by slave ships include mustard greens and kale, introduced from the Mediterranean, and sesame seed, originally of Asian origin but so long used in Africa that it bears the name 'benne' which became the plant's name in the U.S. south. Other plant exchanges underway for millennia before Europeans began enslaving Africans in the 15th century include Taro (Coloasia esculenta), lime (Citrus aurantifolia), the luffa sponge (Luffa spp.), an edible green (Celosia argentea) and banana and plantain (Musa spp.) diffused to Africa in prehistory.

There is as yet no systematic overview of the medicinal species of African origin that are widely used in Caribbean pharmacopoeias. However, the dozens of compendia of herbal medicines now published in the Caribbean and tropical West Africa offer a study of African plant cures, traditionally valued by Caribbean populations.

Polynesian Breadfruit
Breadfruit is a staple Caribbean food, but it's not native to the region. Like many other fruit and plants, it was transplanted. The humble breadfruit is said to have arrived in 1793 brought by Captain William Bligh of the HMS Bounty. Breadfruit (Artocarpus altilis) and its close relative, breadnut (A. camansi), belong to the mulberry botanical family, Moraceae. Within the Caribbean, breadfruit is also known as "cow", "panbwa", "pain bois", "frutapan" and "fruta de pan", whereas, breadnut is also referred to as "chataigne". Jackfruit (A. heterophyllus) is another member of the Artocarpus genus that is known in the region. The seeded breadnut, which is considered as an ancestor of breadfruit, originated in Papua New Guinea in the Western Pacific region. Thousands of years ago, as early peoples moved eastwards across the Pacific with breadnut, the seedless breadfruit developed and became predominant in in the eastern part of the South Pacific. Most of the breadfruit in the Caribbean came from this region.

French navigators first introduced breadnut to the Caribbean and later, in 1793, the famous Captain William Bligh, a British navigator of *Mutiny on the Bounty*, introduced both more breadfruit and breadnut plants from the Pacific to St. Vincent and Jamaica. While most of the breadfruit and breadnut plants in the Windward and Leeward Islands most likely came from plants sent from the botanic gardens in St. Vincent by the early 1800s, in the Windward Islands especially, some might also have been obtained from the nearby French territories, Martinique and Guadeloupe.

The most economically important product of the breadfruit tree is the fruit which is a nutritious, high energy and fiber food source. A 100 g edible portion of boiled breadfruit flesh provides 114 kcal, mainly from carbohydrates, 4.9 g of dietary fiber, 17 g protein, and appreciable amounts of minerals such as calcium, the B vitamins and essential fatty acids. Breadnut seeds are also highly nutritious because they have a high content of both carbohydrate and protein.

Breadfruit is prepared for cooking by boiling, steaming, roasting, baking and frying as it is as versatile as the common white potato. Breadfruit is used to prepare a wide range of dishes and even drinks and it is consumed at any meal. The fruit is processed into commercial products including vacuum-packed, roasted slices, canned slices, and chips, and there is current commercial interest in a flour, and a traditional product with a wide range of uses. The leaves, bark and latex of the breadfruit and breadnut trees have commercial potential for medicinal and insecticidal purposes. The wood of old trees has also been used traditionally for construction and furniture-making.

A Famous Caribbean Herb and Spice

The species Capsicum spread throughout the Caribbean basin in prehistoric times, carried by Amerindians via boat from the Amazon basin to what is now Venezuela to Trinidad, and then through the Lesser Antilles to the Greater Antilles, and finally ending in the Yucatán Peninsula. Capsaicin in chili peppers is the antibacterial, hot chemical and was used before refrigeration to reduce the spoilage of food, so the hotter the pepper, the greater its antibacterial powers.

In folk beliefs, the more pungent a chili pod, the more powerful it is in fighting evil. The East Indian population of Trinidad wraps seven red pepper pods with salt, onion skins and garlic skins in paper, and passes it seven times around a baby to remove *najar*, the evil eye, which is believed to cause unnecessary crying. Also, green chiles are dropped around the doorway to keep away evil spirits. In folk medicine, hot peppers have long been applied to wounds throughout the Caribbean to prevent them from becoming infected, so hotter peppers would work more effectively.

One day in early November 1492, following a reconnaissance of the northern coast of Cuba, Martin Pinzón, the captain of the Pinta, brought Columbus two pieces of bark, claiming he had found cinnamon plantings. But upon inspection of the trees the admiral found that they were not cinnamon. Pinzón also reported that an Indian had been seen carrying some bright red objects that looked like nuts; these were probably native chili peppers, a species of Capsicum. Two envoys sent inland on a journey of several days were unsuccessful in their effort to find the great Khan, but upon returning they reported that they had observed cultivated fields planted with creole peppers, known as ají to the natives. In his own reports Columbus frequently mentioned spices, and in 1493 he took back to Spain samples of leaves, fruits, and branches, of various trees and plants to prove his findings.

In September 1493, two months before he would discover Nevis, Columbus started out on his 2nd voyage with a fleet of 17 caravels and some 1,500 men to establish Spanish power in the New world and continue the search for gold and spices. On this trip the admiral took with him the Spanish physician Diego Chanca, who would describe in vivid detail the flora and fauna of the New World. Dr. Chanca reliably informed about the pungent ají fruits utilized by the natives in Hispaniola to season their yams, meat, and fish. Because of its great "heat" this new spice, called "red pepper" by the Spaniards, caused blisters on the tongue. Presumably it was of the same species of Capsicum as the red pepper fruits reported from northern Cuba during the first voyage. Later this condiment became popular in Hungary as "paprika pepper". Today it is a world celebrated spice.

Dr. Chanca reported examining a medium-sized evergreen tree, with a smooth gray trunk, whose aromatic fruits were characterized by a flavor resembling a combination of cinnamon, nutmeg, and cloves - the allspice or pimento tree, indigenous to the West Indies and Latin America. Columbus and his men were not aware of the importance of these pungent *allspice* berries, and it was not until many years after the death of the admiral that this new spice became popular in Europe. Since the allspice berries resemble peppercorns in shape they were called *pimienta*, the Spanish word for pepper. The high value placed on the true black pepper of India undoubtedly explains why various aromatic and pungent plants found by the early explorers of the Western Hemisphere were called "peppers." Recall, that the British Pound Sterling, in England the Statutes of Ethelred, at the end of the 10th century, required Easterlings (East Germans from the Baltic and Hanseatic towns) to pay tribute that included 10 pounds of pepper for the privilege of trading with London merchants. Some authorities suggest that the word sterling (English currency) is derived from "Easterlings," the early German spice traders in England who sold goods from the East who had to be worth their pound in pepper.

Graman Quassi, Herbalist

Kwasimukamba or Graman Quassi (1692 – 12 March 1787 in Paramaribo) was a Surinamese healer, botanist, slave and later freedman of the 18th century, who is today best known for having given his name to the medicinal plant species *quassia*. Kwasi's roots were among the Kwa speaking Akan people of present-day Ghana, but as a child he was enslaved and brought to the New World. As a slave in Suriname, a Dutch colony in South America, he participated in the wars against the Saramaka maroons as a scout and negotiator for the Dutch, and he lost his right ear during the fighting. Kwasi worked as a healer of some renown, and fared so well that he was able to get his freedom and travel to the Netherlands.

One of his remedies was a bitter tea that he used to treat infections and 'malignant fevers' was by purging intestinal parasites, this concoction was based on the plant Quassia amara. Quassi acquired considerable reputation in the treatment of the malignant fevers of that country, by a secret remedy, which he was induced to disclose to Mr. Rolander, a Swede, for a valuable consideration. Specimens were taken to Stockholm by this gentleman in the year 1756, and the medicine soon became popular in Europe which Carolus Linnaeus named after him, as the discoverer of its medicinal properties. Quassia continues to be used in industrially produced medicines against intestinal parasites today. In contemporary accounts he was described as "one of the most extraordinary black men in Suriname, and perhaps the world".

Quassia bark tea is very proper in dyspepsia, the result of debility of the digestive organs, and is particularly useful in convalescence from alcoholism. The infusion forms an excellent vehicle for alkaline remedies in the acidity of the stomach of gouty and rheumatic habits, and for abuse from the purgatives in the constipation. It is likewise a powerful anthelmintic, destroying the worms, or preventing the formation yet mild as a tea, safe enough for children with pinworms. The editor has used the herb for more than twenty years.

Conclusion

A lot of the medical information in Africa is unknown or has been lost over several centuries, and unfortunately that which has been lost, still most difficult to be retrieved from adequate sources of authentication found in former slave colonies in the New World. When the Africans arrived on the larger islands like Jamaica, Cuba, Hispaniola, exchanges occurred between Africans and Amerindians, resulting in some cases more advanced forms of medicine.

For example, the Haitian nation, which emerged from the first successful slave rebellion of the New World, faced immense political and economic difficulties from the outset. Isolated on the international arena for over half a century, the country was subjected to neo-colonial domination political strife and other factors to create the situation of poverty which still characterizes Haiti today. The thoughts and practices which has given birth to this indigenous medical system seems to be in continuity with the knowledge and the reflections of their African ancestors. A significant contribution came from Amerindian ancestors as well, and European elements also have partially contributed to its development. The Traditional Medical system of Haiti is, thus, part of the people's culture, a people who have found in the reservoir of its heritage the principles, methods and medical knowledge, and combined with acquired knowledge, which are appropriate to their needs and fit their cultural and religious thoughts.

We find a much different story in St. Kitts and Nevis. Two small islands, relatively uninhabited, settled by Europeans with the only culture in mind was to build slave plantations to make money from agricultural factories. Thus, medical tradition except for the African settlements, was virtually non-existent. The medicine practiced by slaves and servants was generally 'folk medicine', and little was recorded. As different from the nearby island of Dominica, where a rural medical system as *bush medicine* has been recorded in *Bwa Mawego*, a community of historically remarkable health, where herbal knowledge was passed on across generations, no such tradition exists in Nevis to the author's knowledge. The medical heritage of Nevis consists mostly of 'simples,' folk and time-tested remedies for common aches and pains, 'simple' bush teas for self-limited complaints, mind you most of all, good common-sense that has helped preserved this lovely island for centuries.

Unlike the Spanish missionaries in Latin America, the British and French contributed little to the medical benefit of the slave and indigenous populations. The British, French, and Dutch Antilles presents no early history of a Florence

Nightingale or Carlos Finlay (Cuba) in the Caribbean. Yet, all of the local population on Nevis is not only familiar with 'bush medicine,' but many regularly drink 'bush tea', made from backyard plants, as a beverage, tonic, and for simple aches and pains. Grandma's *Bush tea* is a Caribbean heritage.

References

- Diet and food production for enslaved Africans. Intl. Slavery Museum.
- http://www.liverpoolmuseums.org.uk/ism/slavery/archaeology/caribbean/caribbean2.aspx
- "Atlantic Slave Trade", http://en.wikipedia.org/wiki/Atlantic_slave_trade
- Beach, Wooster. The American practice of medicine v. 3, 1852. Publisher Charles Scribner
- Digital Archaeological Archive of Comparative Slavery. Jessups Ground.
- http://www.daacs.org/plantations/jessups/
- Finch, Charles, S., "The African Background of Medical Science" in Blacks in Science, Ancient and Modern, edited by Ivan Van Sertima, 2009.
- Graman Quassi. From Wikipedia, the free encyclopedia.
- https://en.wikipedia.org/wiki/Graman_Quassi
- Handler, Jerome S. and JoAnn Jacoby SLAVE MEDICINE AND PLANT
- USE IN BARBADOS. Journal of the Barbados Museum and Historical
- Society Vol. XLI 1993
- Helwig, David, Traditional African Medicine, Encyclopedia of Alternative Medicine, 6 April 2001.
- Morton, J. 1987. Breadfruit. p. 50–58. In: Fruits of warm climates. Julia F. Morton, Miami, FL.
- Newsome, Frederick, "Black Contributions to the Early History of Western Medicine" Blacks in Science, Ancient and Modern, edited by Ivan Van Sertima, 2009
- Roberts-Nkrumah, Laura B. BREADFRUIT AND BREADNUT ORCHARD ESTABLISHMENT. A manual for commercial production. DEPARTMENT OF AGRICULTURE, ST. KITTS AND NEVIS. 2015.
- Robineau-Germosén, I Lionel; Rodríguez, Francisco Morón. Cuban collaboration with the Program for Applied Research and Diffusion of Medicinal Plants in the Caribbean (TRAMIL)/Colaboración cubana con el Programa para la Investigación Aplicada y la Difusión de Plantas Medicinales en el Caribe (TRAMIL). Medical Sciences University of Havana. Central Pharmacological Research Unit. Havana City, Cuba. 2009.
- Rosengarten, F. Jr. 1969. The Book Of Spices. Jove Publishers, NY.
- Savitt, Todd L., Medicine and Slavery. 1978, University of Illinois Press.
- Sheridan, Richard B., Doctors and Slaves: A Medical and Demographic History of Slavery in the British West Indies, 1680–1834, Cambridge: Cambridge University Press, 1985.
- Sylvester, Ayre. BUSH DOCTOR. Forgotten Folklore and Remedies from Jamaica and the Caribbean. LMH Publishing Company (February 1, 2002).

CHAPTER 8. The Pirates of Nevis

The history of the Caribbean holds many mysteries and legends. The most interesting parts of these legends are the pirates of the Caribbean. The Vikings were the first who came in the Caribbean, followed by the conquistadors and explorers, to be followed by the pirates and buccaneers. The central points of their gatherings were the smaller islands of Tortuga, Nevis, and the Bahamas; and their nest egg – Jamaica (Port Royal, home to the privateers). The later part of the 17th and first third of the 18th centuries are considered the "golden age of piracy" when the "masters" of the Caribbean waters were Blackbeard, Captain Kidd, Henry Morgan, Francis Drake, Bartholomew Roberts, Anne Bonny and Mary Read, to name a few.

Piracy is historically an act of robbery or criminal violence by ship or boat-borne attackers upon another ship or a coastal area, typically with the goal of stealing cargo, slaves, and other valuable items or properties. Those who engage in acts of piracy are called pirates. The earliest documented instances of piracy were in the 14th century BC, when the *Sea Peoples*, a group of ocean raiders, attacked the ships of the Aegean and Mediterranean civilizations. Thus, it is a very old act but became famous in the Caribbean. It may be reasonable to assume that piracy has existed for as long as the oceans were used for commerce. As this book portrays, after Columbus 'discovered' the New World, it quickly became the wild, wild West of Europe, and piracy had a lot to do with the historical shaping of the Caribbean as well as Nevis.

The era of piracy in the Caribbean began in the 1500s and died out in the 1830s after the navies of the nations of Western Europe and North America with colonies in the Caribbean began patrolling waters and combating pirates. The period during which pirates were most successful was from the 1650s to 1730s known as the *Golden Age of Piracy*. Piracy flourished in the Caribbean because of the existence of pirate seaports such as the infamous Port Royal in Jamaica, Tortuga next to Haiti, Nassau in the Bahamas, and surprisingly, Nevis.

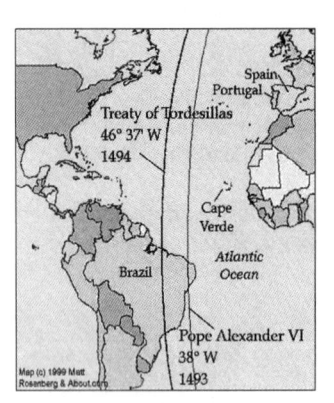

The Caribbean had become a center of European trade and colonization after Columbus' discovery of the New World for Spain in 1492. In the 1493 *Treaty of Tordesillas,* the non-European western world had been divided between the Spanish and the Portuguese along a north-south line 270 leagues west of the Cape Verde off Africa. This gave Spain control of the Americas and Portugal the coast of Africa. The key early settlements were Cartagena in present-day Colombia, Porto Bello and Panama City on the Isthmus of Panama, Santiago on the southeastern coast of Cuba, and Santo Domingo on the island of Hispaniola. In the 16th century, the Spanish were mining extremely large quantities of silver from the mines of Zacatecas in New Spain (Mexico) and Potosí in Bolivia (formerly known as Alto Peru). The huge Spanish silver shipments from the New World to the Old attracted all manner of pirates and contract privateers.

New Spain was a colonial territory of the Spanish Empire, in the New World north of the Isthmus of Panama. It was established following the Spanish conquest of the Aztec Empire in 1521, and following additional conquests, it was made a viceroyalty in 1535. The first of four viceroyalties Spain created in the Americas, it comprised Mexico, Central America, much of the Southwestern and Central United States, and Spanish Florida as well as the Philippines, Guam, Mariana and Caroline Islands. After 1535 the colony was governed by the Viceroy of New Spain, an appointed minister of the King of Spain, who ruled as monarch over the colony. The capital of New Spain was Mexico City.

By the 1560s, the Dutch United Provinces of the Netherlands and England, both Protestant states, were defiantly opposed to Catholic Spain, the greatest power of Christendom in the 16th century; while the French government was seeking to expand its colonial holdings in the New World now that Spain had proven they could be extremely profitable. It was the French Hugenots who had established the first non-Spanish settlement in the Caribbean when they had founded Fort Caroline near what is now Jacksonville, Florida in 1564, although the settlement was soon wiped out by a Spanish, military attack from the larger colony of Saint Augustine. They had also founded colonies in the early 1600's in St. Christopher, Guadeloupe and Martinique.

In England, colonial ventures in the New World was fueled by declining economic opportunities at home and growing religious intolerance for more radical Protestants like the Puritans who rejected the compromise Protestant theology of the established Church of England. After the demise of the English in Saint Lucia and Grenada colonies (1605) soon after their establishment, and the near-extinction of the English settlement of Jamestown in Virginia, new and stronger colonies were established by the English in the first half of the 17th century, at Plymouth, Boston, Barbados, the West Indian islands of Saint Christopher and Nevis, and Providence Island. These colonies would all persevere to become centers of English civilization in the New World. Aided by their governments, English, French and Dutch traders and colonists ignored the treaty to invade Spanish territory: "No peace beyond the line." The Spanish could not afford a sufficient military presence to control this large an area or enforce their trading laws. This led to constant smuggling and colonization in peacetime, and if a war was declared there was even more widespread piracy and privateering throughout the Caribbean, effectively the world's *wild, wild west*.

Thus, the Spanish Caribbean Empire of the 1500s was in decline from the 1600s. The silver had been a double-edged sword, its arrival in Europe providing only a temporary and self-destructive boost to Spain, bringing the envy of others. While in the Caribbean the arrival of European diseases had more than decimated the local populations: the native population of New Spain had fallen by 96% between 1500 and 1600. The Spanish presence in the Caribbean was based on slavery, so while their expansion suffered along with the decline in persons, the newly empty lands were attractive to the more dynamic European nations like the Dutch and English. Also the restrictive Spanish trading regulations came to be more openly flouted, Trinidad becoming a significant port for all nations by trading.

In the 1620s and following the outbreak of the Thirty Years' War in 1618 the Spanish presence in the Caribbean began to decline at a faster rate, becoming more dependent on African slave labor and with a reduced military presence. Meanwhile, other nations began to become more established — Barbados, the first truly successful English colony, was established, as was a colony on Providence Island off the coast of Nicaruagua, which soon became a haven for pirates. The island was known to French and Dutch pirates, but apparently was first visited by English ships in 1628. It had become the premier base for English privateers and other pirates raiding the Spanish Ships for metal coins of gold and silver.

Many of the cities on the Spanish Main in the first third of the 17th century were self-sustaining but few had yet achieved any prosperity. The more backward settlements in Jamaica and Hispaniola were primarily places for ships to take on food and fresh water and thus became havens for pirates. Spanish Trinidad remained a popular smuggling port where European goods were plentiful and fairly cheap, and good prices were paid by its European merchants for tobacco or sugar. The English colonies on Saint Christopher and Nevis, founded in 1623, would prove to become wealthy sugar-growing settlements in time as well as pirate havens.

Nevis was among the list of "Caribee Islands" to which proprietary rights were granted in the King's letter patent of 2 July 1627 to the Earl of Carlisle. The governor, Sir Thomas Warner of St. Christopher, acting in the name of the Earl of Carlisle, gave permission to Anthony Hilton to settle Nevis and appointed him its lieutenant governor. The settlers coming from St. Christopher and the island of Barbuda where they had been raided time and again by the Caribs, prompting them to move to Nevis. Some of the settlers, in addition to their attempt to gain a livelihood through planting tobacco, turned to buccaneering which led to repeated attacks by the Spanish and the destruction of the first plantations (1629). The Spaniards saw the English in St. Christopher and Nevis as trespassers, and when the Spanish Admiral *Fadrique de Toledo* appeared in Nevis (7 Sept. 1629) with 30 armed vessels, the English indentured servants, being badly treated by their masters, deserted to the enemy and Nevis had to surrender. Anthony Hilton left for the island of Tortuga as a developing buccaneer and took with him many settlers from Nevis with him.

The end of widespread conflict in Europe after the thirty years' war (1648) left most of the nations in a dreadful state, especially Spain which had bankrupted. This was reflected in the Caribbean with both a constant influx of European refugees and the shrinking of Spanish power. While the major cities of the region were still Spanish the peripheries were being overrun by other nations' more aggressive expansion. The English had expanded beyond Barbados, with successful colonies on St. Christopher and Nevis, Antigua, Montserrat, and Bermuda. The French were well established on Guadeloupe, Hispaniola and Martinique and they nominally held Tortuga, a noted pirate base from the 1640s. The Dutch had remained an almost baseless trading presence in the area but following the Spanish decline they became established at Curaçao and St. Eustatius.

The Caribbean continued to reflect European policy shifts. As England, France and Holland became stronger they moved from fighting the Spanish over Catholicism to fighting each other over economics. The English began economic sanctions against the Dutch in the 1650s and the two nations were at war three times in the next two decades. Louis XIV was pursuing an aggressive expansionist policy in France. In the 1660s the Spanish Empire had a brief revival with boosted silver output. Basically everyone was fighting everyone else, all the other nations present in the Caribbean. These vagaries were especially apparent in the Caribbean — St. Eustatius changed hands ten times between 1664 and 1674 and many other settlements were damaged by repeated conquest and re-conquest. With the warring European nations providing almost no military support for the colonies, this was a bonanza for privateers, buccaneers, and pirates. Port Royal in Jamaica joined the piracy bases, following the islands capture by the English in 1655. From there it became its infamous pirate port of ill repute and the headquarters for the *Brethren of the Coast*.

While European warfare continued towards the end of the 17th century, affairs in the Caribbean became more settled. The colonies were more important and the adverse economic effects of piracy were more apparent. The English were becoming a much more significant presence and stationed a naval squadron at Port Royale from the 1680s. Privateering was becoming rarer and naval pirate-hunting more common, although the Spanish established a *Costa Guarda* of privateers that patrolled the waters against smugglers and other marauders.

In the Caribbean the use of privateers was especially popular. The cost of maintaining a fleet to defend the colonies was beyond national governments of the 16th and 17th centuries. Private vessels would be commissioned into a 'navy' with a *letter of marque*, paid with a substantial share of whatever they could capture from enemy ships and settlements, the rest going to the crown. These ships would operate independently or as a fleet and if successful the rewards could be fantastic. When Francis Drake captured the Spanish Silver Train at *Nombre de Dios* (Panama's Caribbean port at the time) in 1573 his crews were rich for life. This substantial profit made privateering something of a regular line of business; wealthy businessmen or nobles would be quite willing to finance this legitimized piracy in return for a share of the booty. The sale of captured goods was a boost to colonial economies as well. This confusion between the activities of privateers (legal pirates) and pirates (proper) made the Caribbean waters notorious and rich in stories, legends, crime, and mystique that would last centuries.

Specific to the Caribbean were pirates termed buccaneers. They developed in the 1630s and remained until the effective end of piracy in the 1730s. The original buccaneers were escapees from the colonies, as well as knights and soldiers of Europe after the thirty years war, forced to survive with little support from their crown, so they had to be skilled at boat construction, sailing, military skills, and hunting. In the middle of the seventeenth century, apart from such leading powers as Spain, Portugal, England, France, and the Netherlands, all of a sudden even the Order of St John joined in the global race for colonies as the knights went to sea. The word "buccaneer" is actually from the French *boucaner*, meaning literally *smoked meat*, from the hunters of wild oxen curing meat over an open fire, Amerindian style. They transferred their skills which kept them alive into piracy. They operated with the partial support of the non-Spanish colonies and until the 1700s their activities were made legal, or partially legal, and there were irregular amnesties from participating nations.

Buccaneer is used synonymously with the idea of the 17th-18th century Caribbean pirates, but it actually means something quite specific. When Spain started colonizing the Caribbean in the 16th century, it was initially the only nation to do so. Around the beginning of the 17th century, people from other nations like France, England and the Netherlands started trying to settle in the Caribbean looking for greener pastures, freedom from persecution, and a better life that the plagues had left Europe decimated. The problem was they weren't welcome in Spanish ports because they didn't recognize their right to settle and had no respect for anyone other than devout Catholics. As a result, the only people willing to trade with these settlers and adventurers were social outcasts like mulattos, indentured servants, Amerindians, maroon shipwreck survivors who largely lived in the wild, the pilgrims of the new Americas, and of course the buccaneers and privateers.

Boucaniers is a French term of some ambiguity, but according to Cotgrave's 1611 French/English Dictionary, the closely related word Boucane' translates as a wooden gridiron that these outcasts used to cook meat. Buccaneers started selling supplies like water and meat to the non-Spaniards, who started calling them "Boucaniers." As the story goes, the smell of roasting meat off the beaches would attract the ships to shore, only for the shipmen to find out they were to become the picnic. In addition, the French already had a verb called "boucaner" which meant "to hang around with low lives" or "to imitate a foul tempered, billy goat." These words got meshed together, and the French ended up calling the local outcasts *boucaniers*. From 1620 on, these "boucaniers" started developing reputations as navigators and sharpshooters, which they were, so anyone who wanted to move against the Spanish would want some Boucaniers, or Buccaneers, with them for their combat prowess. By 1680, the term Buccaneer was being used to describe not just the locals but any Pirate or Privateer in general. As a result, the Buccaneer was a Pirate and/or Privateer, sometimes with a *letter of marque*, or other times 'marked,' operating in the Caribbean during the late 17th century and early 18th century.

Nevisians Settle Tortuga

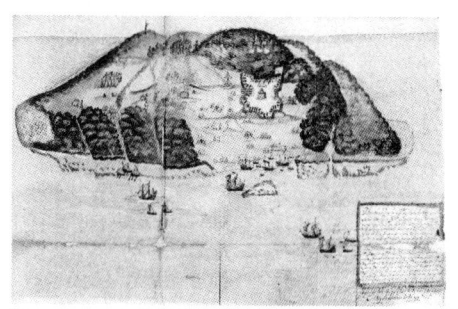

Tortuga or Turtle Island, presently known as *Ile de la Tortue* and located off the Northwest shore of present day Haiti, not to be confused with Isle of Tortuga, a modern day island owned by Venezuela, or the Dry Tortuga owned by the United States. Tortuga is approximately 20 miles long and no more than 4 miles wide, but about twice the size of Nevis' 36 square miles. Tortuga was first discovered and named by the Spanish. The name Tortuga means *Sea Turtle*. It was named this because the island resembles a large, humped turtle. But also keep in mind turtle meat was considered a sailor's delicacy, and any island that harbored them, like Dry Tortuga, also received that name. Despite its immediate proximity to Hispaniola, an island claimed by Spain since the time of Columbus, the French decided to establish a settlement of sorts on the island in 1625. Most of the settlers came from the nearby French colonies and also of St. Christophe and Nevis to escape Spanish war parties.

The Spaniards set to oust these French settlers off Tortuga and the first of these attacks was in 1629 and was only marginally successful. In the same year they also attacked St. Christophe and Nevis. Many of the colonists became the true buccaneers – scavengers and successful hunters of wild oxen and pigs. Rather than fight the Spaniards in open combat, they fled across the narrow channel and began hunting on the northern coast of Hispaniola. Anthony Hilton from Nevis had previously acquired this skill defending it from a Spanish attack in 1629 from Spanish Admiral Fadrique de Toledo. The Spaniards built a fort on Tortuga after they chased away the French but only left the fort with a small garrison to protect it and headed off in pursuit of other Buccaneers. The lightly held fort was easily taken by the original settlers in a counter attack, and the French set about improving the fortifications after the claim of victory. The island would remain a French colony from then on, despite repeated attacks by the Spaniards.

Strategically, Tortuga was a most important island for France. To the Northeast of Tortuga, is Cuba, the last stop of the Treasure Fleet before returning to Spain. France, like most of Europe was at war with Spain for most of the 1600s. Tortuga became a perfect spot to ambush and raid the returning Spanish fleets with their gold and silver. Piracy was given legal status by the colonial powers, especially by France under King Francis I (1515–1547), in the hope of weakening and looting Spain and Portugal's *mare clausum* trade monopolies in the Atlantic and Indian Oceans. This officially sanctioned piracy was known as *privateering*. From 1520 to 1560, French privateers were alone in their fight against the Crown of Spain and the vast commerce of the Spanish Empire in the New World, but were later joined by the English and Dutch once the governments figured out how to profiteer from it, so they legalized it too. This 'perfect storm' developed the golden age of piracy.

Buccaneers on Tortuga (1633-1634)
"The French send a request for a Governor to the Governor of St. Kitts. He sends Jean Le Vasseur to them with men and equipment to further fortify the island. He built the Fort de Rocher on a rocky outcrop of a natural harbour. Tortuga from then on is regularly used by privateers and pirates as a base of operations. In 1633 the governor of Tortuga, also called *association island*, is still Captain Anthony Hilton. In this year the first slaves are imported. 1634 saw the Governor-General of the French West Indies transfer his seat of power from St. Kitts to Tortuga. The Compagnie des Isles d'Amerique takes possession of French Colony on the island."
(Anthony Hilton's letter to his mother. Genealogy.com)

The French Governors of Tortuga would, for a price, offer safe harbor to just about any ship that wasn't Spanish, making it a pirates haven like sleepy Nevis. They were also entrusted with the powers to offer *letter of Marques* to privateers so long as they agreed to attack Spanish ships and split the booty with them. As such, on Tortuga, the Nevis Governor Anthony Hilton, and the pirates joined the developing home of the *Brethren of the Coast*.

The **Brethren of the Coast** were a loose coalition of pirates and privateers commonly known as buccaneers and active in the seventeenth and eighteenth centuries in the Atlantic Ocean, Caribbean Sea and Gulf of Mexico. They were an informal syndicate of captains with *letters of marque and reprisal* who regulated their privateering enterprises within the community of privateers and with their outside benefactors. They were primarily private individual merchant mariners of Protestant background usually of English and French origin.

During their heyday when the Thirty Years War was devastating the Protestant communities of France, Germany and the Netherlands, while England was engaged in various conflicts, the privateers of these nationalities were issued letters of marque to raid Catholic French and Spanish shipping and territories.

Based primarily on the island of Tortuga off the coast of Haiti and the infamous city of

Henry Morgan was perhaps the most famous member of the Brethren and the one usually noted with codifying its organization.

It is believed in 1666 that Henry Morgan arrived on Tortuga as an indentured servant. From here he staged the invasion and sacking of Maracaibo and Gibraltar in 1667. When he returned in May of 1671 he was given a vote of thanks from the Council of Jamaica. Later that year however, he was returned to England for questioning along with Thomas Modyford and imprisoned in the Tower of London in 1672. He was found not guilty of all charges and instead made a *knight*. It is rumored that when Henry Morgan returned to

Port Royal on the island of Jamaica, the original *Brethren* were mostly French Huguenot and British Protestants, but their ranks were joined by other adventurers of various nationalities including Spaniards, and even African sailors, as well as escaped slaves and outlaws of various sovereigns.

Thus, the 'letters of marque and reprisal' was the first instance of the famed 'offshore corporate industry' that would emerge in the Caribbean in the 20th century! As the Templars of Christendom established the first 'traveler's checks', the pirates of the Caribbean (Brethren of the Coast) established the first offshore cooperatives!

the West Indies in the mid 1670's he continued his piracy under a French commission and hid his actions from the British.

Pirate Sir Henry Morgan recruiting

Around this same time (1630), Anthony Hilton, and other Englishmen, set up an English Colony on the island. The English and the French on Tortuga at first were allies against the greater enemy, Spain. This however was short lived as the two start fighting over the imported slaves on the island and who had rights to what property. When the Spaniards got word of this they decided to attack Tortuga and wipe out the divided intruders. They managed to wipe out the English colony but the French and the English survivors once again fled the island only to quickly return. It seems Tortuga really had nothing for the Spaniards because as soon as the interlopers were vacated, the Spaniards left. And once again as the Spaniards left and the like of Buccaneers returned their stake of claim.

By now the buccaneers are *raising Cain* and tobacco while also attacking the Spanish Fleets. By 1641, the French colony has become so well established that the French (Poincy from St. Christophe) send *Jean Le Vasseur* to take control of the island. Le Vasseur managed to expel the English Colony, so to speak. The English Plantation became French in name but most of the population of Tortuga is made of pirates and privateers and these remain on the island with the blessing of the French Government. The pirate fleets offer both protection and income to the small colony. Most of the pirates/privateers are English or French. In order to keep the pirates happy and settled, the French governor imported hundred of prostitutes. So now, as a *waggish observer* in the 17th century West Indies once wrote - that when new colonies were established, the first thing the Spanish did was to build a church, the Dutch to build a fort, the English to build a tavern, and *the French to build a brothel.*

By this time, the pirate/privateer community is firmly established on Tortuga and enjoys the support of the French Government and the brothels. Pirates of any nationality are free to roam the seas around Tortuga under loosely written *Letters of Reprisal* against the Spanish government. Eventually this is frowned upon and the French make efforts to weed their privateer ranks of Dutch Freebooters and

English privateers. The man primarily responsible for this action is Governor Monsieur D'Ogeron. Bertrand D'ogeron had the difficult task of convincing the buccaneers to accept him as governor and to abandon their relations with Dutch rovers. He found the men whom he hoped to convert into colonists dispersed in small and unorganized parties living in a rather primitive fashion along the coasts. The English in turn head for Jamaica and safe harbor while the Dutch head off to Virgin Islands, primarily St. Thomas.

Tortuga Pirates

Among the notable pirates to have ventured into Tortuga is none other than Sir **Henry Morgan** who arrived there in 1660 as and indentured servant. He soon deserted a cruel boss and joined the ranks of Buccaneers as a surgeon, later moving his base of operation to Jamaica. Henry Morgan, a Welshman, was one of the most destructive pirate captains of the 17th century. Although Morgan always considered himself a privateer rather than a pirate, several of his attacks had no real legal justification and are considered piracy. Morgan's most famous exploit came in late 1670 when he led 1700 buccaneers up the pestilential Chagres River and then through the Central American jungle to attack and capture the "impregnable" city of Panama. Morgan's men burnt the city to the ground, and the inhabitants were either killed or forced to flee. Although the burning of Panama City did not mean any great financial gain for Morgan, it was a deep blow to Spanish power and pride in the Caribbean and Morgan became the hero of the hour in England. Henry Morgan had to conceal his activities under French *Letters of Commission* and he actively promoted the island of Tortuga as a base of operations for the Brethren and for the disposal of booty. But Morgan too sailed to the Isla Vache, South-West of Hispaniola, in October of 1668. At the height of his career, Morgan had been made a titled nobleman by the English Crown, Knighted, and lived on an enormous sugar plantation in Jamaica, as lieutenant governor. Morgan died in his bed, rich and respected—something rarely achieved by pirates in his day or any other.

Among the French pirates was none other than **Jean David L'Ollonais**, probably one of the cruelest men to ever hold a cutlass in his hand. Francois L'ollonais was born Jean David Nau in France around 1635. After a period of indentured servitude in Martinique ended in the early 1650's, he spent a time on Hispaniola (now Haiti / Dominican Republic) hunting game with the Buccaneers before moving to nearby Tortuga Island (Isla Tortuga) to pursue the more profitable route of piracy. Tortuga's governor La Place, a pirate himself, gave Nau his own ship around 1655, which he used in cruel pursuit of any Spanish ships and sailors that he found.

Together with Michel le Basque he carries out an attack on the cities of Gibraltar and Maracaibo in 1667. Sometime later in 1667 he sets out again with a fleet of ships to plunder the harbour city Puerto de Cavallo and the town of San Pedro. This same year he dies on the coast of Nicaragua where he and some of his crew were captured by Indians and killed. His merciless treatment earned him the nickname, "The Flail of the Spaniards", but it also produced more resistance when his victims believed death was inevitable - fighting would hurt no less.

By the 1680s, laws were made that English seaman sailing under foreign flags were traitors to the Throne and branded pirates. Several Englishmen sailing from Tortuga under French letters of marque were convicted and hanged for piracy after attacking Dutch ships. When the Spanish gold began to dwindle the buccaneers turned their attention to Jamaican plantations and English Merchant ships. This led to protests from the English government to the King of France. Eventually the buccaneers were privateers only in name and attacked anything that wasn't French. The Governor-general of the French Colonies attempted to bring the buccaneers under control but failed.

Finally, in 1684 the *Treaty of Ratisbone* was signed which formally ended hostility between France and Spain. With the treaty came the withdrawal of all Letters of Marques. From that point on, the Buccaneers who continued attacks were pirates and were quickly hanged. Many of the former privateers were employed by the government of France to hunt down their former *Brethren of the Coast* and would later include an attack on Nevis. While piracy would continue in and around Tortuga for years to come, it no longer enjoyed the status as a Home of the Buccaneers. The pirates found that it was better in the Bahamas with its many small islands upon which to hide.

Captain "Red Legs" Greaves of Nevis
West Indian Pirate, 1670-80. Robin Hood of the Caribbean.

According to legend, Red Legs Greaves was not only a successful buccaneer, but also a lucky one. He managed to survive his life as a pirate and live to ripe old age providing charity on Nevis where he retired thanks to a royal pardon. What makes this history even the more remarkable was how his life began...

Greaves was born in Barbados, the son of Scottish slaves. In the 1935 Errol Flynn movie **"Captain Blood"** there is a scene at the beginning of the movie where several men are tried for treason and eventually sold into slavery. This was a common practice in England and was the case of the parents of Greaves. Apparently Greaves' father was the on the wrong side of the Civil war when Cromwell came to power, as were many people in Scotland and Ireland. *Redleg* is a term used to refer to poor whites that migrated to the islands of Barbados, St. Vincent, Grenada, Nevis and a few other Caribbean. Their forebears came from Ireland, Scotland and the West of

England mostly as indentured servants and workers in the 17th and 18th centuries. In this case however, it was 'white' slave labor, the first slaves of the Antilles.

A short time after the elder Greaves arrived in Barbados as a slave, young Greaves was born and while the new baby boy had nothing to do with the Civil War in England, he paid for the sins of his father and was a slave from the moment of birth. At first, life as a slave was at least tolerable because Greaves had a kind master. But his life took a turn for the worse after his parents as well as his master died and the orphaned boy was sold to another slave master who reputedly delighted in punishment.

While still in his teens, Greaves one night he swam across Carlisle Bay in attempt to find his freedom. Greaves stowed away aboard a ship hoping to sail off to a safe harbor. Unfortunately the ship belonged to a notorious pirate known as *Captain Hawkins*. Hawkins was known throughout the Caribbean as an unusually cruel captain, who found joy in torturing his captives and mistreating women. He rarely offered quarter to ships he attacked and was feared by even his own crew. The only reason his crew remained loyal to him was because he had a knack for finding and looting treasure.

Greaves' childhood as a slave led him to despise Captain Hawkins. Greaves refused to kill for no reason and would not partake in torturing prisoners. It didn't take long for the two men with distinctly different moral codes to come to terms. While it is said that the two men had a duel over the issue, it is more likely Hawkins attacked Greaves for not following his orders and bloody fight ensued. In the end, Greaves managed to terminate Hawkins and the crew which had lived in fear of the cruel Hawkins immediately elected Young Greaves the new Captain.

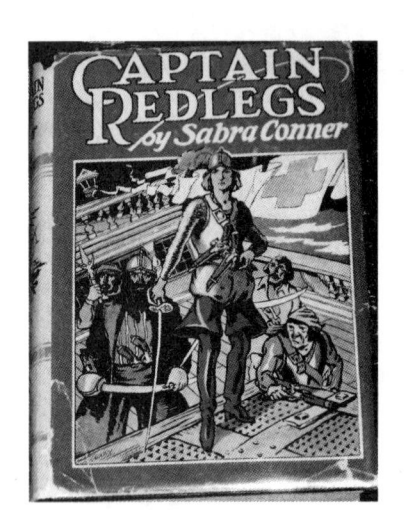

Greaves in turn drew up a new set of Ship's Articles which gave stiff penalties for maltreatment of prisoners and women and willingness to offer quarter. Much to the delight of his crew, what followed was a period of the highest piratical success. As his reputation spread throughout the Caribbean, "Red Leg" Greaves became known for his humanity and morality. He never tortured his prisoners, nor ever robbed the poor, nor maltreated women. He was a true 'Robin Hood' of the Caribbean.

His greatest success of all was his capture of the Island of Margarita, off the coast of Venezuela. On this occasion, after capturing the Spanish Fleet, he turned the guns of their warships against the forts, which he then stormed, and was rewarded by a huge booty of pearls and gold. And as was true to his form, he didn't sack the town, or rape and torture the

Spaniards, he just took the money and left.
Having made off with enough money to last a lifetime, Greaves retired to the respectable life of a plantation on the Island of **Nevis**. The story would end at this point but unfortunately for Greaves, one of his former victims happened to cross his path and turned him in for the bounty. As was typical of the time he was quickly escorted, tried and found guilty in the infamous Port Royal, Jamaica, and sentenced to be hanged. In chains, he was cast into a dungeon to await execution, when the great earthquake came which destroyed and submerged the evil town in 1680, and one of the few survivors was Greaves. Greaves was rescued by a whaling ship and in turn he joined the crew and served them remarkably well. Later he would turn pirate hunter and received a pardon for his earlier crimes after assisting in the capturing a gang of pirates that had been ravaging the whaling fleets.

After Greaves became a legally free and pardoned man he once again retired to a plantation becoming well known for being a charitable and kindly gentleman who gave generously to many public institutions. Greaves died of old age, universally respected and missed by all in his community of Nevis. Red Legs was without a doubt the luckiest pirate, since he was able to retire a wealthy man after starting life as a slave.

Greaves got his nickname "Red Legs" from his heritage. The kilt wearing Scots were known for going bare legged in any weather and this lifestyle led to "red legs" in the Caribbean sun. Red Legs was a common nickname for the Scots and the Irish.

In popular culture
1. He is a character in the 2005 sci-fi bestseller Farlight by Michael Swanson.
2. He is a character in the 2002 book Mortimer the Magic Monkey by Allan D. McCune.
3. Jorun "Red Legs" Greaves is faction officer of Angel Cartel in EVE Online.

CAPTAIN KIDD

William Kidd (ca. 22 January 1645 – 23 May 1701) was a Scottish sailor who was tried and executed for piracy after returning from a voyage to the Indian Ocean. A life lived in the age of imperialism known for its building of European empires, Captain William Kidd was either one of the most notorious pirates in history, or one of its most unjustly vilified and prosecuted privateers, depending upon published perspective. Legends and fiction surround this character; his actual career, however, was punctuated by just a handful of skirmishes, followed by a desperate quest to clear his name. Some modern historians deem his piratical reputation unjust, as there is evidence that Kidd acted only as a privateer.

William Kidd served aboard a twenty-gun brig that anchored in the Leeward Islands of St. Christopher in 1689. Kidd and his compatriots, including a man named Robert Culliford, absconded with the ship, sailing her over to **Nevis**. The ship was rechristened the *Blessed William*, and Kidd became her captain. As a result of election by the ship's crew, or by appointment of Christopher Codrington, governor of the island of Nevis, or both, Captain Kidd and the Blessed William, an experienced leader and sailor by that time, became part of Codrington's small fleet assembled to defend Nevis from the French, with whom the English were at war. The governor did not pay the sailors for their defensive services, telling them instead to take their booty from the French. At that time, Kidd and his men attacked the French island of Marie-Galante, south of Guadaloupe, destroying its only town and looting the area, and gathering for themselves something around 2,000 pounds Sterling.

Marauding Pirates were constantly disrupting English shipping traffic. To solve this problem it was decided that Captain Kidd would sail to pirate infested waters and take pirates into custody. Captain Kidd would then "recover" the booty the captured pirates had plundered from other ships, and would divide it among himself and several investors, who would include King William of England.

Kidd's fame springs largely from the sensational circumstances of his questioning before the English Parliament and the ensuing trial. Captain Kidd was arrested upon his return to New York by the former sponsor of his privateering enterprise, Governor Lord Bellomont. He was taken back to England and put in the notorious Newgate Prison in London, to await his trial. The trial was held on the 8th and 9th of May, 1701. Captain Kidd was found guilty at Old Bailey, London, England. History records his actual depredations on the high seas, whether piratical or not, were both less destructive and less lucrative than those of many other contemporary pirates and privateers.

Among Kidd's officers was his quartermaster, Hendrick van der Heul. The quartermaster was considered 'second in command' to the captain in pirate culture of this era. Van der Heul is noteworthy because he may have been of African descent. This fact would make him the highest ranking black pirate so far identified. Van der Heul went on to become a master's mate on a merchant vessel, and was never convicted of piracy.

Captain Kidd was hanged on May 23rd, 1701 at Tilbury Point Execution Dock. Following tradition, the crowds passed him rum and Captain Kidd was blind drunk when he swung from the gallows. It was said that Captain Kidd died hard, as the rope broke from his weight and he fell to the ground. He was tied up a second time, rehung, and then died. This is why there is a legend of Captain Kidd being hung twice. After he was dead, his body was put in a harness of iron hoops (a gibbet) and chains so that all mariners could observe his rotting, crow-pecked corpse for more than an hour, as they swept around that wide and desolate part of the Thames River. This was a warning to other seamen regarding what happens to

Pirates. Captain Kidd was tarred so as to hold the skeleton together longer, thus his body was totally blackened before the dirt.

BBC NEWS 7 MAY 2015 - CAPTAIN KIDD'S TREASURE FOUND IN MADAGASCAR
Underwater explorers in Madagascar say they have discovered treasure belonging to the notorious 17th-Century Scottish pirate William Kidd. A 50kg (7st 9lb) silver bar was brought to shore on Thursday on the island of Sainte Marie, from what is thought to be the wreck of the Adventure Galley. The bar was presented to Madagascar's president at a special ceremony. US explorer Barry Clifford says he believes there are many more such bars still in the wreck.

Bartholomew Sharp — The Unlucky Pirate Who Threw Away Millions in Silver

A 17th Century sea captain (fl. 1679–1682), buccaneer, and adventurer, Sharp commanded an ill-fated two-year voyage in 1679 to capture Spain's treasure fleet off the Pacific coast of South America. Sharp was, apparently, one of the party of buccaneers, French and English, which in 1679 captured and sacked Porto Bello on the Spanish main.

In order to reach the distant ocean, the party actually landed on the Caribbean side of Panama, abandoned their own ships and marched overland to seize Spanish vessels in Bay of Panama. With their new fleet, the party of 331 men sailed out to find a fortune in treasure.

Sharp's tiny armada spent months cruising the west coast of the continent in search of vessels to plunder; they failed to find any prizes of value. The restless crew soon deposed their captain for his lack of results. Sharp managed to regain command however after the sailors tired of their new skipper. At long last, with the men of the expedition once more on the verge of mutiny, a lookout finally spotted a large galleon flying Spanish colors. The English vessels closed for battle.

Following a brief engagement, Sharp and his men captured the enemy ship. But instead of a king's ransom in jewels and gold, the only booty recovered were 700 slabs of an unknown dull grey metal. Assuming it was tin, the frustrated crew tossed all of it overboard, saving one portion to cast into musket balls. Sharp and scabby his crew sailed for home and the journey was a treacherous one – the small fleet was nearly lost as it navigated around the stormy Magellan Straits. When they finally returned to the Caribbean more than two years after their expedition began, there was more bad news: the entire band was now wanted for piracy by English authorities. Word of their Pacific voyage had been conveyed from Panama to Europe, at which point the Spanish ambassador to London lodged a formal complaint. Hoping to avoid yet another war with Spain, the Crown agreed to bring the voyagers to justice.

As Sharp's party sailed into Barbados, the captain and crew were shocked to discover an English frigate waiting for them. Putting back out to sea, they next tried to make port in Antigua, but were refused entry by local officials. Eventually, they landed at **Nevis**. It was then that the crew made a shocking discovery —

those musket balls they had fashioned themselves from that unknown Spanish metal weren't made of tin at all; they were in fact silver. And so were the 700 slabs of unknown metal they sent to the bottom of the ocean. The entire haul was worth an estimated £150,000 at the time, which would be equal to tens of millions of dollars today.

On his return to England, Sharpe was arrested at the instance of the Spanish ambassador, and tried for piracy; but in the absence of legal evidence was acquitted. His journals and 'waggoners,' carefully written and drawn (Sloane MSS. 44, 46a and b, and 47), suggest that he was permitted to live in peace and comfort. Lack of evidence was the only thing that helped them escape the hangman's noose. Sharp ended his adventuring days and retired to the Danish Island of St. Thomas. He was arrested again and imprisoned for unpaid debts and died behind bars in 1702. His brief career as an adventurer was recorded in a book entitled: The Dangerous Voyage And Bold Assaults of Captain Bartholomew Sharp and Others; by Basil Ringrose, London, 1684. Thus Nevis has landed the two most lucky and unlucky pirates known to Caribbean History.

Bartholomew (Black Bart) Roberts

Born John Roberts on 17 May 1682 in Little Newcastle, Wales. He was the most successful pirate of the so-called "Golden Age of Piracy," capturing and looting more ships than pirates like Blackbeard, Edward Low, Jack Rackham and Francis Spriggs put together. He was to become known as Black Bart after taking command of the Bart on which he was previously the navigator. At the height of his power, he had a fleet of four ships and hundreds of pirates. His success was due to his organization, charisma and daring. He was to become known as Black Bart after taking command of the Bart on which he was previously the navigator.

In 1719 Roberts was a sailor serving as third mate on the slave-ship Princess, when she was captured by pirates off the Gold Coast. The raiders were led by Hywell Davis, and a reluctant Roberts was press-ganged into joining the pirate crew. It was on Davis' ship the Royal Rover that they sailed to Principe with the intention of taking the Portuguese governor for ransom. The plot was discovered and Davis was ambushed and killed.

The pirates regrouped, attacked and plundered the island, in revenge for Davis' death and then sailed for Brazil, capturing countless ships and much booty. On his new ship, the Fortune, Roberts even instigated a pirate code, sworn on a Bible, setting out rules and regulations for their conduct.

Back in the Caribbean, Roberts carried on raiding but eventually came across stiff resistance in the form of two well-armed ships from Barbados. Severely damaged, the Fortune, limped to Dominica for repairs. Rumors that pirates who had taken advantage of the 1698 royal pardon were on surrendering denied the benefits of the pardon only increased mistrust and antagonism; the pirates resolved "no longer to attend to any offers of forgiveness but in case of attack, to defend themselves on their faithless countrymen who may fall into their hands." In 1722 Captain Luke Knott was granted £230 for the loss of his career, after turning over 8 pirates, "his being obliged to quit the Merchant service, the Pirates threatening to Torture him to death if ever he should fall into their hands." It was by no means an empty threat - in 1720 pirates of the crew of Bartholomew Roberts "openly and in the daytime burnt and destroyed... vessels in the Road of Basseterre [St. Kitts] and had the audaciousness to insult H.M. Fort," avenging the execution of "their comrades at **Nevis**".

Roberts then sent word to the governor that "they would Come and Burn the Town [Sandy Point] about his Ears for hanging the Pyrates there." Roberts even had his own pirate flag made showing him standing on two skulls labeled ABH and AMH - 'A Barbadian's Head' and 'A Martinican's Head' - later that same year he gave substance to his vendetta against the two islands by hanging the governor of Martinique from a yardarm. As bounties were offered for the capture of pirates, the pirates responded by offering rewards for certain officials. And when pirates were captured or executed, other pirate crews often revenged their Brethren of the Coast, attacking the town that condemned them, or the shipping of that port. This sort of solidarity shows that there had developed a real pirate community, and that those sailing under 'the banner of King Death' no longer thought of themselves as English or Dutch or French but as pirates of the Caribbean.

Having created havoc in the West Indies, Roberts crossed back to Africa in the spring of 1721, where he finally met his match, in the form of HMS Swallow. Dressed in his finery, as usual, on 10th February Roberts attempted to out manoeuvre Swallow, but was hit in the throat and killed. To prevent the Navy capturing his body, his crew wrapped his corpse in a sail, weighted it down and threw it overboard, never to be recovered, nor all his booty. Roberts' death was seen by many as the end of the age of piracy.

Roberts owed his success to many factors, including his personal charisma and leadership, his daring and ruthlessness, and his ability to co-ordinate small fleets to maximum military effect. Wherever he was, commerce came to a halt, as fear of him and his men made merchants stayed in port. Roberts is a favorite of true pirate buffs. He was mentioned in Treasure Island, that classic of pirate literature. In the movie "The Princess Bride," the name "Dread Pirate Roberts" is a reference to him. He often appears in pirate video games and has been the subject of several novels, histories and movies.

THE JOLLY ROGER
The enigmatic image of the skull and crossbones is deeply entrenched in the minds of millions around the world as the symbol of piracy, death and even poison. Whenever we see a pirate ship on television, cinema or in comic books we also see an extremely ancient symbol - the skull and crossbones. This however, was not a

symbol of death or indeed poison but instead it profoundly symbolized life in so many aspects.

Popular Notions of the Skull and Crossbones Flag

The origin of this or icon name is unclear. Jolly Roger had been a generic term for a jovial, carefree man since at least the 17th century and the existing term seems to have been applied to the skeleton or grinning skull in these flags by the early 18th century. In 1703, a pirate named John Quelch was reported to have been flying the "Old Roger" off Brazil, "Old Roger" being a nickname for the devil.

1798 Jolly Roger Flag

Jolly Roger is the traditional English name for the flags flown to identify a pirate ship about to attack during the early 18th century known as the "Golden Age of Piracy". The flag most commonly identified as the Jolly Roger today, the skull and crossbones symbol on a black flag, was used during the 1710s by a number of pirate captains including Black Sam Bellamy, Edward England, and John Taylor and it went on to become the most commonly used pirate flag during the 1720s.

The first recorded uses of the skull-and-crossbones symbol on naval flags date to the 17th century. It possibly originated among the Barbary pirates of the period, which would connect the black color of the Jolly Roger to the Muslim black flag. But an early reference to Muslim corsairs flying a skull symbol, in the context of a 1625 slave raid on Cornwall, explicitly refers to the symbol being shown on a green flag. There are mentions of Francis Drake flying a black flag as early as 1585, but the historicity of this tradition has been called into question.

17th and 18th century colonial governors usually required *privateers* to fly a specific version of the British flag, the 1606 Union Jack, distinguishing them from naval vessels. Before this time, British privateers such as Sir Henry Morgan sailed under English colors and recorded at the London Public Record Office.

An early use of a black flag with skull, crossbones, and hourglass is attributed to pirate captain Emanuel Wynn in 1700, according to a wide variety of secondary sources. Reportedly, these secondary sources are based on the account of Captain John Cranby of HMS Poole.

With the end of the War of the Spanish Succession in 1714, many privateers turned to piracy. They still used red and black flags, but they decorated them with their own designs. Edward England, for example, flew three different flags: from his mainmast the black flag with skull and crossbones; from his foremast a red version of the same; and from his ensign staff the English national flag.

Just as variations on the Jolly Roger design existed, red flags sometimes incorporated yellow stripes or images symbolic of death.

Templar and Masonic History

Many researchers of Templar and Masonic history have pointed out the links between this symbol and the one used by the Knights Templar on their ships. Some historians take into account and point to the fact that the Templars had at one time the world's biggest naval fleet in the 13th century, and that they were well known for acts that we would call today 'piracy'. The Knights of Malta were also well known for piracy as they protected Malta and were in fact the very similar as the Templars - having been formed or joined by the remnants of the dissolved Templars, once the Knights began occupying the islands of Rhoades and Malta after defeats in the Holy Land.

These new Templars or Knights of Malta were accused on several occasions of piracy and henceforth we have tales of piracy on the high seas. There is a direct link therefore between the creation or use of the skull and crossbones by the Knights Templar and our modern day idea of it being a symbol of piracy. The skull and crossed bones were adopted as an emblem of the ancient Templars between the third and fourth crusade. The legend is one based on love, and is handed down as thus:

According to legend, a Templar fell in love with a beautiful noblewoman of Maraclea. She died before they could be married, but he could not endure to be separated from her, and dug up the body, and with full ceremonies married what was left of the corpse. After the body was reburied and he returned home, a voice came to him in a dream and told him to return in nine years. When he returned, he found only the skull and two large leg bones preserved enough to be moved. The voice spoke to him again and told him to guard and keep them always, and he would be successful in all his undertakings. Thereafter he prospered greatly and defeated all his enemies.

The skull and bones was passed on to the Templars at his death, and as mentioned was credited with their rise to affluence and power. Thus, deeply rooted in the heritage of the ancient Templars, the Knight Templar apron draws its symbolism from the past, to create a link between those ancient Templars and the modern Masonic Knight Templar. I note, in the George Washington Masonic Memorial in Virginia, USA, there is an anteroom with a large portrait of the Colonial period Grand Master Lafayette wearing the Templar Apron bearing the 'skull and crossbones.' The same apron images have also been found elsewhere worn by Masons.

PIRATES, BUCCANEERS, & PRIVATEERS ASSOCIATED WITH NEVIS

Pirates, Smoke and Pots

The claim that Nevis was a haven for pirates in the 17th and 18th centuries may be hard to convince the skeptics. Some of the earliest historical archaeological fieldwork carried out in the Caribbean focused on skeletal remains of slaves. Yet as posited at the outset of this book, the study of pottery is without doubt one of the most important tasks taken on by any archaeologist. The material cultural focus of much Caribbean historical archaeology has made a number of significant contributions, most notably in the study of earthenware ceramics. A great wealth of information can be gained from the study of pottery, despite its inanimate state. Pottery is to culture what bones are to existence. Pottery is beyond *prima facie evidence* proving some basic facts, and it cannot be easily refuted or dismissed when found.

The archaeological evidence from Nevis reflects this great complexity of Caribbean prehistory and also modern history. Although the broad outlines of the region's chronology are fairly well established, there is considerable uniqueness about Nevis that can be deduced from pottery digs. Archaeologists researching a site where Caribbean pirates were thought to "laid their hats" have found that the drunken men not only 'smoked tobacco like the devil' but also kept fine pottery. These were the real sort of *Pirates of the Caribbean*.

It is interesting to first take note the life of real Caribbean pirates which lend us a facet of understanding life on Nevis in its earliest days, just discovered, with no telegraph or radio, no electricity, no grocery store, just the sun, rain, wind and moon...

Until the publicity and documentaries of the recent attacks on cruises ship off the coast of Somalia, pirates terrorizing the high seas have been mostly the stuff of legend, children's books, and Hollywood fantasy. But piracy, particularly in the Caribbean, was at one time a very real and dangerous problem. Men with names such as Blackbeard, Calico Jack, Captain Kidd, Captain Hawkins, and Black Bart pillaged and plundered ships and seaport towns, offering violent retribution to those who resisted and seizing fortunes at will. Island wars and battles at sea were fought because of piracy. Readers can get to know the real characters, the battles they fought, and watch nations rise up to stop them, as well as separate fact from fiction in the world premiere *TRUE CARIBBEAN PIRATES* which appeared on The History Channel, 2006.

After Christopher Columbus landed in the West Indies in 1492, Spain and its powerful navy established a dominating presence in the region during the 16th century. Vast riches in gold and silver were mined and stolen in the New World that soon drew the attention of England, France, and Holland for a claim to the booty. The Caribbean would become a free-for-all as these competing nations summonsed maritime law, claim to lands, and worst of all "privateering," basically the use of freelancing pirate (mercenary) sailors to fight battles, disrupt trade, and rob from the Spanish—all in an effort to establish a presence in the Caribbean without having to pay, out-of-pocket, for a formal, national real navy to stake righteous claim.

The temptation of Spanish treasure in open, unchartered waters, stretched the thin line between privateer and self-made pirates to an entrepreneurial breaking point. One of the most famous privateers to *cross the line* into piracy was Sir Henry Morgan. Commissioned by the British Governor of Jamaica to command more than 1,500 buccaneers, he responded by becoming one of the first true great pirates, leading daring attacks and conquests of Spanish colonies at Portobello and Panama and gaining a reputation for brutal acts such as hanging men by their genitals to get them to give up their possessions. In 1668, Morgan quickly captured Puerto Príncipe (now Camagüey), Cuba, and in an extraordinarily daring move—stormed and sacked the well-fortified city of Portobello on the Isthmus of Panama. In 1669 he made a successful raid on wealthy Spanish settlements around Lake Maracaibo on the coast of Venezuela. Finally, in August 1670, with 36 ships and nearly 2,000 buccaneers, Morgan set out to capture Panamá, one of the chief cities of Spain's American empire. Crossing the Isthmus of Panama, he defeated a large Spanish force (January 18, 1671) and entered the city, which burned to the ground while his men were looting it. On the return journey he deserted his followers and absconded with most of the booty.

From the piracy heydays, beginning around 1670, the cycle of privateers and quasi-legal pirates continued for decades, until an extraordinary event changed everything in the Caribbean. "Universal Peace, true and sincere Amity in America," the Treaty of Madrid (Godolphin Treaty) between Spain and England, 18 July 1670 was ratified. Under the terms of the treaty, Spain recognized English possessions in the Caribbean Sea: "all those lands, islands, colonies and places whatsoever situated in the West Indies." Spain confirmed England was to hold all territories in the Western Hemisphere that it had already settled; however the treaty did not define what areas were settled. England took formal control of Jamaica and the Cayman Islands after the treaty was signed. Spain also agreed to permit English ships freedom of movement in the Caribbean. Each country agreed to refrain from trading in the other's territory, and both countries agreed to limit trading to their own possessions. England agreed to suppress piracy in the Caribbean. Because Morgan's raid on Panamá had taken place after the conclusion of a peace between England and Spain, he was arrested and transported to London (April 1672). Nevertheless, relations with Spain quickly deteriorated due to continued piracy, and in 1674 King Charles II knighted Morgan and sent him out again as deputy governor of Jamaica, where he lived as a wealthy and respected planter until his death.

But suddenly, tens of thousands of privateers and sailors were out of a job, and thus began the age of the outlaw pirates went into full swing. From the maritime crimes from Morgan to Calico Jack, and even on to female pirates such as Anne Bonny and Mary Read, who were far more notorious, and every bit as dangerous, as their male counterparts, is the true story of piracy's Golden Age. Tale after tale of true pirate lore that brings to life the unique reality of brazen disregard of almost every societal rule, disrespect for governmental authority, and unmatched thirst for adventure and brutality, all motivated by a true desire to be free and live their way on the open seas. Understanding the pirates' true motives and methodology for plying their trade, and dispelling time-honored myths such as those of treasure maps and buried booty brings a much better understanding of Caribbean life during these formative years of plantations and slavery.

From historical records, scientists had known that by 1720 these Caribbean pirates occupied a settlement called "Barcadares," a name derived from the Spanish word for "landing place." One well documented place, located 15 miles up the Belize River, in a territory supposedly controlled by the Spanish, the site was used as an illegal logwood-cutting operation for pirates to obtain lumber for repair of ships. The records indicate that a good portion of its occupants were pirates taking a land-lubbing to stave off some boating fever, or a break from life at sea. This is what small islands like Nevis, Antigua, and Tortuga were noted for. Their living conditions were more than rustic to say the least, but private. There were no houses, and the men slept on raised platforms with a canvas over them to keep the mosquitoes off while sleeping under a cool, Caribbean breeze. They hunted and gathered a good deal of their food and smoked meat like a true buccaneer. Should another boat approach, smelling the whiff of barbeque, and tempted to land ashore, you can only imagine the picnic.

Captain Nathaniel Uring, a merchant seaman who was shipwrecked on Belize and spent more than four months with the inhabitants, described this in the book - *The Voyages and Travels of Captain Nathaniel Uring* (reprinted in 1928 by Cassell and Company) as a "rude drunken crew, some which have been pirates, and most of them sailors." Their "chief delight is in drinking; and when they broach a quarter cask or a hogshead of Bottle Ale or Cyder, keeping at it sometimes a week together, drinking till they fall asleep; and as soon as they awake at it again, without stirring off the place." Eventually Captain Uring returned to Jamaica and, in 1726, published an account of his adventures.

Heather Hatch, an archaeologist who is a doctoral student at the Nautical Archaeology Program, Texas A&M University, performed an analysis comparing the artifacts found at the Barcadares site with that of two British colonial sites, on the island of **Nevis**. "The Barcadares is the only clearly pirate-associated site from this period excavated to date," Hatch wrote in her report, recently published as a chapter in the book "The Archaeology of Maritime Landscapes"(Springer Science and Business Media, 2011).

She is researching 18th century piracy, examining pirate flag symbolism as an expression of group identity, and searching for markers of pirate identity at previously excavated archaeological sites. Her present research focuses on understanding the nature of maritime identity, or *maritimity*, and examining whether this can be seen in the archaeological record. "There are few pirate sites to examine, period. The few pirate shipwrecks that have been excavated are embroiled in debates over ethics and identification," she wrote. [Shipwrecks Gallery: Secrets of the Deep]

The pirates, while at sea, would've had a lot of time on their hands, time they likely spent smoking heavily, Hatch said. "They're not going to be sword fighting all the time," Hatch said. "There's a lot of down time when you're a pirate, when you're sitting around in your ship, when you're waiting for prey, waiting for someone to attack or when you're sailing from point A to point B." She also pointed out that "pirate activity wasn't regulated on a ship the same way it was on a merchant ship or navy," and that pirate crews were larger and "generally speaking that there was less work for everyone to do."

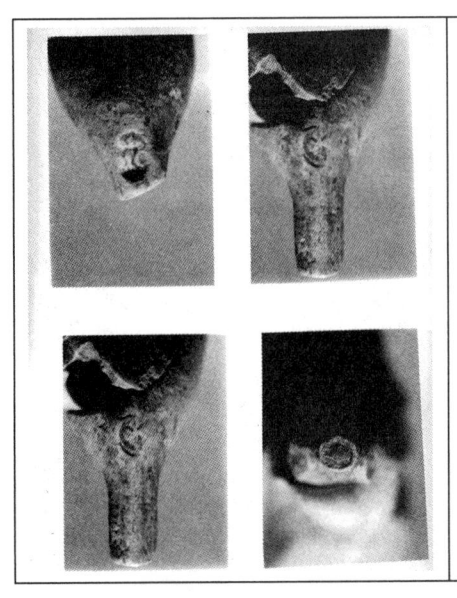

Both Nevis sites were excavated by Marco Meniketti, who is now a professor at San Jose State University. The Ridge Complex site consisted of a sugar mill and related dwellings, while the Port St. George site, on the southern coast of the island, was used to process and transport sugar. About 36 percent of all the artifacts at the Barcadares are made up of tobacco pipes (shown here), indicating that the pirates were heavy smokers. The differences between the Barcadares and the two non-pirate sites, also occupied during the 18th century, on Nevis are striking. One stark difference between the sites was the sheer amount of tobacco use at the Barcadares. Pipes make up 36 percent of the artifacts found at the pirate site, compared with 22 percent at the Ridge Complex and 16 percent at Port St. George. Hatch told that she is not aware of another site from this period with such a high proportion of tobacco pipes.

Pirate pottery
In addition to finding smokes, Hatch's analysis revealed differences in ceramics found. The pottery on the two Nevis sites is made from diverse materials, including various types of tough, practical stoneware. However, more than 65 percent of the pirate ceramics is made up of delftware — a soft, decorative material that was finished with a glaze. It is less sturdy than stoneware and not terribly practical for people living in a remote location.

The Nevis pirate site also had a small amount of Chinese porcelain that was transported half way across the world and would have been part of some booty. The pirates likely either captured it themselves or traded with someone who did. Finamore believes that the porcelain and delftware would have been prized possessions for the pirates. "They're sort of copying the appearances of upper class societies such as how the captains would live." Hatch agrees, "I do think it was a matter of wanting to display that they could have these nice things," she said. It would have made a point that, even out in Belize, they had "access even to these sorts of fancy pottery types that you might find in the bigger cities in the colonial world."

While the pirates liked glittering pottery, they liked it mainly in two forms – bowls or porringers. The pirates who lived at the two Nevis sites, on the other hand, had a mix of plates, storage jars, saucers, tankards and mugs, among other objects. It's possible that some of the tableware was made of wood, and has since decomposed. Another possibility, the researchers suggest, is that the pirates simply didn't feel a need for it. "You can use a bowl for anything you can use a plate for pretty much. But you can't use a plate to eat, for example, cold soup," Hatch said. Unlike the people of Nevis, the pirates would have eaten more informally and probably ate communally out of the same bowls.

Nevis sites excavated by Marco Meniketti. The Ridge Complex site consisted of a sugar mill and related dwellings, while the Port St. George site, on the southern coast of the island, was used to process and transport sugar.

As for why no cups were found at the Barcadares site, Finamore and Hatch suggest that the pirates could have drank from wooden containers. However, the explanation could be even simpler. "I don't think they would have any qualms whatsoever about drinking straight from the bottle," Hatch said. Finamore recalled that after he had found the Barcadares site, he shared the location with Emory King, a well-known Belize historian who has since died. King told him that in the 1960s the bend in the river where the site is located was known as a great place for bottle diving. "People had gone out there, dived into the river, and pulled out very old bottles," Finamore said. These bottles would not have been thrown away after a one-time use. "The nearest bottle manufactory, from the Barcadares site, was a long, long way away." But despite the value of the bottles, and perhaps while under the influence of alcohol, the pirates would simply throw them into the river.

Conclusion

In the past, I have never read nor heard of any pirates of fame associated with Nevis until I began to research this book. I have yet to talk to any Nevisian who knew that the first Governor of Nevis, Anthony Hilton, was actually a buccaneer, in fact, almost no one knows who our first Governor was. Historical records about pirates are rare material. Much of what is known comes from government records including court trials, trading logs, maps, and the few first-person accounts written during a particular time period. This information rarely contains details pertinent to what is needed to fully identify or learn about the early Caribbean settlers. Thanks to the internet and thorough search engines, and archaeologists, some valuable information has come to light. The simple fact is that the vast majority of pirates' names remain unknown. Suffice it to say, however, the early history of Nevis involved a lot of pirates after Columbus' landing. A lot of Nevis' early history in fact rotates around piracy, slavery, and maritime adventures. Were it not for the fortitude and spirit of independence of the pilgrims, pirates and slaves, Nevis and the Caribbean as it is today would not be!

References

- Brethren of the Coast. From Wikipedia, https://en.wikipedia.org/wiki/Brethren_of_the_Coast
- Burns, Sir Alan. History of the West Indies. London, 1954
- Cawthorne, Nigel. A History of Pirates: Blood and Thunder on the High Seas. Edison: Chartwell Books, 2005.
- Defoe, Daniel. (Captain Charles Johnson) A General History of the Pyrates. Edited by Manuel Schonhorn. Mineola: Dover Publications, 1972/1999.
- Gosse, Philip. The Pirates' Who's Who. New York: Burt Franklin, 1924.
- Jarus, Owen. Caribbean Pirate Life: Tobacco, Ale ... and Fine Pottery. Live Science Contributor | September 1, 2011
- Kongstam, Angus. Piracy the Complete History. Osprey, 2008.
- Konstam, Angus. Pirates: Predators of the Seas. Skyhorse Publishing, 2007.
- Laughton, John Knox. Sharpe, Bartholomew. Dictionary of National Biography, 1885-1900, Volume 51
- Malesic, Tony. "GREAVES, Captain, alias "Red Legs." West Indian Pirate.
- http://www.genealogy.com/forum/surnames/topics/greaves/291/
- Masefield, John. ON THE SPANISH MAIN (or, some English forays on the
- isthmus of Darien. with a description of the buccaneers and a short account of old-time ships and sailors). Methuen & co. London. 1906
- Piracy in the Caribbean. https://en.wikipedia.org/wiki/Piracy_in_the_Caribbean
- Preston, Diana and Michael. A Pirate of Exquisite Mind. Explorer, Naturalist, and Buccaneer: The Life of William Dampier. Walker Publishing Company, 2004.
- Pringle, Patrick. Jolly Roger: The Story of the Great Age of Piracy. 1953.
- Roberts, Patrick, et al. "The men of Nelson's navy: A comparative stable isotope dietary study of late 18th century and early 19th century servicemen from Royal Naval Hospital burial grounds at Plymouth and Gosport, England." American Journal of Physical Anthropology
- Treaty of Madrid (1670). https://en.wikipedia.org/wiki/Treaty_of_Madrid

CHAPTER 9. Emancipation

18th Century Nevis

Due to its small size and tolerant populace, pirates had been finding refuge on Nevis for nearly one hundred years. The era of piracy during which pirates were most active from the 1650s to 1730s was known as the *Golden Age of Piracy*. In 1706, Pierre Le Moyne d'Iberville, the French Canadian founder of Louisiana in North America, decided to drive the English out of Nevis and thus also stop pirate attacks on French ships. He considered Nevis the region's headquarters for piracy against French trade and he would use French pirates to raid the island and decimate its economy for more than a century.

The Failed French Invasion of Nevis

Pierre Le Moyne d'Iberville was only 25 years old when, on August 10, 1686, the chevalier Pierre de Troyes entrusts him with the command of the posts which have just fallen to the French around Hudson Bay. D'Iberville becomes a freebooter (pirate or lawless adventurer) marauding around the Nelson River, he captured two English ships. These seizures allow him to avoid starvation and to resupply Fort Monsoni. When he returns to Québec by sea near the end of October 1687, his ship is overloaded with a booty of furs and English merchandise.

D'Iberville believed that the presence of the English at Fort Nelson augured the loss of *New France*. On August 5, 1689, the residents of Lachine were attacked and massacred by him and his troops. On February 18, 1690, an attack on Corlaer (Schenectady, New York) ends with the pillaging and burning of the town and the massacre of approximately 60 townspeople. Dreaming of giving North America to France, d'Iberville argues for the establishment of a French colony at the mouth of the Mississippi river: "If France does not seize this most beautiful part of America and set up a colony, ... the English colony which is becoming quite large, will increase to such a degree that, in less than one hundred years, it will be strong enough to take over all of America and chase away all other nations." His plan was to strangle the New England colonies between Canada in the north, the Gulf Mexico and Louisiana in the south and the Mississippi River in the west. On March 2, 1699, he succeeds where Robert Cavelier de La Salle failed: travelling by sea, he discovers the mouth of the Mississippi. Three consecutive expeditions, in 1699, 1700 and 1701, allow him to build the forts of Maurepas (Biloxi), Mississippi and Saint-Louis (Mobile). In 1702, having won the trust of the native Amerindians, the now commander of Louisiana leaves that colony, never to return.

The last years in his history was his personal freebooting to secure French domination in America by driving out of the Antilles the determined English buccaneers who conducted successful raids against the interests of France. By 1689, the infamous Captain Kidd was a member of a French-English pirate crew sailing and looting the Caribbean, during a voyage of which, Kidd and other crew members mutinied, ousting the captain and sailing to the British colony of **Nevis**. There they renamed the ship *Blessed William*, and Kidd became captain either as a result of election by the ship's crew, or by appointment of Christopher Codrington, governor of the island of Nevis or both. In any case, Captain Kidd and the Blessed William, an experienced leader and sailor by that time, became part of Codrington's small fleet assembled to defend Nevis from the French, with whom the English were at war. The governor did not pay the sailors for their defensive services, so as a privateer, Kidd and his men attacked the French island of Marie-Galante, destroying its only town and looting the area, and gathering for themselves something around 2,000 pounds Sterling and now bringing the ire of the French to the attention of Nevis as a pirate stronghold island. In September 1696, Kidd had set course for the Cape of Good Hope but we assume pirates remained on Nevis. Three privateers were employed by the British Crown to help protect ships in Nevis' waters. One of them, Captain Frances, who was of African descent. He commanded 100 men and a 20-gun ship moored off Nevis' waters.

In 1705 King Louis XIV put Iberville in charge of a large fleet, which was to attack the British colony of Nevis in the Caribbean to end the piracy. At the beginning of 1706, d'Iberville began spreading fear throughout the English Antilles. He planned to terrorize, pillage and claim the island of Nevis for France. When Queen Anne's War with England broke out in 1702, d'Iberville became commander of an eight-ship naval squadron. Bouts of malaria kept him sporadically sidelined over the next three years as he was unable to accomplish much. By 1706, d'Iberville had recovered sufficiently to assume control of a 12-ship task force headed for Nevis.

During d'Iberville's invasion of Nevis, French buccaneers were used in the front line, infamous for being ruthless killers after the pillaging during the wars with Spain where they gained a reputation for torturing and murdering non-combatants. In the face of the invading force, the English militiamen of Nevis fled like cowards. Some planters burned their plantations, rather than letting the French have them, and hid in the mountains. It was the courageous enslaved Africans who held the French at bay by taking up arms to defend their families and Nevis. The slave quarters in Charlestown had been looted and burned as well, as the main reward promised the freebooters on the French side in the attack was the right to capture as many slaves as possible and resell them in Martinique for their booty, which they did.

During the onslaught, it was estimated that 3,400 enslaved Nevisians were captured and sent off to Martinique, but about 1,000 brave souls, poorly armed and militarily untrained, held the French troops at bay, by "murderous fire" according to an eyewitness account by an English militiaman. He wrote that "the slaves' brave behaviour and defence there shamed what some of their masters did, and they do not shrink to tell us so." After 18 days of fighting, the French were driven off the island. Among the Nevisian men, women and children carried away on d'Iberville's ships, six ended up in Louisiana, the first persons of African descent to arrive there in that part of the Americas. Those were the conditions of

Nevis at the beginning of the 18th century. Nevis was already beset with swashbuckling slaves, engaged in daring and romantic adventure with ostentatious bravado of a Hollywood film. But were it not for the Africans held captives by the cowardly English, Nevis may well be a colony of France, would not be what it is today, an independent nation.

Nevis' Unknown Soldier
A monument at the Crusader Museum in dedication to the services of an unknown warrior and to the common memories of all Nevisians killed or taken hostage in the 18 day war of 1706. This is a monument dedicated to Nevis Africans who have died without their remains being identified, having defended the island from the attack of the French pirates led by the infamous Captain d'Iberville in 1706. Had it not been for this bravery, Nevis today may not have become independent and effectively an overseas collectivity of France.

One consequence of this invasion was the collapse in the economy of the island due to the destruction of the plantations and infrastructure and the capture of a significant portion of the workforce. The island underwent a period of profound famine and hunger. One solution, that was to have lasting consequences, was that surviving slave families were granted small plots of land to tend and grow crops of their own. They were still obliged to work under very severe conditions for their European slave owners, but the *smallholdings* would play an important part in the economy and livelihoods of the slaves who could tailor their crops and diets more appropriately and gain a semblance of self-sufficiency and dignity, which they did.

Shortly after looting and larceny, d'Iberville sailed to Havana, apparently to sell French iron. He dies there, on board the *Juste*, on July 9, 1706, laid down sick by an epidemic or infectious fever that had been weakening him since 1701. The remains of this man-of-ilk, the burial records identify him as "El General Dom Pedro Berbila" were laid to rest in the church of San Cristobal in Havana. He was 45 years old. The investigation which had been started shortly before his death, revealed that the "El Cid" (Warrior) of Canada was a greedy, ruthless pirate and that his lust for conquest had as much to do with his desire for financial and personal gains as it did with his supposed dedication to France. A final note on his notorious reputation occurred soon after, when it was revealed that he had embezzled funding from his recent expedition pillaging Nevis. His widow was obliged to make amends to the state and pay back money from the largess of booty she inherited.

Mathew, then governor of St Kitts, he had reported to London 'that Nevis has quite lost its trade, and is a desert Island to what it was Thirty Years ago'. One consequence of the French attack was a collapsed sugar industry and during the ensuing hardship on Nevis, small plots of land on the plantations were taken over by the enslaved families in order to prevent loss of life due to starvation. With the absentee plantation owners, the import of food supplies for the workers dwindled to near nothing. Decades of struggle began and between 1776 and 1783, the food supplies failed to arrive altogether due to the rebellions in North America, and it is recorded that 300–400 enslaved Nevisians starved to death. The *Queen of the Caribees* was no more.

Calendar of State Papers Colonial, America and West Indies: Volume 23, 1706-1708. Originally published by His Majesty's Stationery Office, London, 1916. May 11/12. 318.
Extract of the Paris Gazette, May 22, 1706. Comte de Chavagnac ravaged St. Christophers from Feb. 21 to March 2 (N.S.), when he returned to Guardeloupe with a great booty. The damage inflicted on the enemy is estimated at 3 millions. On the 7th March (N.S.) the Sieur d'Iberville, arrived at Martinique with another squadron of the King's ships. He embarked 1,100 inhabitants, or flibustiers, of that Island, and having joined the Comte de Chavagnac made a descent in the night of April 1st upon Nevis. He turned the enemy out of several advantageous positions and from the Fort of the Point, where they had retired with the greater part of their artillery, and seized 22 ships which were anchored under the Fort. On April 4 (N.S.) he marched to attack them in the mountains, where they were entrenched in a position, the approaches to which were almost inaccessible; but he called upon them to surrender, and they accepted his terms. The principal conditions were that the Commander, the soldiers and all the inhabitants without distinction of age or sex should be prisoners of war, and that they should give up all their negroes. The value of the rest of the booty is not yet known; but there are more than 7,000 negroes, about 30 armed vessels, and we are assured that these two Islands will not be able to regain their former state in ten years time. These two expeditions have not cost us 50 men, killed and wounded, etc. Endorsed, Recd. Read May 22, 1706. French. 2 pp. [C.O. 152, 6. No. 46.]
May 16. Bermuda. 323. Lt. Governor Bennett to W. Popple. The vessell that gives the opportunity of sending this, just touched here from Barbados. I transmit the enclosed duplicate [? April 22], concluding it will arrive sooner than the original. Besides I do not find by the Captain that at Barbados they have so particular an account of Nevis as therein related. He likewise tells me it's concluded there Antigua is taken. My reason to the contrary is that the Master that brought my letter from Antigua [see April 22] told me that a sloop lay ready, in case the French made any show of landing there, to bring several gentlewomen of that Country here, but I have heard nothing of them; it may be the vessel has been intercepted: he added that the Enemy was on shore on Nevis when he sailed from Antigua, March 30, and by a letter from Barbados I find they were there on April 10. In that letter it is also said that Nevis surrendred on articles, but I fear it was taken, for that day (being Good Friday) the French attacked and took the forts, they landed their men, and at night great fires were seen supposed to be the town and plantations of Canes...
[May.] 355. Merchants and Planters concerned in Nevis and St. Kitts to Sir C. Hedges. Recount the invasions of the French Feb. 11, and March 22. The damage done to Nevis, by a modest computation, amounts to a million of money, besides all H.M. Forts, with 100 cannon and all warlike stores. Two days before their departure they forced the inhabitants' consent to deliver 1,400 negroes or 42,000l. by Oct. 8, taking as hostages 4 of the principal inhabitants. Propose speedy reliefe in respect to that article; the inhabitants, not being able

to comply, will be forced to desert the Island, as some have already done, the Enemy having threatned, if not performed, to use the utmost extremity of fire and sword, and will send all the men to New Spaine and the women and children among the French. Pray that sufficient ships of war and regular forces, guns, warlike stores and provisions be sent there, the enemy destroying and carrying away all provisions and live cattell that are proper for subsistance; soe that the poor distressed inhabitants will starve unless releived by H.M., the merchants tradeing there being wholly disabled to supply them. That H.M. take into her princely compassion the deplorable condition of her distressed subjects for the further reliefe of their great losses, etc. Signed, Jos. Jory, Rich. Meriwether, F. Duport, John Tonstall, Jasper Wall, Joseph Martyn, Ja. Walker, Saml. Ball, Dan. Alford. Endorsed, May, 1706. 1¼ pp. [C.O. 152, 39. No. 110.]

During much of the seventeenth century, Nevis enjoyed considerable prosperity, escaping the British-French warfare that engulfed St. Kitts, serving as the entry point for the slave trade into the Leeward Islands, and boasting the largest European population in the Leeward islands. Toward the end of the century however, in 1680 the first of a series of disasters visited the island in the form of a devastating earthquake. During the century that followed, one violent occurrence after another: hurricanes, warfare, starvation, and epidemical disease contributed to the erosion of Nevis' early prosperity. The small land holdings of Nevis were consolidated into about 100 plantations by 1700. The white population, which was around 3500 in 1660, by 1710 had dropped to about 1300 after the earthquakes and the French invasion of d'Iberville.

Nevis was the premier landing point for enslaved Africans in the Leeward Islands between 1675 and 1700, and Bristol was the most important British slaving port in England. *Mountravers*, also known as 'Pinney's Estate', was a medium-sized sugar plantation on the Caribbean island of Nevis. It was made up of several estates and tracts of land.

From the seventeenth century until slavery was abolished in 1834, more than 850 enslaved people are now known to have lived on Mountravers and its constituent parts. Successive members of the Pinney family owned the plantation, among them John Pretor Pinney, who settled in Bristol, England, in 1784. His family home in Bristol is now the city's Georgian House Museum.

Slave Resistance

In the Caribbean and in many slave societies in the Americas, one of the most important aspects of resistance to slavery was the retention of African culture or melding African, American and European cultural forms to create new ones such as the Kweyol languages (Antillean Creole). The importance of African culture – names, craftsmanship, languages, scientific knowledge, beliefs, philosophy, music and dance, was that it provided the psychological support to help the captives resist the process of enslavement and retain some dignity. The act of plantation enslavement involved attempts to break the will and ignore the humanity of slaves in what was known as 'seasoning'. Obvious examples of resistance would be the use of Vodun (Voodoo) religious beliefs in the Haitian Revolution and the employment of Obeah to strengthen the Jamaican Maroons in the struggles against the British. Rebel leaders such as Nanny in Jamaica and Boukman and Mackandal in St Domingue (Haiti) were also religious or spiritual leaders. Religious beliefs should perhaps be seen as also providing the enslaved Africans a way of understanding the world and giving them a holistic belief system, a coping mechanism as well as a means of resistance.

Enslaved Africans resisted and rebelled against their stations in many different ways. Each expression of resistance by enslaved individuals or groups counted as acts of rebellion. The many instances of resistance show that slaves were not just victims of slavery who accepted their situation. Instead they proved their strength and determination in fighting for their freedom. Uprising, or rebellion, was the most dramatic and violent way that slaves could resist their enslavement. Less obvious methods of *resistance* occurred on the plantations. For example, slaves could steal from their owner, robbing him of his property and profit. They could damage machinery, so that it was put out of action and needed either lengthy repairs or costly replacement. The slaves could avoid work, by working as slowly as they dared, or by pretending to be sick. All these acts of resistance carried the threat of punishment if they were found out or confessed.

There were other ways of attacking slave owners. Many enslaved African women had knowledge of medicines made from plants and could use their skills against owners. Plantation owners were therefore anxious that the female slaves who cooked their food might poison them. It is known in the islands that West Indian 'weedwomen' would use the juice of the manchineel apple for poison. The little death apple, or *Columbus death apple* -- because he recorded the first encounter with it when some of his men died after eating it -- is one of the most poisonous and deadly plants in the world. Every part of the tree is toxic. Arson and murder were also ever-present threats in the plantation owners' minds. Edward Huggins, a sugar grower on the island of Nevis, had a reputation as a brutal slave owner. His slaves made five attempts on his life for the brutal punishments he meted out. Sometimes violent acts turned against themselves by committing infanticide, self-mutilation and suicide.

Enslaved Africans also fought against slavery by keeping their African cultures and traditions alive in words, names, music and beliefs. Slave owners often tried to control this. Slaves' stick drumming was banned by plantation owners on the Caribbean island of St Kitts (except at Christmas time). Such activity was seen as a threat by the owners which would rouse a riot. They knew that if the slaves developed a common sense of identity through African culture and traditions, they would be more likely to join together and rebel against their owners. Drumming metal pots and pans was an important part of many African musical and religious traditions that led to steelpan music.

In the Caribbean and in many slave societies in the Americas, one of the most important aspects of resistance to slavery was the retention of African culture or melding African, American and European cultural forms to create new ones such as the Kweyol languages (Antillean Creole). The mainly Christian plantation owners also did not want their slaves taking part in any religious activity that was not Christian. African religions were very different from Christianity and the slave owners were suspicious of them. So, even playing the drums, or continuing to practice their religious beliefs were methods by which the slaves could resist and challenge slavery.

> **'To Take the Island for Themselves'**
> In the summer and autumn of 1725, tensions were running high in the British West Indian island of Nevis. This island, one of four which constituted the federated colony of the Leeward Islands (the others being Antigua, Montserrat, and St. Kitts), was home to approximately 1500 white and 6000 black people, of whom almost all of the latter were slaves of the former. During these months, masters and bonds people alike looked daily to the skies, hoping for rainfall which would end the drought under which the island suffered. As Governor John Hart informed imperial authorities in London, Nevis was 'in a most deplorable Condition from the Dry weather'. Local planters had been obliged to import drinking water from the nearby islands of Montserrat and Guadeloupe 'which was Sold at fifteen Shillings a Hogshead which has occasioned the loss of many of the Cattle and Negroes'. (1) As planters agonized over the threat that the dry weather posed to their sugar crops, their slaves' already difficult lives became still harsher, as they laboured beneath the blazing sun and struggled to survive on ever-decreasing amounts of food and water. By September, at least some of them appear to have reached their breaking point, and apparently conspired to 'cut off all the whites, and take the island for themselves'. (2) Upon being informed of this turn of events, Governor Hart left his base at Antigua, the capital of the Leewards, and made his way to Nevis, where, after he had jailed ten of the alleged conspirators and sentenced two others to be burnt to death, he pronounced the 'Negroes' to be 'sufficiently terrified' that they no longer constituted a threat to the island's security. (3)
>
> Reading the rebels: currents of slave resistance in the eighteenth-century British West Indies
> Natalie Zacek, School of History and Classics, University of Manchester
> V. L. Oliver, The History of the Island of Antigua (London, 1894), i. xcvi. (1)
> K. Mason, 'The World an Absentee Planter and His Slaves Made: Sir William Stapleton and His Nevis Sugar Estate, 1722-1740', Bulletin of the John Rylands Library, 75 (1993), 129. (2)
> Hart to Board of Trade, January 1726, in London, National Archives of Great Britain, CO 152/15/1 (Board of Trade: Original Correspondence, Leeward Islands, 1725-1727). (3)

The Black Dogg Coin of Nevis

By the end of the 17th century the number of inhabitants and, consequently, the number of merchants in major colonial cities had grown to the extent that the use of barter, wampum and other money substitutes was too cumbersome even for small transactions. Local merchants found it increasingly difficult to sell daily staples with money substitutes. For example, bakers could not efficiently sell bread if they needed to count strands of wampum and examine each bead to insure it was not flawed, nor could they be expected to spend time bartering with a customer when there were other individuals waiting to be served.

British law prohibited the export of regal gold and silver coins, however there was no law against exporting British coppers (either regal or token coinages). Additionally, the situation in the colonies was well known that British coppers traded above their face value in the colonies. For these reasons new settlers as well as English visitors brought small change copper coins with them when they traveled the waters to the colonies. In addition to personal caches a few bulk shipments made their way over whereby individuals hoped to make a profit by exchanging copper coins to the colonies. In 1681 Mark Newby brought a large quantity of Saint Patrick coppers to New Jersey and in 1682 a group of Quakers brought some three hundred pounds worth of halfpence and farthings to Philadelphia. From these trading centers, coins made their way to the Caribbean colonies.

A dog or a **black dogg** was a coin in the Caribbean of Queen Anne of Great Britain, made of pewter or copper, typically worth 1½ pence or 1/72 of a dollar. The name comes from the negative connotation of the word dog (ugly) as they came from impure silver with a dark, oxidized color. Black dogs were also called "stamps" or "stampees," as they were typically the coins of other colonial powers—French coins worth 2 sous or, equivalently, 24 diniers—stamped to make them British currency. A dog and a stampe were not necessarily of equal value and worth in the islands varied according to the deal. In 1797, however, a "black dog" was equated with a "stampee." Mary Prince's slave narrative tells of slaves in Antigua buying a "dog's worth" of salted fish or pork on Sundays (the only day they could go to the market).

In 1672 Britain had demonetization trade tokens and initiated production of British regal coppers. Copper half-pence's were minted in 1672, 1673 and 1675, they were then replaced with tin coinage. Tin half-pence's were issued from 1685-1692. It is clear some of these coppers were circulating in American from a very early date. The "**Black Dogg**" was a popular coin used in the West Indies. It is explained in a letter from Col. Joseph Jorye to William Popple, the Secretary for the Council of Trade and Plantations in London. In August of 1700 Jorye had been appointed as the Agent for the colony of Nevis and was required to explain some points concerning laws passed in Nevis during 1698 and 1699. Regarding a law of April 1, 1698 concerning rates of liquors for taverns and for the passing of Black Dogs, Jorye explained to Popple in a letter of September 13, 1700:

I have made inquiry about Sowse [that is, sous] commonly called Blackdoggs; they are in France, 60 to the crown, and with us abroad three half-pence each. I find not many, but only a conveniency for change, for in paying 20 or 30 pieces of eight, they may not have more than one paid in Blackdogs. So far it cannot prejudice commerce, considering they have no half-pence nor farthings, our nation's coin, amongst them. (Cecil Headlam, ed., Calendar of State Papers, Colonial Series, America and the West Indies. 1700. Preserved in the Public Record Office, London: 1910)

The Black Dogg dollar was the currency of Nevis until 1830. The currency consisted of counter-stamped Spanish and French colonial coins. The dollar was subdivided into 72 black dogs, each of 1½ pence a piece. Around 1801, coins were issued for 1, 4, 6, 7 and 9 black dogs with the word "Nevis" and the denomination stamped on them. The 1 black dog coins were countermarked on French Guianan 2 sous, whilst the 9 black dogs were made from Spanish colonial 1 real coins. In 1830, the sterling was established as the official currency of Nevis island.

Since 1935, dollars have once more circulated on Nevis, first the British West Indies dollar, then the East Caribbean dollar.

Slavery Abolition Act 1833

The Slavery Abolition Act 1833 was an Act of the Parliament of the United Kingdom abolishing slavery throughout the British Empire with the exceptions "of the Territories in the Possession of the East India Company", Ceylon, now Sri Lanka, and Saint Helena; the exceptions were eliminated in 1843. The Act provided for compensation for slave-owners.

In May 1772, Lord Mansfield's judgment in the Somersett's Case emancipated a slave in England, which helped launch the movement to abolish slavery. The case ruled that slavery was unsupported by law in England and no authority could be exercised on slaves entering English or Scottish soil. In 1785, English poet William Cowper wrote:
We have no slaves at home – Then why abroad?
Slaves cannot breathe in England; if their lungs
Receive our air, that moment they are free.
They touch our country, and their shackles fall.
That's noble, and bespeaks a nation proud.
And jealous of the blessing. Spread it then,
And let it circulate through every vein.

By 1783, an anti-slavery movement to abolish the slave trade throughout the Empire had begun among the British public. In 1793 Lieutenant-Governor of Upper Canada John Graves Simcoe signed the Act Against Slavery. Passed by the local Legislative Assembly, it was the first legislation to outlaw the slave trade in a part of the British Empire.

On 1834 in Nevis, 8,815 slaves were freed. However, only slaves below the age of six were actually freed. Former slaves over the age of six were re-designated as "apprentices" required to work, 40 hours per week without pay, as part of compensation payment to their former owners. A four-year apprenticeship program followed the abolishment of slavery on the plantations. In spite of the continued use of the labor force, the Nevisian slave owners were paid over £150,000 in compensation from the British Government for the loss of property, whereas the enslaved families received nothing for 200 years of labor. One of the wealthiest planter families in Nevis, the Pinneys of Montravers Plantation, claimed £36,396 (worth close to £1,800,000 today) in compensation for the slaves on the family-owned plantations around the Caribbean. Full emancipation was finally achieved for all Nevisians at midnight on 31 July 1838. The first Monday in August is celebrated as Emancipation Day and is part of the annual Nevis *Culturama* festival.

Because of the early distribution of plots and because many of the planters departed from the island when sugar cultivation became unprofitable, a relatively large percentage of Nevisians already owned or controlled land at emancipation. Others settled on crown land. This early development of a society with a majority of small, landowning farmers and entrepreneurs created a stronger middleclass in Nevis than in Saint Kitts where the sugar industry continued until its closure in 2006.

Eden Brown Estate

A 1740 plantation, with a great house and other outbuildings has a history unlike many of the other plantations, and some believe it is haunted including the author who toured the house. The Eden Brown ruins, which are on the Mannings Estate, are considered to be haunted because of a tragedy that happened there in the early 19th century, which left a beautiful young woman without a husband, and possibly without a brother too.

A duel took place at the house in 1822, the night before the wedding of Julia Huggins, between her betrothed and the best man, who was her brother. A recent discovery of an old letter has shown that the bridegroom survived, and he went to propose to another woman. However, her father forbade her from marrying a "murderer." As the story goes, Julia spent the rest of her days as a recluse in the house, and can still be heard today as she wanders through the ruins. Local residents claim they can feel the presence of "someone" whenever they go near the eerie old house with its shroud of weeds and wildflowers. Though memorable more for the story than the hike or ruins, it's always open, and it's free. The house still commands spectacular views over the sea, and on a clear day Antigua and Montserrat can be seen from the Gallery.

Mary Prince

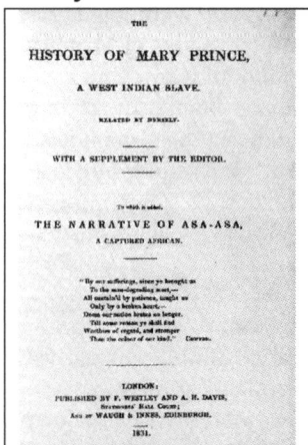

Mary Prince (c. 1788–after 1833) was born in Devonshire Parish, Bermuda, to an enslaved family of African descent. While she was later living in London, her autobiography, *The History of Mary Prince* (1831), was the first account of the life of a black woman to be published in the United Kingdom. Belonging to the genre of slave narratives, this first-hand description of the brutalities of enslavement, released at a time when slavery was still legal in Bermuda and British Caribbean colonies, had a galvanizing effect on the anti-slavery movement. It went through three printings in the first year. Prince had her account transcribed while living and working in England at the home of Thomas Pringle, a founder of the Anti-Slavery Society. She had gone to London with her master and his family in 1828 from Antigua.

Alexander Hamilton

Alexander Hamilton (1755 or 1757 – 1804) was an American statesman and one of the Founding Fathers of the United States. He was an influential interpreter and promoter of the U.S. Constitution, as well as the founder of the nation's financial system, the Federalist Party, the United States Coast Guard, and The New York Post newspaper. Hamilton was born out of wedlock in Charlestown, British West Indies, to a mother of French Huguenot and British ancestry, and a Scots father, James A. Hamilton, the fourth son of Scottish laird Alexander Hamilton of Grange, Ayrshire. Orphaned as a child by his mother's death and his father's abandonment, he was taken in by an older cousin, and later by a prosperous merchant family. He was recognized for his intelligence and talent, and sponsored by a group of wealthy local men to travel to New York City and pursue his education. Hamilton attended King's College (now Columbia University), choosing to stay in the Thirteen Colonies to seek his fortune.

This two-story Georgian style building was the birthplace of Alexander Hamilton in 1757. Hamilton lived on the island until the age of nine. He was naturally an outspoken advocate of the emancipation of slavery.

The building today, known as Hamilton House, houses one of the island's two museums on the first floor. The second floor is the meeting room for the Nevis House of Assembly. The lovely stone building was built around 1680, but was destroyed in an earthquake in 1840, and was restored in 1983. Its historic value coupled with its beautiful setting on Charlestown harbor make it an island treasure and a delightful place to spend an afternoon in the Museum and grounds.

Born in Nevis, in 1755, Hamilton had a childhood marked by waste and brutality. At sixteen, his mother, Rachel Faucette, the daughter of an Englishwoman and a Frenchman, inherited her father's Nevis plantation and was married off, to Johann

Michael Lavien, an older Danish man in St. Croix, who had aspirations to be a planter. When she ran away from the marriage and their child, her husband had her locked up for several months. After her release, Rachel fled to St. Kitts, where she met James Hamilton, a Scot, who, having failed to distinguish himself at home, had come to seek his fortune in the land-rich West Indies. Eventually, Rachel took James to Nevis, where Alexander, their second son, was born. Because she'd never divorced Lavien, Alexander was considered illegitimate, a stigma that haunted him for the rest of his life, along with the myth that he was part black (which, as Ron Chernow writes, in "Alexander Hamilton," his 2004 biography, "probably arose from the incontestable truth that many, if not most, illegitimate children in the West Indies bore mixed blood").

By the time Hamilton was a teenager, he had no parents at all. James had deserted the family, and Rachel had died of a fever. Lavien, still her legal husband, claimed her estate for their son, leaving the two Hamilton boys, whom he called "whore-children," penniless. Hamilton, then in St. Croix, found work as a clerk and a slave inspector, and it was there that he had his first stroke of luck, precipitated, by a disaster. In August, 1772, a hurricane blew through the Virgin Islands, wiping out homes, property, and people. A vivid letter that Hamilton wrote about the catastrophe found its way into a newspaper and impressed a local clergyman, who, with Hamilton's employers, arranged his passage to New York, where it was hoped that he would study medicine and then return home to minister to his people. But, once Hamilton boarded that ship, he never went back to the Caribbean.

References

- America and West Indies: May 1706, Pages 125-141. Calendar of State Papers Colonial, America and West Indies: Volume 23, 1706-1708. Originally published by His Majesty's Stationery Office, London, 1916. http://www.british-history.ac.uk/cal-state-papers/colonial/america-west-indies/vol23/pp125-141
- Pierre Le Moyne d'Iberville. Relation de la prise et capitulation de l'isle Nieve appartenant aux Anglois, par M. d'Iberville en 1706. Manuscript.
- Gillingham, Harrold. Counterfeiting in Colonial Pennsylvania, Numismatic Notes and Monographs, number 86, New York: American Numismatic Society, 1939, pp. 6-7.
- Greely, Adolphus Washington. Explorers and travelers. New York, Scribner 1904.
- Meniketti, Marco G. Sugar Cane Capitalism and Environmental Transformation: An Archaeology of Colonial Nevis, West Indies (Caribbean Archaeology and Ethnohistory) 2nd ed. Edition, Kindle Edition
- Nevisian dollar. https://en.wikipedia.org/wiki/Nevisian_dollar
  Mary Prince. https://en.wikipedia.org/wiki/Mary_Prince
- Scott, Kenneth. Counterfeiting in Colonial Pennsylvania, Numismatic Notes and Monographs, number 132, New York: American Numismatic Society, 1955, pp. 9-10.
- Snelling, Thomas. A View of the Copper Coin and Coinage of England, London: printed for T. Snelling, 1766.
- Brady, Jeremiah D. "The French Tradition: The Colonial Period (exclusive of Canada)" in Theodore V. Buttrey, Jr., ed. Coinage of the Americas New York: American Numismatic Society, 1973, pp. 71-75 on p. 71 and illustration 102 on p. 72.
- Reed, Charles. The First Great Canadian, Pierre Le Moyne d'Iberville. Chicago, 1910.
- Slavery Abolition Act 1833. From Wikipedia, the free encyclopedia.

CHAPTER 10. Independence - "Bones in our rice, pepper in our soup"

The passage Columbus' Ships took arriving to Nevis in 1493.

The eclectic nature of contemporary societies on Saint Kitts and Nevis, and the varied origins of the Afro-Caribbean populace has produced a longing for independence and freedom, but its short history does not seem to posit deeply held *cultural symbols* as one would find in long standing cultures. Two miles apart, a populace consisting of Afro-Caribbeans who are largely descendants of the sugar plantations, with the remainder made up of descendants of British settlers and later migrants formed contemporaneous yet varied island cultures. English being the official language, but a local dialect, referred to as *Kittitian* on Saint Kitts and *Nevisian* on Nevis, is used in the family, at social gatherings, and among men socializing, together galvanized of sorts, unique and not identical indigenous cultures since the 17th century. Both islands easily converse and intermingle with each other daily, but there are aspects uniquely Nevisian and uniquely Kittitian. Only living on the islands for some time will make this evident.

Sugar was still the dominant plantation crop in the Eighteenth Century and the rise of the 13 Colonies on the Atlantic seaboard provided new markets to sell to. The Southern Colonies also provided new markets for the slave traders. Antagonism with the French did not abate as both the Austrian War of Succession from 1740 to 1748 and the Seven Years War of 1756 - 1763 saw the Caribbean become a battleground for the French and British fleets once again. The rise in the skill and power of the Royal Navy meant that the British were becoming more successful at holding their ground and capturing nearby French islands using Nevis as an important supply port and safe harbor.

The American Wars of Independence were to be even more challenging to the Nevis island economy as a combined American, French and Spanish effort against the British saw the island cut off for long periods of time. Unable to sell its wares and unable to import foodstuffs, the plantation economy showed its lack of resilience and once again famine and hunger plagued the island. In 1782 the island surrendered to the French without a firing a shot in defence. A large French fleet under Admiral de Grasse was en route to St. Kitts to root out the British there and saw the opportunity to seize the weakened island of Nevis. Fortunately, the war was drawing to a close and it was soon returned to British control by the Treaty of Paris ending the War of Independence in 1783.

Barely a decade had elapsed until the British and French were once again fighting each other in the Revolutionary and Napoleonic Wars. Once more the sugar islands of the Caribbean became a major theatre of operations. It was complicated by the fact that slave revolts in Haiti raised tensions amongst the aristocratic elites on other sugar islands who were concerned that some of the Revolutionary ideas from Europe might spill over into the slave economies. The French assaulted the island twice in both 1805 and 1806 under the direction of Napoleon's youngest brother, Jerome Bonaparte. Both of these were repulsed with the enhanced defenses of Fort Charles playing a prominent role. Yet by 1854, all forts on Nevis were abandoned.

Interestingly, a certain young Captain Horatio Nelson was based on Nevis in the 1780s and married the widow of a plantation owner there by the name of Frances Nisbet. It was common for Royal Naval personnel to spend long periods of time in the Caribbean. In 1784 he received command of the frigate HMS Boreas with the assignment to enforce the Navigation Acts in the vicinity of Antigua. The Acts were unpopular with both the Americans and the colonies. Nelson served on the station under Admiral Sir Richard Hughes, and often came into conflict with his superior officer over their differing interpretation of the Acts. The captains of the American vessels Nelson had seized sued him for illegal seizure. Because the merchants of the nearby island of Nevis supported the American claim, Nelson was in peril of imprisonment; he remained sequestered on Boreas for eight months, until the courts ruled in his favor.

In the interim, Nelson met Frances "Fanny" Nisbet, a young widow from a Nevis plantation family. Nelson and Nisbet were married at Montpelier Estate on the island of Nevis on 11 March 1787, shortly before the end of his tour of duty in the

Caribbean. The marriage was registered at Fig Tree Church in St. John's Parish on Nevis. Nelson returned to England in July, with Fanny following later.

The Napoleonic Wars would offer another profound threat to the sugar island economies. Namely, the introduction of sugar beet as a replacement for sugar cane. Unable to break the British blockade, the French sought a replacement for sugar and found that sugar beet could be grown in Europe and processed to make sugar also. It took a few years for the rest of Europe to follow France's lead, but within the first few decades of the Nineteenth Century, the price of sugar was collapsing and the sugar islands were losing their monopoly on cane sugar.

Nevis was politically united with Saint Kitts and Anguilla in 1882, and they became an associated state with full internal autonomy in 1967, though Anguilla seceded in 1971 'without firing a shot'. Together, Saint Kitts and Nevis became independent on 19th September 1983. On 10th August 1998, a referendum on Nevis to separate from Saint Kitts had 2,427 votes in favor and 1,498 against, falling barely short of the two-thirds majority needed to emancipate and leaving its scars and lamentations.

Old Charlestown, capital of Nevis, c. 1870

Before 1967, the local government of Saint Kitts was also the government of Nevis and Anguilla. Nevis had two seats and Anguilla one seat in the government. The economic and infrastructural development of the two smaller islands was not a priority to the colonial federal government seated in St. Kitts which would leave to develop lasting frustrations.

When the hospital in Charlestown was destroyed in a hurricane in 1899, planting of trees in the squares and refurbishing of government buildings of Saint Kitts took precedence over the rebuilding of the only hospital in Nevis would fester lasting resentments. After five years without any proper medical facilities, the leaders in Nevis initiated a campaign, threatening to seek independence from Saint Kitts. The

British Administrator in Saint Kitts, Charles Cox, was unmoved. He stated that Nevis did not need a hospital since there had been no significant rise in the number of deaths during the time Nevisians had been without a hospital which is hard to imagine. Therefore, no action was considered needed on behalf of the government, and besides, Cox continued, the Legislative Council regarded "Nevis and Anguilla as a drag on St. Kitts and would willingly see a separation". Finally, a letter of complaint to the metropolitan British Foreign Office gave results and the federal government in Saint Kitts was ordered by their superiors in London to take action. The Legislative Council took another five years to consider their options while Nevis suffered further. The final decision by the federal government was to not rebuild the old hospital after all, but to instead convert the old Government House in Nevis into a hospital, named Alexandra Hospital after Queen Alexandra, wife of King Edward VII. A majority of the funds assigned for the hospital could thus spent on the construction of a new official government residence in Nevis.

Electricity was not introduced in Nevis until 1954, when two generators were shipped in to provide electricity to the area around Charlestown, depriving the rest of the island to remain in utter wilderness. In this regard, Nevis fared better than Anguilla, where no paved roads, no electricity and no telephones were not put up until 1967. However, electricity did not become available island-wide on Nevis until as late as 1971. Up until that time, Nevis was living in the dark.

NEVIS-ISLAND-BWI-KEN JARVIS-HAM RADIO OPERATOR - c. 1940-1950

It is only since the end of the 20th century that an ambitious infrastructure development program has been introduced - including upgrading of the island's electrical generators, a transformation of the Charlestown port to be more people and tourist friendly and safe; construction of a new deep-water harbor for cargo with regular shipments from Miami; resurfacing and widening the Island Main Road; and a new airport terminal and control tower (Vance W. Amory International Airport).

THE BIRTH OF ELECTRICITY ON NEVIS

Can you imagine what Nevis was like without electricity? Charlestown had six gas lamps, but, by 9pm they all would go out and plunge the town into darkness. Luckily for everyone, there were no criminals about in those days, and we always looked forward for the moonlight.

Bertram Roach had recently returned from Trinidad where he worked at the US Navel base. He was so good at his job that he was awarded a Navy "E" for efficiency.

His friend Frederick Liburd was in the Army and attached tot he Signalling Division. After he left the army, he joined the Police Force in St Kitts-Nevis. They were close pals at The Charlestown Boys School. Frederick told Bertram that the electricity would be introduced to Nevis soon and that the Management were looking for men to work in Nevis on the project there. Bertram was preparing to return to Trinidad and, therefore he was not interested, but Frederick convinced him to consider the proposition. Having considered it, he made the application and was accepted for the training.

Bertram went over to St. Kitts for his training. At that time, St. Kitts was changing over from Direct Current to alternating current. In the meantime, Frederick got a transfer from the police force to the Electricity Department and joined Bertram for his training in St Kitts.

At the end of their training, they were sent back to Nevis. Their boss was one Mr. Mills from England. They both started preparing the poles for planting. That involved putting on cross arms, and insulators. Having done that , they then started to plan the positions where the poles were to be planted and to run the wires. They also started the process of employing the workmen.

In the meantime, the power station was being built. On completion, Bertram was assigned to the Power Station, and Frederick was in charge of the lines.

The electrification of Nevis started in 1954, and from that time the process of development started at a slow pace, and such development continues up to the present day.

When you put your switch on, and your lights come on , and your fridge, stove, radio, television and all other electrical equipment work, you must remember those two men-- Bertram Roach, and Frederick Liburd (deceased). They lightened your darkness. You must also remember those two men and also James Phillips(otherwise known as Ghandi) who gave them additional assistance with the shifting of the heavy electrical poles. Mr Bertram Roach is now a writer and currently living in Nevis on retirement, and sadly, Mr Frederick Liburd has passed away quite recently, after a short retirement in Canada.

Having done a fair stint of work in Nevis, Bertram emigrated to England in 1955 where he spent forty four years. During that period of time, he pursued a course of studies in the field of Power Station Operation and was successful in being awarded a City & Guilds Certificate/Diploma in that field.

Article: Courtesy from Betram Roach (2017)

Modernized classrooms and better equipped schools, as well as improvements in the educational system, have contributed to a leap in academic performance on the island. The pass rate among the Nevisian students sitting for the Caribbean Examination Council (CXC) exams, the Cambridge General Certificate of Education Examination (GCE) and the Caribbean Advance Proficiency Examinations is now consistently among the highest in the English-speaking Caribbean.

An African baobab tree by a ruin at Montravers Estate, a former plantation that produced, on average, 110 "hogsheads" (30,000 kg) of sugar and around 7,250 gallons (33,000 liters) of rum each year.

After d'Iberville's invasion in 1704, records show Nevis' sugar industry in ruins and a decimated population begging the English Parliament and relatives for loans and monetary assistance to stave off island-wide starvation. The sugar industry on the island never fully recovered and during the general depression that followed the loss of the West Indian sugar monopoly it once hosted, and Nevis fell on hard times and the island became one of the poorest in the region. The Queen of the Caribees remained poorer than Saint Kitts until 1991, when the fiscal performance of Nevis edged ahead of the fiscal performance of Saint Kitts for the first time since the French invasion. The European Commission's Delegation in Barbados and the Eastern Caribbean estimates the annual per capita Gross Domestic Product (GDP) on Nevis to be about 10 percent higher than on St. Kitts.

The major source of revenue for Nevis today is tourism. During the 2003-2004 season, approximately 40,000 tourists visited Nevis. A five star hotel (The Four Seasons Resort Nevis, West Indies), another four exclusive restored plantation inns, and several smaller hotels, are currently in operation.

Offshore Corporate Services
The introduction of legislation has made offshore financial services a rapidly growing economic sector in Nevis in the 1990s. Incorporation of companies, international insurance and reinsurance, as well as several international banks, trust companies, asset management firms, have created a huge boost in the economy. During 2005, the Nevis Island Treasury collected $94.6 million in annual revenue, compared to $59.8 million during 2001. In 1998, 17,500 international banking companies were registered in Nevis. Registration and annual filing fees paid in 1999 by these entities amounted to over 10 percent of Nevis' revenues. The offshore financial industry gained importance during the financial disaster of

1999 when Hurricane Lenny damaged the 4 Seasons resort on the island, causing the hotel to be closed down for a year and 400 of the 700 employees to be laid off.

Politics Today
The political structure for the Federation of Saint Kitts and Nevis is based on the Westminster Parliamentary system, but it is a unique structure in that Nevis has its own unicameral legislature, consisting of Her Majesty's representative (the Deputy Governor General) and members of the Nevis Island Assembly. Nevis has considerable autonomy in its legislative branch. The constitution actually empowers the Nevis Island Legislature to make laws that cannot be abrogated by the National Assembly. Nevis has its own premier and its own local government, the *Nevis Island Administration*. In addition, Nevis has a constitutionally protected right to secede from the federation, should a two-third majority of the island's population vote for independence in a local referendum.

The federal prime minister is the leader of the majority party of the federal House of Representatives in Saint Kitts, and his cabinet conducts the affairs of state. The prime minister and the cabinet are responsible to the Parliament.

Nevis' Secession movement
Nevisians often cite an air of independence and uniqueness as an island community, one that is only palpable after living there for some time. During much of the seventeenth century, Nevis enjoyed considerable prosperity, escaping the British-French warfare that engulfed St. Kitts. Toward the end of the century, in 1680, however, the first of a series of disasters visited the island in the form of a devastating earthquake. After d'Iberville's French invasion in 1704, records show Nevis' economy in ruins. During the century that followed, one violent occurrence after another: hurricanes, warfare, and epidemical disease contributed to the erosion of Nevis' early prosperity, yet they remained independent. During the same period, St. Kitts was transformed into one of the most successful of Britain's Caribbean sugar colonies. Despite this reversal of fortunes, the Nevis island continued to administer itself apart from St. Christopher.

For Nevisian history, difficulties with the politics of St. Kitts date from the decision taken by the British government in 1882 to reunite their island with St. Kitts and Anguilla for administrative purposes. From Nevis' earliest European settlement in 1628 by the buccaneer Hilton, by a party that set off from the new colony of islands of St. Christopher, Barbuda, Barbados, St. Martin, and even Tortuga is traceable. For the first century and a half of their colonial history, the islands were mostly administered separately and at times jointly, and the divide has not fully ended.

In an outline of Nevisian political history written in 1992, a member of the Nevis Reformation Party, whose platform was secessionist at the time, includes this note after the entry of the 1882 event:
"Following this union Nevis as it was became a colony of St. Kitts and
despite that it continued to have representatives on the Presidency they

had very little authority. As a result the quality of life in Nevis as well as its economy went into a great decline."

This is the community theme in Nevis today with reference to the political bondage of the island to St. Kitts - that the prosperity of Nevis island, unimpeded to that time, had declined since amalgamation 1882 with little independent growth. The Kittitian view differs markedly from that in addressing the implications for St. Kitts of having to take on the political and financial burdens of Nevis and Anguilla. The impression overall is that St. Kitts was obliged, in 1882-88, to take on a Nevisian lingering economy that has proved to be a burden ever since. St. Kitts has not been able to satisfy Nevis' needs in the past one hundred years of this ill-fated union and will be even less likely to be able to do so in the future.

A signal event occurred in 1970 that galvanized an opposition in Nevis. The *Christena*, a ferry operated by the government to transport goods and passengers daily across the narrow channel between the two islands, sank on its way from St. Kitts to Nevis. The ferry was seriously overloaded with passengers returning from August holiday outings in St. Kitts, and 227 souls perished.

An acquaintance of the author who was on duty with the US Coast Guard recounted his arrival to the scene at the early morning hours of the disaster and stated he had never seen so many sharks in Caribbean waters. The tragedy struck nearly every family in Nevis, and the government was blamed for an abrogation of responsibility for the safety of the vessel. Two months later the Nevis Reformation Party (NRP) was formed, and it organized and led protests of the mishandling of the Christena case. From its inception the NRP articulated a secessionist position, a stance that eschewed any continuing involvement of Nevis in the two-island state.

In January 1976 the Nevis Council had passed a resolution that read:
Be it resolved that the people of Nevis through the Nevis Local Council
call upon the Central Government of the State to introduce the necessary
Legislation in order to give to the island of Nevis its own Legislative
Council as expressed by the people of Nevis at the recent elections.

Simeon Daniel, leader of the opposition at the time (and the author's solicitor) followed this with another resolution introduced to the House of Assembly that called for Nevisian autonomy and legislation leading to the secession of Nevis from the state. Finally, following unsuccessful attempts at island, state, and colonial levels to achieve this separation, the NRP organized a "referendum" in Nevis on secession. On August 18, 1977, Nevisian voters gave their verdict: 4,193 for secession, 14 against. Premier Robert Bradshaw of the Federation declared the exercise null and void.

The frustration of Nevisians and the animosity that characterized the relationship between Daniel and Bradshaw may be indicated in this passage of a letter in which the former invokes a prominent piece of Nevisian lore:
The people of Nevis have grown accustomed to the neglect, spite and disregard for their political, social and economic welfare meted out to them over a quarter of century at the hands of your Government. You must see to it that your promise of **"Bones in our rice, pepper in our soup"** is fulfilled during your lifetime, but we will not be beaten into submission.

Address for the 38th Anniversary of Anguilla Day
Written by: Public Relations, Govt. of Anguilla
May 30, 2005
Today once again we come together to celebrate that chain of events which led to the liberation of our people from a hostile relationship with the central government of the then unified state of St. Kitts-Nevis and Anguilla. It was a relationship that threatened to keep our people in a state of underdevelopment for a very long time. The seriousness of that threat was borne out in statements attributed to the leader of that central government that he would put "bones in our rice and pepper in our soup". And that he would make Anguilla a desert.

Simeon Daniel, now Nevis' first Premier after gaining independence in 1983 and former leader of the Nevis Reformation Party (NRP); and Vance Amory, Premier and leader of the Concerned Citizens Movement (CCM), made sovereign independence for Nevis from the Federation of Saint Kitts and Nevis part of their parties' agenda. Since independence from the United Kingdom in 1983, the Nevis Island Administration and the Federal Government have been involved in several conflicts over the interpretation of the new constitution which came into effect at independence. During an interview on Voice of America in March 1998, repeated in a government issued press release headlined "PM Douglas Maintains 1983 Constitution is Flawed", Prime Minister Denzil Douglas correctly called the constitution a "recipe for disaster and disharmony among the people of both islands". Both Daniel (now deceased) and Amory, failed in their mission.

A crisis developed in 1984 when the People's Action Movement (PAM) won a majority in the Federal elections and temporarily ceased honoring the Federal Government's financial obligations to Nevis. Consequently, cheques issued by the Nevis Administration were not honored by the Bank, public servants in Nevis were not paid on time, and the Nevis Island Administration experienced difficulties in meeting its financial obligations. Among other issues of inequality, there is also substantial support in Nevis for British Overseas Territory status similarly to Anguilla, which was formerly the third of the tri-state Saint Christopher-Nevis-Anguilla colony.

Legislative motivation for secession
In 1996, four new bills were introduced in the National Assembly in Saint Kitts, one of which made provisions to have revenue derived from activities in Nevis paid directly to the treasury in Saint Kitts instead of to the treasury in Nevis. Another bill, The Financial Services Committee Act, contained provisions that all investments in Saint Kitts and Nevis would require approval by an investment committee in Saint Kitts. This was controversial, because ever since 1983 the Nevis Island Administration had approved all investments for Nevis, on the basis that the constitution vests legislative authority for industries, trades and businesses and economic development in Nevis to administrated by the Nevis Island Administration.

All three representatives from Nevis, including the leader of the opposition in the Nevis Island Assembly, objected to the introduction of these bills into the National Assembly in Saint Kitts, arguing that the bills would affect the ability of Nevis to develop its offshore financial services sector and that the bills would be detrimental to the Nevis economy. All the representatives in opposition in the National Assembly shared the conviction that the bills, if passed into law, would be unconstitutional and undermine the constitutional and legislative authority of the Nevis Island Administration, as well as result in the destruction of the economy of Nevis.

The constitutional crisis initially developed when the newly appointed Attorney General refused to grant permission for the Nevis Island Administration to assert its legal right in the Courts. After a decision of the High Court in favor of the Nevis Island Administration, the Prime Minister gave newspaper interviews stating that he "refused to accept the decision of the High Court". Due to the deteriorating relationship between the Nevis Island Administration and the Federal Government, a Constitutional Committee was appointed in April 1996 to advise on whether or not the present constitutional arrangement between the islands should continue. The committee recommended constitutional reform and the establishment of an island administration for Saint Kitts, separate from the Federal Government.

The Federal Government in Saint Kitts fills both functions today and Saint Kitts does not have an equivalent to the Nevis Island Administration. Disagreements between the political parties in Nevis and between the Nevis Island Administration and the Federal Government have prevented the recommendations by the electoral committee from being implemented. The problematic political arrangement between the two islands therefore continues to date.

Nevis has continued developing its own legislation, such as The Nevis International Insurance Ordinance and the Nevis International Mutual Funds Ordinance of 2004, but calls for secession are often based on concerns that the legislative authority of the Nevis Island Administration might be challenged again in the future.

Fiscal motivation for secession
The issues of political dissension between Saint Kitts and Nevis are often centered around an imbalance in the economic structure. As noted by many scholars, Nevisians have often referred to a structural imbalance in Saint Kitts' favor in how funds are distributed between the two islands and this issue has made the movement for Nevis secession a constant presence in the island's political arena, with many articles appearing in the local press expressing concerns such as those compiled by Dr. Everton Powell in "What Motivates Our Call for Independence":

- Many of the businesses that operate in Nevis are headquartered in Saint Kitts and pay the corporate taxes to Saint Kitts, despite the fact that profits for those businesses are derived from Nevis.
- The vast majority of Nevisians and residents of Nevis depart the Federation from Saint Kitts. This meant that departure taxes are paid in Saint Kitts.
- The bulk of cargo destined for Nevis enters the Federation through Saint Kitts. Custom duties are therefore paid in Saint Kitts.
- The largest expenditure for Nevis, approximately 29 percent of the Nevis Island Administration's recurrent budget, is education and health services, but the Nevis Island Legislature has no power to legislate over these two areas.
- Police, defense and coast guard are a federal responsibility. Charlestown Police Station, which served as the Headquarters for police officers in Nevis, was destroyed by fire in December 1991. Police officers initially had to operate out of the ruin, until the Nevis Island Administration managed to raise the resources to re-house the police.
- Nevis experiences an economic disadvantage because of a highly and persistent preferential treatment by the federal government for development of Saint Kitts. The division of foreign aid and various forms of international assistance toward development and infrastructure are especially contentious issues. Lists showing the disparities in sharing have been compiled by Dr. Everson Hull, a former Economics professor of Howard University, and are available online.

Another referendum on secession from the Federation of St. Kitts and Nevis was held in 1998. Although 62% voted in favor of secession, a two-thirds majority would have been necessary for the referendum to barely succeed.

Parishes of Nevis
The island of Nevis is divided into five administrative subdivisions called parishes, each of which has an elected representative in the Nevis Island Assembly. The division of this almost round island into parishes was done in a circular sector pattern, so each parish is shaped like a pie slice, reaching from the highest point of Nevis Peak down to the coastline.

The parishes have double names, for example Saint George - Gingerland. The first part of the name is the name of the patron saint of the parish church, and the second part of the name is the traditional common name of the parish. Often the parishes are referred to simply by their common names. The religious part of a parish name is sometimes written or pronounced in the possessive: Saint George's Gingerland. The five parishes of Nevis are:

Saint George Gingerland   Saint John Figtree   Saint Thomas Lowland
Saint James Windward   Saint Paul Charlestown

Religion in Nevis

As was the custom at that time, the Church followed the flag – the colonists both of sections undertook to provide for the spiritual needs of their people. The first Church of England clergyman in St Christopher was the Reverend John Featley, who arrived in 1625 and became the rector at Old Road. He was followed by others and it seems unlikely that the presence of any of them was widely welcomed. No proper parishes were established until 1655, by which time there were three churches on the leeward side and the two on the windward side. Whether there were then, or at any time in the next twenty years, five parish priests in residence seems most unlikely. Nor is it likely that Nevis or Anguilla were better served. Although Nevis was divided into five parishes around 1670 it is very doubtful if more than one or two clergymen were present at any time during the next thirty or forty years. In 1671 four parishes on Nevis were without ministers.

Around 1670 a small congregation of Quakers had been established on Nevis. As they refused to participate in Church of England services, to bear arms or to swear oaths, their presence was greatly resented, and reportedly they were forced to live and worship under a variety of restrictions. When two missionaries accompanied by a Quaker planter from Barbados arrived in late 1671 they were welcomed by 'several honest tender friends', but refused permission to remain on the island by the Governor. After this, being prevented from proselytizing and being 'frequently victimized', the Quakers on Nevis had little future and by the end of the century had left the island. This was seen as a pity because they were the only Christian denomination at the time that saw African slaves as fellow human beings and prepared to do something to improve their living conditions.

Nevis being less troubled by the wars of the seventeenth century was one of the main reasons why Nevis was able to make the transition from tobacco to sugar and prosper so rapidly was because of the presence of a mercantile community larger and being more progressive and tolerant than that on any of the other islands. While three members of this community, as agents for the *Royal African Company*, provided the planters of Nevis with the choice pick of the slaves sent to the Leeward Islands, others supplied all the goods and services needed to produce sugar. Some of them, once they had made enough from such trading activities, bought land or took over existing estates and became planters themselves.

Among these merchants, and probably leading the rest with their business acumen, were a number of Jews of Sephardic heritage who had arrived around the middle of the 17th century. They were descended from families who had gone to the early Dutch settlements in Brazil after the expulsion of Jews from Spain and Portugal in the fifteenth century, and then been forced to leave when Brazil was claimed by Portugal, another Catholic stronghold. Some of those who had moved to Barbados, eventually found life too restricted or business prospects too limited, had sought better opportunities in a less-crowded island like Nevis. There they were welcomed, and by 1690 were so well established that Charlestown possessed a synagogue and a Jewish school. The earliest tombstone in the still extant Jewish cemetery dates from 1679.

Accusations about Jews trading with slaves, such as those already encountered in Jamaica and Barbados, were also made in Nevis. A description, by Nevis historian Karen Fog Olwlg, of the market where the slaves sold their produce explains that: While the market seems to have been patronized primarily by the white population during the 17th century, during the 18th century, when the white population of small farmers and laborers had virtually disappeared from Nevis, the market became entirely dominated by the slaves...It was held Sunday morning in Charlestown...Negroes bring fowls, Indian corn, yam...It is no longer acceptable for the white population to trade at the markets, perhaps because they were held primarily by slaves, and on Sundays, and Robertson, noted that only Jews and lesser sort of Christians traded with slaves.

One of the most popular historic sites on the island of Nevis is the Jewish Cemetery located on Government Road in Charlestown. The nineteen surviving grave markers spanning the period from 1679 to 1730 are the most visible reminder of the island's former Jewish community. In the cemetery the visitor may gaze upon carved inscriptions in Hebrew, English, and Portuguese that bear testimony to the experiences of an uprooted and persecuted religious group whose forced exodus drove them across oceans and from continent to continent.

As it happened in the West Indies, Jews were respected all the time they were in the plantations and provided help with their skills in tropical agriculture. Once they were in the cities engaged in commerce, they were seen as unfair competitors, and they fostered limitations of their rights and a series of disabilities, removed only in the 19th century. With the gradual depopulation of Nevis, and the movement of Jews from Barbados, the percentage of Jews in Nevis rose to one-quarter of the white population of Charlestown, although that meant only about 70 persons. The decline of the Nevis Jewish population began in the second half of the 18th century. The sugar trade declined, and Nevis Jews had to look for new prospects. The last grave in the cemetery is that of Jacob Vas Mendes, dated 13 November 1768. Most Nevis Jews joined the Sephardic Jewish congregations in the British colonies of North America.

By the beginning of the 19th century there was little trace of the Jews. The main body of the white population consisted of masons, blacksmiths, poor cotton growers, seamen, fisherman, and tavern keepers. "It looks as though the Jews had almost deserted the island" (Richard Pares, A West India Fortune, London, 1950).

The Fig-Tree Church where Admiral Nelson married Fanny Nisbet

It is not known what the Established Church thought of the presence of a synagogue on Nevis, as the Church of England had only a marginal role in the society of any the Leeward Islands during the seventeenth century. Religious fanaticism dominated in every island except Nevis, as many of the settlers had left England - and France - to escape persecution or to be able to follow their own method of worship. In 1671 the inhabitants of Nevis were said to be loyal Anglicans.

Arrival of the Methodists
Dr. Thomas Coke of England reports in the book *A History of the West Indies* (1801), "on business solely of a missionary nature, reached the island of St. Christopher's ; from which, in company with other ministers employed on the same important errand, on the 19th of January 1787, he went with some recommendatory letters to that of Nevis. We were received with the greatest civility, and even with politeness; but every door seemed to be completely shut against our ministry. In this island the Moravian brethren had established no mission; so that, by viewing the gospel through an improper medium, the inhabitants might probably have apprehended, that its operations on the minds of the slaves would tend to lessen that subordination which is inseparably connected with their relative situations in life. Our letters of recommendation were apparently useless as to the object of our visit... In this opinion, however, we found soon afterward that we were much deceived... soon received an invitation from a Mr. Brazier, a gentleman in the island of Nevis, and a member of the

assembly, to come over and preach to his negroes. Early in the year 1789, the Author being then in the West indies, we again made two visits to Nevis; and found, to our great joy, that God had so disposed the hearts of the people, that the slaves were willing to hear the word, and their rulers to permit the gospel to be preached.

To two or three gentlemen, particularly the Judge of the Admiralty, we felt ourselves greatly obliged, for the comfortable accommodations which we found, and for that civility and politeness which they so readily manifested on the present, as well as on the former occasion. From this period we may date the introduction of the gospel into the island. At this time we formed a little class of twenty-one catechumens, and provided for their instruction before our departure, by leaving them to the care of Mr. Owens, one of our missionaries, who was appointed to take upon him the charge of the mission throughout the whole colony. Towards the close of the year 1790, in company with other missionaries, I again visited this island, and was received with the greatest hospitality by many friends; particularly by Mr. Ward, the Judge of the Admiralty, whose kindness 1 have already had an occasion to mention.

In the month of June 1803, a letter from Nevis was written by Mr. Edward Turner... "I have been," Mr. Turner observes, " in this island nearly four months, and feel an attachment to my situation. I trust, I have grown in grace, and in the knowledge and love of God, since I came hither; and I have reason to believe that my labors have not been in vain. Two white persons, and sixty or seventy blacks, have joined us since our arrival. Our congregations are not only large but I generally increasing. Many respectable white people attend our preaching, and behave with the utmost propriety... " Last Thursday, Brother Joseph Taylor landed on our little friendly isle. He appears to be a young man of deep piety, and, I hope, will be an useful and acceptable preacher."

Such was the state of religion in the island of Nevis in the year 1803. On the 18th of May 1804, the same pleasing prospects continued to bloom before the missionaries, to excite their future exertions; while past successes presented them with an ample recompense for all their toils.

** Sunday, in the West Indies, is the common market-day.
But so visible is the change which has being wrought here, that many now shut up their shops, and keep the Sabbaths of the Lord by attending to his service. The negroes who used to spend that sacred day in dancing, drinking, etc. which generally ended in fighting, now attend the house of God, and learn to sing his praise. This is the Lord's doings and it is marvellous in our eyes..."

It was early in the year 1805, that the island of Nevis, in conjunction with others, was invaded by the French. The Methodists, in common with others, were involved in this disaster, and had to share in the public calamity. An event so serious could not fail to create an alarm, and spread consternation through the whole territory. Disorder and confusion must have been felt ill every department, particularly in the religious, because the tumults of war are not congenial with the mild dominion of the Prince of Peace." [Coke, Thomas LLD. A HISTORY OF THE WEST INDIES, CONTAINING THE NATURAL, CIVIL, AND ECCLESIASTICAL. 1801.]

The records of the Island show that in St. Kitts as in Nevis there were planters who encouraged their slaves to accept baptism. During the rectorship of the Revd. John Julius Kerie (1812 – 1825) the St. George's Church Registers record large numbers of slave baptisms on the plantations, particularly on Buckley's, the estate of Abednego Matthew. Mr. Matthew was one of the richest of the Basseterre planters and a devout Churchman. The same of Mr. Cottle in Nevis, for it is said that one of the fields of the estate was called, Negro Church field.

The Cottle Church was built by Thomas Cottle (1761-1828) owner of the Round Hill estate, Nevis. The church and its grounds are being preserved for the public as a contribution to the cultural heritage of the island of Nevis. The people of St. Kitts and Nevis today are generally devoutly religious, especially the older population. Several historic Anglican churches remain on Nevis, and fifty percent of the country's population still practices the religion. Most other people belong to other Christian denominations, though there are some Rastafarians and Bahá'í followers. An old Jewish cemetery on Nevis shows that there was once a Jewish population as well, but currently there is no active Jewish community in the country.

Today, the people of Nevis fill their churches not only on Sundays but throughout the week for functions, clubs and meetings. Religious expression is part of their everyday lives and many a meeting begins with a short prayer. Churches cater for a great variety of worshippers from Methodists, Anglicans and Roman Catholics to the diverse modern expressions of non-conformity. Churches abound on the island of Nevis, services are lively and exuberant with much singing and dancing but also considerable time for the essential sermons. Churches also run clubs for the elderly and arrange outings for their members and youth. The islanders enjoy a very sociable and friendly lifestyle, regularly visiting friends on other islands.

References
- Coke, Thomas LLD. A HISTORY OF THE WEST INDIES, CONTAINING THE NATURAL, CIVIL, AND ECCLESIASTICAL. 1801.
- Hubbard, Vincent K. Swords, Ships, and Sugar: A History of Nevis to 1900, 1993.
- Iles, John Alexander Burke. An Account Descriptive Of The Island Of Nevis, West Indies. Fletcher and Son, Printers 1923.
- Merrill, Gordon Clark. The Historical Geography of Saint Kitts and Nevis, 1958.
- Midgett, Douglas. Pepper and bones: the secessionist impulse in Nevis. New West Indian Guide/ Nieuwe West-Indische Gids 78 (2004), no: 1/2, Leiden, 43-7
- Nevis. From Wikipedia, https://en.wikipedia.org/wiki/Nevis

CHAPTER 10. The Culture of St. Kitts/Nevis

The culture of St. Kitts and Nevis, two small Caribbean islands forming one country, has grown mainly out of the West African traditions brought in during the colonial period. British influence remains in the country's official language, English, while some islanders speak an English-based Creole. There is also a local dialect. Due to television and many islanders living in the America, Canada, and England, western culture has increasingly influenced native lifestyle (some feel to its detriment and peril).

A *festival* is an event ordinarily celebrated by a community and centering on some characteristic and unique aspect of that community and its religion or traditions. It is often marked as a local or national holiday or *mela* (fair). Next to religion and folklore, a significant origin is agricultural. Food is such a vital resource that many festivals are associated with harvest time. Religious commemoration and thanksgiving for good harvests are blended in events that take place in autumn, such as Halloween in the northern hemisphere and Easter in the southern.

Festivals often serve to fulfill specific communal purposes, especially in regard to commemorations or thanksgiving. The celebrations offer a sense of belonging for religious, social, or geographical groups, contributing to group cohesiveness. They may also provide entertainment, which was particularly important to local communities before the advent of mass-produced entertainment. Festivals that focus on cultural or ethnic topics also seek to inform community members of their traditions; the involvement of elders sharing stories and experience provides a means for unity among families.

Both islands of St. Kitts and Nevis have traditional dances, music, garb, and tales, but neither one is committed to a constellation of symbols that could identify a *cultural identity*. Instead, the richness and variety of the cultural backgrounds is celebrated in a *series* of festivals throughout the year. The roots of those festivals go back to the seventeenth century, when they were often associated with Christmas and May Day celebrations. A strong association with Christmas remains, partly because of Christian tradition and partly from the holiday visits of many Kittitians and Nevisians living elsewhere who visit home during that period.

Festivities
As in all other Caribbean nations, the culture on St. Kitts and Nevis is festive and vibrant. Carnivals and celebrations play an important role in island life. At Christmas time, Carnival is in full swing on St. Kitts. The opening gala takes place in mid-December, with events going on until a few days after New Year's. Among these events, crowd favorites include the Miss Caribbean Talented Teen Pageant, the Junior Calypso Show, and the National Carnival Queen Pageant. Of course, there are also plenty of parades full of people wearing colorful, spangled costumes.

Apart from St. Kitts Carnival, the island of Nevis has its own unique festival, *Culturama*. Celebrated on the weekend of Emancipation Day, it began in 1974 when some islanders feared that their native folk art and customs were being lost. They started Culturama to reconnect people with their traditional culture. In addition to arts and crafts, the five-day-long celebration includes dances, music, drama, and religious sacrifices. Parties, boat rides, swimsuit contests, and street jams have also become part of the festivities.

The idea of Nevis Culturama festival was conceived in February 1974 during a meeting of the Nevis Dramatic and Cultural Society (NEDACS). The main point discussed during this meeting was the general decline in the customary folklore troupes on parade during the then Christmas festival.

It was felt that much of the customary indigenous Christmas traditions and activities were dying and that there was an urgent need to revive these traditions so that they can be handed down from generation to generation thereby ensuring the posterity of Nevis' rich cultural heritage.

Music of St. Kitts & Nevis
The music of Saint Kitts and Nevis is known for a number of musical celebrations including Carnival (December 17 to January 3 on Saint Kitts). The last week in June features the *St Kitts Music Festival*, while the week-long *Culturama* on Nevis lasts from the end of July into early August. These celebrations typically feature parades, street dances and salsa, jazz, soca, calypso and steelpan music.

Music Genres
A music genre is a conventional category that identifies pieces of music as belonging to a shared tradition or set of conventions. Caribbean music genres are diverse. They are each syntheses of African, European, Indian and Indigenous influences, largely created by descendants of Africa along with contributions from other communities. *Afro-Caribbean music* is a broad term for music styles originating in the Caribbean from the African diaspora. These types of music usually have West/Central African influence because of the presence and history of African people and their descendants living in the Caribbean, as a result of the trans-Atlantic migration. Some of the styles have gained wide popularity outside of the Caribbean include baithak gana, bouyon, cadence-lypso, calypso, chutney, chutney-soca, compas, dancehall, jing ping, parang, pichakaree, punta, ragga, reggae, reggaeton, salsa, soca, and zouk. Caribbean music, as from Puerto Rico, is also related to Central and South American music styles.

The complex deep origins of Caribbean music are best understood if you have knowledge of Western Hemisphere colonial immigration patterns, the resulting melting pot of people each of its nations and territories, and thus resulting influx of original musical influences. Colonial Caribbean ancestors were predominantly from West Africa, West Europe, and India. In the 20th and 21st centuries immigrants have also come from Taiwan, China, Indonesia/Java, and the Middle East. In addition, neighboring Latin American and North American (particularly hip hop and pop music) countries have naturally influenced Caribbean culture and vice versa. Although there are musical commonalities among Caribbean nations and territories, the variation in immigration patterns and colonial hegemony tend to parallel the variations in musical influence. Diverse languages from Spanish, Portuguese, English, Hindustani, Tamil, Telugu, Arabic, Chinese, Hebrew, Yiddish, Yoruba, African languages, Indian languages, Amerindian languages, French, Indonesian, Javanese, and Dutch are one of the strongest influences.

Indo-Caribbean music is most common in Trinidad, Guyana and Suriname, makes contributions to popular music and is very important. The most well-known is the Indo-Trinidadian chutney music tradition. Chutney is a form of popular dance music that developed in the mid-to late 20th century. Baithak Gana is a similar popular form originating in Suriname. Modern Indian film music, filmi, is also renowned among Indo-Caribbeans.

Due to the diversity of peoples, divisions between Caribbean music genres are not well-defined, because many of these genres share common relations and have influenced each other in many ways and directions. For example, the Jamaican *mento* style has a long history of conflation with Trinidadian *calypso*. Elements of calypso have come to be used in mento, and vice versa, while their origins lie in the Afro-Caribbean culture, each uniquely characterized by influences from the Shango and Shouters religions of Trinidad and the Kumina spiritual tradition of Jamaica.

Carnival music

Carnival in Saint Kitts and Nevis features music quite prominently during holidays. Big Drum and string bands accompany folk performers. Other instruments include shack-shack (a tin can with beads inside), *baha* (a blown metal pipe), triangle, fife, guitar and *quarto*.

Iron bands were introduced to Saint Kitts Carnival in the 1940s, when bands used makeshift percussion instruments from the likes of car rims. Ensembles of local, collaborative musicians formed during this era, playing drums, saxophones, bass guitars and trumpets and these included the Silver Rhythm Orchestra, Brown Queen, Music Makers, Esperanza and Rhythm Kings. The following decade saw the introduction a Trinidadian style called steelpan, brought by Lloyd Matheson, C.B.E., then an Education Officer. The first steelpan band was Roy Martin's Wilberforce Steel Pan. Other bands included the Eagle Squadron, Boomerang, Casablanca, Boston Tigers and The Invaders. Modern Carnival in Saint Kitts and

Nevis did not begin until the late 1950s. In the 1960s, brass bands dominated first Carnival, then much of popular music.

The Quarto Pals of St. Kitts

Calypso

Calypso is a style of music from Trinidad and Tobago, consisting of highly lyrical songs that frequently makes topical comments on the ruling classes and social issues of the day. Calypso music originated during the slave trade by slaves who lived on the sugar plantations. During slavery, calypso was used for commentary against the oppression and brutal treatment suffered by the slaves at the hands of their masters. This form was called Caiso (Ka-ee-sow) meaning "the town cry", while the singer/composer was called the "Caisonian". This singing was then nicknamed "calypso" by the European slave masters, who called it after the mythological sea nymph calypso because of its melodic ability to captivate its listeners.

Calypso was a nymph in Greek mythology, who lived on the island of Ogygia, where she detained Odysseus for several years. She is generally said to be the daughter of the Titan Atlas. Calypso is remembered most for her role in Homer's Odyssey, in which she keeps the fabled Greek hero Odysseus on her island to make him her immortal husband.

Calypso means "I will conceal" and probably relates to the time when she was a major goddess. The author of the Odyssey is not the same person as the author of the Iliad, even though both are called Homer.

The caisonians were then pressured by their masters to sing songs to entertain them in return for certain privileges and an ease of tasks, and for money during the post-emancipation period.

Calypso was subsequently commercialized in Trinidad, where it was sung mainly for entertainment in shows called "calypso tents" during the Trinidad carnival celebrations. From Trinidad, calypso spread across the Caribbean, and became a major part of Kittitian and Nevisian music with the introduction of formal calypso competitions In the 1950s. Prominent early calypsonians from this period included Mighty Kush, Lord Mike, Elmo Osborne, Lord Harmony, King Monow and the Mighty Saint. By the 1980s, calypso had begun to peak in popularity on Saint Kitts and Nevis, while the two dominant performers were the rivals Starshield and Ellie Matt.

Soca music (also known as the soul of calypso) is a genre of Caribbean music that originated within a marginalized subculture in the Trinidad and Tobago in the early 1970s, and developed into a range of styles in the 1980s and later. Soca was initially developed as a sound research experiment. The project was started in 1970 at KH Studios sea lots under the project name " South Caribbean Sound ". The purpose was to find a way to record the complex calypso rhythm in a multi-track era. The song "Trinidad Boogie" by The Last Supper (Robin Imamshah 1970) is generally considered to be the first recording out of this initiative, and was used by the studio as a template for all subsequent versions of the sound. Soca is an offshoot of kaiso/calypso, with influences from chutney, cadence, funk, soul and Rock.

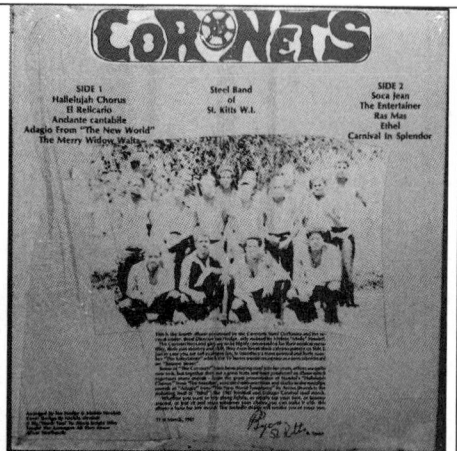

The Coronets Steel Band of St. Kitts

Steelpans

Steelpans (also known as steel drums or pans, and sometimes, collectively with other musicians, as a steel band or orchestra) is a musical instrument originating from Trinidad and Tobago. Steel pan musicians are called pannists. French planters and their slaves emigrated to Trinidad during the French Revolution (1789) from Martinique, including a number of West Africans, and French creoles from Saint Vincent, Grenada, Saint Lucia and Dominica, establishing a local community before Trinidad and Tobago were taken from Spain by the British. The celebration of carnival had arrived with the French. Slaves, who could not take part in carnival, formed their own, parallel celebration called canboulay.

Stick-fighting and African percussion music were banned in 1880, in response to the Canboulay Riots. They were replaced by bamboo sticks beaten together, which were themselves banned in turn. In 1937 they reappeared in Laventille, transformed as an orchestra of frying pans, dustbin lids, and oil drums. These steelpans are now a major part of the Trinidadian music scene and are a popular section of the Canboulay music contests. In 1941, the United States Navy arrived on Trinidad. The pannists, who were associated with lawlessness and violence, helped to popularize steelpan music among the soldiers, which began its international popularization.

Cuisine

With its rich soil, St. Kitts and Nevis grows a wide variety of fresh produce. Seafood and meats such as goat add to the diet. The style of cooking is fairly simple, flavored much like other West Indian cuisine. Goat water stew, perhaps the country's most well-known dish, mixes goat, breadfruit, green pawpaw (papaya), and dumplings (also known as "droppers") in a tomato-based stew. Another favorite dish is cook-up, or *pelau*, which combines chicken, pigtail, salt-fish and vegetables with rice and pigeon peas. Conkies bear a large similarity to tamales, though instead of having filling rolled inside the dough, the cornmeal is mixed together with grated sweet potato, pumpkin, coconut, and a few other ingredients; after wrapping the dough in banana leaves, they're boiled rather than steamed. Sweets tend to be simply made, sometimes with nothing more than fruit, like tamarind or guava, and sugar.

Rum is as popular on St. Kitts and Nevis as it is throughout the Caribbean. The Brinley Gold Company manufactures rum on St. Kitts, with such distinctive flavors as coffee, mango, and vanilla. But the national drink is actually Cane Spirits Rothschild (often abbreviated to CSR), distilled from fresh sugar cane. Belmont Estate and St. Kitts Rum also make rum on the island. In addition several of the beach bars will provide moonshine rum produced by individuals with homemade stills. Many villages on Nevis hold cookouts on Friday and Saturday nights, where people come together to eat, drink, play games like dominoes, and have a good time.

Arts and crafts

Artists of St. Kitts and Nevis create works inspired by their own native traditions, life on the islands, and African roots. Pottery is especially notable, both red clay pieces and pieces fired with colorful glazes and indigenous designs. Paintings often depict tropical landscapes, portraits of islanders, or cultural traditions like clowns performing. Other crafts include rug weaving, wooden items such as carvings, batiks and sculptures, and leather work.

Sports and games

Hearkening back to its British occupation, the country's most loved sport is cricket. Local, regional, and even international matches are played. Horse racing is also popular, particularly on Nevis. The monthly races are festive events, with music and barbecue adding to the fun spirit. Mountain biking, golf, and soccer are other pastimes. St. Kitts also hosts an annual triathlon, which has become increasingly popular since its inception seven years ago. There is also an annual swim across the channel between St. Kitts and Nevis. A local hash association exists as well, with hashes occurring roughly every third Saturday.

Kim Collins, the 2002 Commonwealth and 2003 World Championship 100m winner, is from St. Kitts and Nevis.

References

- Culture of Saint Kitts and Nevis. From Wikipedia, the free encyclopedia.
- https://en.wikipedia.org/wiki/Culture_of_Saint_Kitts_and_Nevis
- List of Caribbean music genres. From Wikipedia, the free encyclopedia
- https://en.wikipedia.org/wiki/List_of_Caribbean_music_genres
- Music of Saint Kitts and Nevis. From Wikipedia, the free encyclopedia
- https://en.wikipedia.org/wiki/Music_of_Saint_Kitts_and_Nevis

CHAPTER 11. SUMMARY

The Caribbean community today represents probably the largest territory of various cultures in the entire Western Hemisphere. Its history is recent with **Nevis** being one of the few islands that was 'settled' but not colonized by displacement of its indigenous peoples. The island was truly 'discovered' by Columbus without intention of any colonization on the day he landed in November of 1493. The island was already blessed with peacefulness and has remained so.

Colonialism is the establishment of a colony in one territory by a political power from another territory, and the subsequent maintenance, expansion, and exploitation of that colony. The term is also used to describe a set of unequal relationships between the colonial power and the colony and often between the colonists and the indigenous peoples and this dramatically is exemplified by the Colonization of the Americas.

The European colonial period was the era from the 16th century to the mid-20th century when several European powers claimed lands and established colonies in Asia, Africa, and the Americas. At first the countries followed a policy of exploitive mercantilism, designed to strengthen the home economy at the expense of rivals and the lands so occupied. The colonies were usually allowed to trade only with the mother country which in turn fostered independence, piracy and lawlessness. By the mid-19th century, however, the powerful British Empire gave up mercantilism and trade restrictions and introduced the principle of free trade, with few restrictions or tariffs. Colonies were then granted forms of independence.

European colonization of the Americas actually began as early as the 10th–11th century, when West Norse sailors explored and briefly settled limited areas on the shores of present-day Canada. These Norsemen were Vikings who had discovered and settled Greenland, then sailed the Arctic region of North America alongside Greenland, and down alongside Canada to explore, pillage, and settle. According to Icelandic Sagas, violent conflicts with the indigenous population ultimately made the Norse abandon those settlements.

For nearly two centuries, the Knights Templar accumulated riches of the Near East while marching under the banner of Christ in the Crusades. In addition to the silks, bullion, spices and other valuables, the Templars claimed as spoils of war, the wealth of countless dukes, barons, viscounts and other lords which flowed into the Order's coffers as the flower of European nobility rushed to join the ranks of the holy warriors. The massive fortune collected by the Templars generated awe and jealousy of the Church. The wealth of a medieval order of knights, who were dissolved by the papacy in 1307, more than a century before Christopher Columbus's historic voyage, found a home in the New World. The prevailing theory among true believers is that during the Templar's final days, a fleet of the Order's ships sailed from La Rochelle, France to the safety of Scotland. The treasure then rested at Kilwinning Abbey until Sir Henry Sinclair and a group of Scottish knights spirited the wealth away to Oak Island off Canada's coast, hiding the riches on the island for their progeny to eventually recover.

Few people know that there was a successful expedition to the New World in the 1390s, led by Henry St. Clair and members of the prominent Zeno family of Venice. The Sinclair family, which owned a fleet of ships, actually made a number of voyages across the Atlantic. They brought the treasure and built the *Money Pit*, to Oak Island undetected. Henry Sinclair and the Templars embarked at the end of the fourteenth century in a fleet of ships bound for Iceland then past the declining communities in Greenland following old Viking routes. These would eventually lead them to Vinland, the fabled settlement established by the Vikings in the New World – roughly corresponding to Nova Scotia. It is claimed that the local Mi'kmaq Indians still tell tales of white-skinned people who came from lands over the seas in their folklore. Some of their art incorporates a red cross pattée on a white background, as does their tribal emblem.

The following quote is from the Catholic Encyclopedia online under "Crusades": "The Conquistadores, who ever since the fifteenth century had been going forth to discover new lands, considered themselves the auxiliaries of the crusade."

Extensive European colonization, however, began in 1492, when a Spanish expedition headed by Christopher Columbus sailed west to find a new trade route to the Far East but inadvertently landed in what came to be known to Europeans as the "New World". Running aground on the northern part of Hispaniola on December 5, 1492, which the Taino people had inhabited since the 7th century, the site became the first European settlement in the Americas. European conquest, large-scale exploration, colonization and industrial development soon followed. Columbus' first two voyages (1492–93) reached the Bahamas and various Caribbean islands, including Hispaniola, Puerto Rico, Cuba and St. Kitts/Nevis. In 1497, sailing from Bristol on behalf of England, John Cabot landed on the North American coast, and a year later, Columbus's third voyage reached the South American coast. As the sponsor of Christopher Columbus's voyages, Spain was the first European power to settle and colonize the largest areas, from North America and the Caribbean to the southern tip of South America.

The island of Nevis began not as a colony, per se, but as an isolated island settlement. Genuinely founded by Columbus in 1493, there were no other inhabitants on the island with maritime claim as Spanish territory. The English settlers, however, were the first to arrive, followed by the French, exiled persons seeking freedom, Jewish people from Barbados who were exiled from Spain, as well as slaves held in captivity and pirates seeking refuge.

Other powers such as France also founded colonies in the Americas: in eastern North America, a number of Caribbean islands, and small coastal parts of South America. Portugal colonized Brazil, tried colonizing of the coasts of present-day

Canada, and settled for extended periods northwest (on the east bank) of the River Plate. The Age of Exploration was the beginning of territorial expansion for several European countries. Europe had been preoccupied with internal wars, and was slowly recovering from the devastation and loss of population caused by the bubonic plague; thus the rapid rate at which it grew in wealth and power was unforeseeable in the early 15th century.

Eventually, the entire Western Hemisphere came under the ostensible control of European governments, leading to profound changes to its landscape, population, plant and animal life. The American Revolution was a political upheaval that took place between 1765 and 1783 during which the Thirteen American Colonies maintained by force of arms their refusal to submit to the authority of the King and Parliament of Great Britain, and founded the independent United States. The Mexican War of Independence was an armed conflict, and the culmination of a political and social process which ended the rule of Spain in 1821 in the territory of New Spain. In the 19th century alone over 50 million people left Europe for the Americas, some fed up with oppression and others seeking riches and fortune. The post-1492 era is known as the period of the *Columbian Exchange*, a dramatically widespread exchange of animals, plants, culture, human populations (including slaves), communicable disease, and ideas between the American and Afro-Eurasian hemispheres following Columbus's voyages to the Americas.

Most people think in terms of the "Crusades" having been conducted in the Holy Land of Jerusalem from the eleventh through the thirteenth centuries. However, the Crusades actually continued throughout the sixteenth century in the Americas. According to the Webster's Revised Unabridged Dictionary (1913) a "Crusade" includes "any enterprise undertaken with zeal and enthusiasm; as, a crusade against intemperance". It is well known that the Knights Templar, along with other Orders of Knights who were also known as Crusaders, among other things protected Catholic Christians who were on a pilgrimage to the Holy Land in Israel. The Knights also protected the Holy Land in Jerusalem and equally in Spain.

To understand the explorations that took place in America, the reader needs to understand that it was not only a search for gold and silver, but it was also a spiritual battle with principalities operating behind the Spaniards. And to understand the principalities operating behind Columbus, Ponce de Leon, Cortez, Menendez, DeSoto, and others you need to understand the relationship between the Knights, the Crowns, and the Church, and how that relates to America.

Carol Delaney, author of *Columbus and the Quest for Jerusalem* (Free Press/Simon and Schuster, 2011), a cultural anthropologist and long-time professor at Stanford University, concludes that most people misunderstand the purpose of Columbus' voyage. Everybody knows that Columbus was trying to find gold, but they don't know what the gold was for: to fund a crusade to take Jerusalem back from the Muslims before their perceived end of the world. A lot of people at the time thought that the apocalypse was coming because of all the signs unfolding: the plague, famine, changes in weather, and earthquakes. And it was believed that before the end, Jerusalem had to be back in Christian hands so that Christ could return in judgment. Columbus actually calculated how many years were left before the end of the world. He seemed to think of his whole voyage as a mission, which was part of this apocalyptic scenario. Believing he was traveling to Asia, Columbus particularly wanted to convince the Grand Khan of China, who had already expressed interest in Christianity, to convert. He thought that the Grand Khan could help with the crusade to take Jerusalem by marching from the east, while the Europeans marched from the west.

After Columbus, the Spanish King halted all attempts to establish colonies in what is now known as America. The first non-Spanish settlement attempt in the Caribbean occurred on Saint Christopher, when French Huguenot refugees from the fishing town of Dieppe, Northern France, established a harbor on the island's north coast, which they also named Dieppe, in 1538. However, only months after the founding, the settlement was raided by the Spanish and all the inhabitants were deported.

In 1564 the Hugenots again established Fort Caroline in Florida. When Spain found out that the French Huguenots had successfully established a colony in Florida, the King of Spain commissioned Menendez as his Adelantado (Governor) and as a Knight in the Order of Santiago to sail to Florida and convert or remove the French Huguenot heretics. Menendez set foot on what is now Florida, he claimed the land in the name of Spain and the Roman Catholic Church, and announced the establishment of America's oldest city - St. Augustine. Then to protect Spain's interest, he offered the heretics to repent, and upon refusing he and his troops killed the French Huguenots as well as enslaved the Native American Indians.

Though the Spaniards claimed Nevis and St. Christopher as part of their empire early on with Columbus' landing, they never settled the two islands. The privateer Sir Francis Drake found them uninhabited in 1585, and no sighting of 'Indians' was recorded by the first wood-cutters in the 1590s. On another arrival of an English ship in 1622, Thomas Warner stepped ashore on St. Christopher, nearly 30 years after Columbus, and settled the island for planting of tobacco. On July 22, 1628, Hilton and his men landed on Nevis near Charlestown. The Spaniards considered the English in St. Christopher and Nevis as trespassers and pirates. Thus, when Spanish Admiral *Fadrique de Toledo* appeared in Nevis (7th Sept. 1629) with 30 armed vessels, the English indentured servants on Nevis had to surrender. Once the Spanish left, however, the islands were again quickly resettled by the English and the French and would never return to the Spanish Main.

Saint Christopher had suffered heavily from a Spanish raid in 1629, from which nearly all of the island's inhabitants fled as the Spaniards pillaged. The Hospitaller Crusader colonization from Malta to the Americas occurred during a 14-year period in which the Knights of St. John possessed four Caribbean islands: Saint

Christopher, Saint Martin, Saint Barthélemy, and Saint Croix. The Knights' presence in the Caribbean grew out of their order's close relationship with the French nobility and the presence of many members in the Americas as French administrators.

Phillippe de Longvilliers de Poincy, founder of the Hospitaller colonies, began in 1639 as the appointed governor under the *Compagnie des Îles de l'Amérique*. King Louis XIII of France soon after made Poincy his Lieutenant-General for the entire Caribbean of French holdings. Poincy would establish St. Christophe as a prime sugar agricultural producer. Nevis meanwhile remained relatively independent under semi-autonomous rule from England. It would become the greatest sugar producer of the entire western world and major slave trading port into the 18th century and earn the title 'Queen of the Caribees.'

As the Age of Exploration of the Caribbean would wane with most all territories discovered, mapped, and claimed by European crowns, shipment of goods, slave trading, and piracy would replace the exploring ships. The Golden Age of Piracy begins; sugar becomes the planters gold; and slave labor the machine to make money.

From a standpoint of world history, the Caribbean poses an abrupt and recent beginning, coupled with the brutal modes of occupation, agriculture, slavery, piracy, hurricanes, and desolation among the colonizing forces beginning with the Vikings and later the knights and conquistadors. We could thus say, the *American Crusade* led by Knights of the Christian military orders would forever change the world as we know it, once again.

References

- Delaney, Carol. Columbus and the Quest for Jerusalem. New York: Free Press/Simon and Schuster, 2011
- Freller, Thomas. Knights, Buccaneers, and Sugar Cane: The Caribbean Colonies of the Order of Malta.
- L'Abbe de Vertot. The History of the Knights of Malta. London, 1728.
- Knights Hospitaller. From Wikipedia, the free encyclopedia.
- https://en.wikipedia.org/wiki/Knights_Hospitaller
- McWilliams, Charles. The Medical Cross. The Achievements, Medical, Political and Social Works of the Orders of St. John of Jerusalem, Knights Hospitaller. SMOKH. 2007.
- Phillippe de Longvilliers de Poincy. From Wikipedia, the free encyclopedia.
- https://en.wikipedia.org/wiki/Phillippe_de_Longvilliers_de_Poincy

NEVIS HOSPITALLER • CRUSADER MUSEUM, CHAPEL, MONASTIC LIBRARY, GIFT SHOP

Open for Tours • http://hospitallers-americas.org/ • (869) 469-9564

APPENDIX

LIFE ON NEVIS IN THE 20TH CENTURY - BERNICE AND EUNICE BROWNE - March 8, 2017 (Interview by Marilyn Curtis, Nevis)

Bernice and Eunice Browne were born in New River Path to Arnold Browne (1909) and Beryl Browne (1911) who also were born in Nevis. Bernice and Eunice have generously shared some tidbits of their growing up experiences and what it was like living and going to school in the late 1930's as Nevisian children. Their mother, Beryl, was a seamstress as well as the mother of nine children. Their father, Arnold, was known as a very successful fisherman.

During different holidays the fishermen took great pride in entering their boats in a local boat race. It was customary to bet on different boatmen to win the race. One year their father entered his boat, Perseverance, and no one bet on his boat, but the boat won and it upset some of the other fishermen. It upset someone enough to poison their father and he passed away after thirteen agonizing days of suffering.

This left their mother, Beryl, as sole caretaker of all nine children with no income. Beryl was a strong and strict taskmaster, which was the way she kept her children safe and cared for. They had about five acres of land at River Path that they all tended. "All our mother had was what people gave her to grow and she would plant the seeds or plants they gave her and when the crop came in she would pay them 2 for 1 of everything the crop yielded." The sugar cane we grew would go to the miller and they would make molasses. We used it mostly for the animals. It was long hard work for the whole family but it helped to sustain them as they grew up.

The boys in the family tended to the animals and brought in wood for the fire to make their own charcoal for cooking. They all helped to carry water from the distant river with a bucket at a time on their heads. Eunice shared how they would wad up cloth or leaves to form a ball to help rest the bucket on their head. She remembered how sad she was for her sister when she got all the way to the gate and the bucket tipped and spilled all the water after all her hard work of carrying the bucket.

Their mother worked very hard and was very strict. They were not allowed to go out of our yard to play with others...mother said there was enough of us to entertain each other. If we were to tell a joke our mother would give us a smack. In those times one could expect a lashing for just about anything. She also would not allow us to dance even when the neighbor man played his wonderful drums.

We had a cellar where we kept the barrels of sugar cane and it contained our shower. After meals we stored any leftover porridge down there to keep it for the baby. There were times when the meals weren't really filling. One time Bernice went to the cellar and was so hungry she ate the last of the porridge that had been saved. When mother found out she confronted Bernice and she told mother she had seen a mouse coming out of the porridge pot...but Bernice got in trouble anyway because she couldn't tell a lie...and still can't.

We went to Gingerland Girls School and then later we went to Zion School. We got free meals for lunch as children who were in need. We walked from River Path to Zion. We had no money to buy shoes. Most of the children had no shoes. At mango time we would save the seeds from the mango's and get the Clima sticky cherries and glue three stones together and put them on the bottom of our feet. The streets were tared and it was so hot that the hot pitch would bubble up and burn us so we put the mango pits on our feet to protect them.

Some of the rich people had socks and shoes so we made our own with the mango pit shoes.

At our school we were in one room for prayers and then we had different classrooms for seniors and primary students. The teachers were very good. Eunice got to 7th Standard at about age 10 or 11. She loved reading so the Headmaster said to mother that if she didn't mind he would hold Eunice after school to train her to be a teacher. When Eunice was 12 or 13 she took an exam to be a teacher and she became a student/teacher.

We were taught English, math, and health/hygiene. The teacher would have everyone in a circle and if we didn't get an answer right we got licks. Bernice shared that if she got lashed in the a.m. she had a bad day all day. The teachers were allowed to do that as much as they wanted then.

You were to arrive when the school door was closed, but promptly at 9:00 a.m. when they opened the door they would let the children in and they would close the door. The children that were still on the road walking would be considered late and they would get lashed. It was to learn that when you grow up that punctuality was very important. Each class had its own teacher. First thing we did to start our school day was singing and the bible. We went from 9 a.m. to 3. p.m.

Before we left for school we had to make beds, feed the pigs and chickens and let them out and tie up the donkeys and so on. We had to get up early before school to make sure all our shores were done first. Our mother would wake us and if we didn't get right up we would get whipped. We also had to make sure the yard was tidy so it looked good. We used a machete and we swept the yard with the big coconut branches. If we were late for school we'd be in trouble at home and at school. There was a lot to do as children and that's why some children would fall asleep during school time.

Bush tea was used for healing various illness. For colds we would make lemon grass tea and often used the lime bush leaves. Soursop helped us to sleep. Mother would make up a big pot of tea made from various bush leaves and we slept really well.

Nearly every night we had a lot of mosquito's. We would pick soursop leaves and mother put them in the coal pot in the room and the smoke would clear the room of mosquito's.

When the smoke cleared we'd close the windows. No mosquito's combined with the soursop tea had us sleeping beautifully.

The village people really helped each other. You always said good afternoon to the elders or they would lash you for being rude. Everyone knew each other and many times they were related family members. They would say, "Come here Eunice" and if she was cooking something she would put whatever she was cooking on a leaf for you to eat. It was always a delightful treat even if it was a piece of potato.

We didn't have to worry about robberies or locking our doors back then. At Christmas time people would bake in a stone oven outside and would often share their baked items...they were very kind. The boys also knew how to bake and they would look for wood to help the people with their fires.

We ate the Calabash tree nuts when they were ripe Then we scrapped it out and put it to dry in the sun. They were large and that is what we used as our bowl. We each took care of our own Calabash bowl. We'd also get a small Calabash nut, bore holes in it and put a stick through it to use to dip the water out of a bucket.

Dishes were shipped in by boat and sold in the market. The clay pots we used were made locally. Because we grew sugar cane on the island, the children could gather the cane and take it to the New River factory and get some sugar cane juice.

We went into Charlestown maybe once at holiday times. We had to walk which was about five miles one way.

Back then the five parishes had a government man overseeing the needs of each parish. He came around on horseback and he'd shout out to the people and they would talk. He'd see how clean everything was kept and he checked to see if there was anything needed. All the trenches were clean and well done with no garbage strewn or bush un-kept. It was always very tidy...not like today.

When we became an independent country everything changed. The plantations supplied work for the grownups and we thought they were treated fairly until they stopped producing sugar cane in Nevis. Then the

Plantation owner called all the workers together and locked them in a building and burned all the workers to death (Golden Rock) and returned to England.

They stopped doing sugar cane when we were children. Nothing has replaced it. They used to grow cotton at the same time. There was no demand for cotton after a while. We paid people to work our land and pick the cotton.

Girls were not supposed to ride the donkeys. Our sister, Aretha, had to go to the clinic because she had trouble with her feet and Bernice had a sore leg so they got on the donkey and as he was going up the hill he decided to buck and one flew over the top and one over the back...Bernice said she never wanted to ride again.

When Bernice was nine years old she spent six months in the hospital and missed a full year of school because of the sore on her foot. After all of that she returned home not healed. There was a man from Brown Hill who treated her foot with a special salve that finally healed her foot. They never knew what caused the sore.

It was very strongly enforced that children should be seen but not heard...so some never got over speaking up even as adults. Eunice still spoke up even if there were consequences, but Bernice would hide and would not be forthright. Eunice said she would often say things just to provoke her mother. Our mother was very out front. She would have us go to the tree to pick a switch for our own punishment and if it was not the right size, we would get an extra lashing.

If someone gave us money, Eunice would hide it under a stone outside because mother said it was not good to take money. If we found money, even a penny, we would have to turn it over to the police and if no one claimed it in a month we would get to go back and get it from the police and keep it.

When we would go on a walk Eunice would tell Bernice she should dance...mother would have objected. Eunice would dance in the field, but Bernice never felt comfortable dancing.

In our village there was a drummer and from time to time he would drum and the village people would dance, but mother would not let us move a muscle. Our sister danced with one of the men and she was beaten harshly by our mother. She said you have to set an example for your brothers and sisters.

We don't know a lot of our relatives even if they spell their names the same.

The women were always the strong part of the island. Many people will still sit on the walls and tell stories of times past. If someone died they had to carry all their clothes, bed sheets and wash it in the River. The river was very important to us. When someone died the whole village would help each other.

Bernice was 18 when she went to England. Eunice couldn't go because she was bringing in the money for the home. Britain had employment openings for the common wealth so they could get workers. Bernice said it was scary and exciting as she sailed for 17 days to get to England. They had a set-up in place to go to the employment office to fill out forms about what your family did. As a female they aligned you to what your mother did. My mother was a seamstress and I did not like sewing but because of being under age I had to stay there for four months as a seamstress. Then I saw an ad to be a conductress. I passed their written test and became a conductress making four times more money than as a seamstress.

Bernice saved as much as she could to help her mother and others to come to England. At that time there was no way to make money on Nevis with no sugar and no cotton.

Years later after raising her family Bernice decided to come back to Nevis and now declares, "It is my time to be on holiday and to enjoy the sun. It is just too cold in England."

Eunice came on holiday some time later and says that by the time she got to Antigua and felt the sun she knew she would never live in England again. She quit her high level, good paying job even after they begged her to come back. She also declares, "I love the sun."

FILMS ABOUT or ASSOCIATED with ST. KITTS/NEVIS & PEOPLE

Dr. June Goodfield - the premiere of her film - shot in Nevis - ***The Time Detective***. Accomplished British historian and author Dr. June Goodfield, who fell in love with Nevis since her first visit in 1985, was applauded by Acting Premier of Nevis and Minister of Tourism Hon. Mark Brantley for the production of her film "The Time Detective," based on the island's history, based on her novel "Rivers of Time." Published: 17 January 2017

That Hamilton Woman, (also known as Lady Hamilton and The Enchantress), is a 1941 black-and-white historical film drama, produced and directed by Alexander Korda for his American company during his exile in the United States. Set during the Napoleonic Wars, the film tells the story of the rise and fall of Emma Hamilton, dance-hall girl and courtesan, who married Sir William Hamilton, British ambassador to the Kingdom of Naples. She later became mistress to Admiral Horatio Nelson.

The story begins with an ageing, alcoholic woman (Vivien Leigh) being clapped into debtors' prison in the slums of Calais. In a husky, despairing, whiskey-soaked voice, the former Lady Hamilton narrates the story of her life to her skeptical fellow inmates.

In one of the early scenes that launches the flashback, Emma, well past her prime, looks into a mirror and remembers "the face I knew before," the face of the young, lovely girl who captured the imagination of artists. When Horatio Nelson (Laurence Olivier) arrives in Naples, Emma is soon deeply attracted to him and is impressed by his passionate insistence on resisting Napoleon's dictatorial rule. She leaves Sir William to live with Nelson, who is also married. Their idyllic life together is threatened by the continuing war and their infidelity to their spouses. Nelson leaves to confront Napoleon's navy in the decisive Battle of Trafalgar. After his death in the battle, she succumbs to alcoholism and spirals down into poverty and oblivion.

Captain Kidd is a 1945 adventure film starring Charles Laughton, Randolph Scott and Barbara Britton. It has entered the public domain because the producers neglected to renew the copyright in 1972. In 1699, pirate William Kidd (Charles Laughton) loots and destroys the London galleon The Twelve Apostles. He and three confederates bury the stolen treasure on a remote island. He then presents himself at the court of King William III (Henry Daniell) as an honest shipmaster seeking a royal commission as a privateer after striking his colors to a pirate. The King sends Kidd and his ship the Adventure Galley to the waters near Madagascar (where The Twelve Apostles met its fate) to rendezvous with the ship Quedagh Merchant and provide an escort back to England. On the voyage home, Kidd schemes to rid himself of his three close associates (to avoid sharing the booty) and Mercy, whom he rightly suspects. Mercy is really the vengeance-seeking son of Admiral Lord Blayne, the slandered captain of The Twelve Apostles. The King's men have found the booty looted from The Twelve Apostles after searching Kidd's cabin. Kidd is tried, condemned, and hanged.

Hot Resort (1985) - Young guys on the make get a job at a resort hotel in the Caribbean. A group of young men get jobs at a Caribbean resort, but choose to spend more of their time chasing girls and avoiding their boss than taking care of guests. The blandly titled "Hot Resort" definitely falls into that last category, ... He only made one other film after the bad taste from this one faded away. You get shots of the island St. Kitts where it was filmed of yesteryear. Rare film.

The Dread Pirate Roberts is a fictional character in the novel **The Princess Bride** (1973) and its 1987 film adaptation. A pirate of near-mythical reputation, the Dread Pirate *Black Barts* Roberts is feared across the seven seas for his ruthlessness and sword fighting prowess, and is well known for taking no prisoners. It is revealed during the course of the story that Roberts is not one man, but a series of individuals who pass the name and reputation to a chosen successor once they are wealthy enough to retire. When the time comes, "Roberts" and his chosen successor sail into port and discharge the crew. Then they hire a new crew, the ex-Roberts staying aboard as first mate and referring to his successor as "Captain Roberts". Once the crew grows accustomed to the new Roberts, the previous captain leaves to enjoy his retirement.

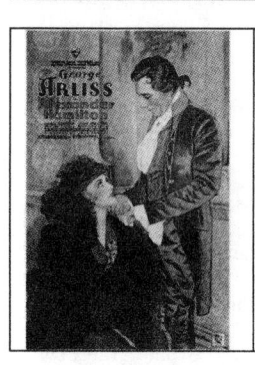

Alexander Hamilton (1931). With the end of the Revolutionary War in 1783, General George Washington took Colonel Hamilton with him into the newly formed government. While the main disagreements in the early days was over paying the soldiers who had fought in the War, Hamilton also dedicated his energies towards a national bank so that the United States would be able to trade with other countries. He fought eight long years for his Assumption Bill while considering the new Residence Bill. While he is engaged in running a clean treasury, his arch rival, Senator Roberts, takes every opportunity to slander and cast Alexander as a dishonorable man.

Island Hoppers Nevis
Pro Surfer Scott Marvin joins the Island Hopper crew to check out the tiny island of Nevis. Just off the coast of St Kitts, Nevis is a tiny dot on the map with plenty of interesting and unknown surf spots. Reef breaks and Point breaks, Rain Forests and abandoned Sugar Mills, Nevis has many interesting highlights.

Lance & Lexi find an archeological crew who gives them some insight on the islands rich history. The crew also takes an amazing hike through the rain forest to the top of Nevis Peak. 2009

MUSIC FROM or ABOUT ST. KITTS/NEVIS & PEOPLE

"ELLIE MATT AND THE G.I.'S BRASS - HAVING A JOLLY GOOD TIME" LP FULL-LENGTH RECORD ALBUM/1973 WIRL RECORDS #W 047/BARBADOS IMPORT. TRACKS INCLUDE...
BIG THING TROUBLE
RAINORAMA
MY CONCERTO
FUNDAMENTAL REGGAE
HAVING A JOLLY GOOD TIME
MEDLEY
ONLY A FOOL BREAKS HIS OWN HEART
HARD OLD WORLD
IRON HAND
ALL DAY ALL NIGHT

CORONETS STEEL BAND OF ST KITTS
THIS IS ON A PRIVATE LABEL

SIDE 1:
HALLELUJAH CHORUS, EL RELICARIO, ANDANTE CANTIBILE, ADAGIO FROM THE NEW WORLD, THE MERRY WIDOW WALTZ

SIDE 2:
SOCA JEAN, THE ENTERTAINER, RAS 30.00MAS, ETHEL, CARNIVAL IN SPLENDOR

The Quarto Pals of St. Kitts

HOSPITALLER / CRUSADER MUSEUM GIFT SHOP (Newcastle)
(Tours/Open – Tuesday-Friday (869) 469-9564; email: jadecenter2@hotmail.com

Museum: A specialty building which houses objects of historical, scientific, artistic, and cultural interest, exhibited for the public and tourists of Nevis with special emphasis on Crusader, Nevisian and Caribbean History. On display are life-size statues of historical personalities with accompanying texts including Brother Gerard (first Hospitaller); Captain Kidd; the Unknown Solder, Christopher Columbus; Hippocrates; etc. Featured are short video narratives; posters; regalia; pictures, murals, tapestries, commemorative plates, memorabilia, relics, etc.; and other artifacts of interest. This is the only such museum of its kind in the West Indies.

Virtual Museum mini-tour: www.hospitallers-americas.org

Chapel of the Sacred Medical Order, Knights of Hope www.smoch.org
A chapel for campus meetings, prayer room, Christenings, Investitures, Baptisms and weddings of members of the Church of Hope, a Special Diocese of the Church of the East, Brazil. Chapel includes exhibits authentic replicas of relics: Shroud of Turin, Spear of Destiny (Lance of Longinus), The Antioch Chalice of the Holy Grail; all famed of Templar Legends.

Monastic Medical Library: A specialty 'reference library' for the history of medicine, monastic medicine, complementary medicines, basic medical sciences, and associated subjects. Serving the field and as testament to the history of monastic (Christian) medicine as part of the Sacred Medical Order's role in preserving this tradition. This is the only such Museum of its type in the West Indies. Open to the public as a reference library (only). Books are not available for lending.

Taíno Exhibit: Ameridians once native to Nevis, the original, pre-Columbian inhabitants of the island.

Hospitaller/Crusader Museum Grand Opening: June 9th, 2017